Workers and
Their Wages

Workers and Their Wages

Changing Patterns in the United States

Marvin H. Kosters, editor

The AEI Press

Publisher for the American Enterprise Institute
WASHINGTON, D.C.

1991

Distributed by arrangement with

University Press of America, Inc.
4720 Boston Way   3 Henrietta Street
Lanham, Md. 20706   London WC2E 8LU England

Library of Congress Cataloging-in-Publication Data

Workers and their wages : changing patterns in the United States /
  Marvin H. Kosters, editor.
     p.   cm.
    Consists of analyses and commentaries presented at a
  conference at the American Enterprise Institute, Washington, D.C., on
  November 3, 1989.
    ISBN 0-8447-3747-X
    1. Wages—United States—Congresses. I. Kosters, Marvin H.
  HD4975.W76 1991
  331.2′1′0973—dc20   91-13513
                                              CIP

1 3 5 7 9 10 8 6 4 2

AEI Studies 520

The AEI PRESS
Publisher for the American Enterprise Institute
1150 Seventeenth Street, N.W., Washington, D.C. 20036

Printed in the United States of America

Contents

CONTENTS

FIGURES

CONTENTS

Foreword

Trends in real wages for different groups of workers were very uneven during the 1980s. This uneven performance contrasted with that of the 1950s and 1960s, when the trend of average wages was a fairly reliable indicator of how well most workers were faring. The strong increases in real wages that most workers experienced then may have muted concerns about the poorer relative performance of some groups of workers. Differences among groups remained small when real wages stagnated in the 1970s. The large increase in earnings of high-wage workers in the 1980s dramatically shifted relative wages—a change that was striking in both its size and its direction compared with the gradual earlier changes.

The remarkable changes in wage patterns that emerged in the 1980s gave rise to considerable public discussion about their causes and consequences and about policies to offset them. Among the proximate causes suggested were employer offers of mainly low-wage jobs, declining union bargaining power, and federal government policies that were too market-oriented to protect workers' wages or to prop them up. Suggested consequences included a shrinking middle class and persistent poverty because too many jobs paid wages too low to support middle-class living standards. Policies that were proposed for consideration generally emphasized programs that could provide more high-wage employment opportunities for less-skilled workers or more direct approaches to raising their wages and incomes.

These essays describe and analyze the major, broad changes in wage relationships during the 1980s. The analyses examine the influence of changes in the supply and demand for workers' skills, as measured primarily by years of schooling and work experience. A major goal of the research was to identify and to explain the underlying causes of these changing relative wage patterns. The studies attempted to develop explanations that are more unified and comprehensive than those that emphasize many separate, particular circumstances influencing the changes.

The focus on the role of education provides a useful frame

for structuring the analyses. The most pervasive change in wage relationships that is apparent in all the studies is the increase in wage differentials for workers with different levels of schooling. During the 1980s the wage premiums for additional schooling increased across the entire schooling spectrum to levels much larger than experienced earlier.

Schooling levels for the work force as a whole were upgraded less rapidly during the 1980s than in the 1970s, and this slowdown in the growth of the supply of workers with more schooling was one factor influencing schooling wage premiums. The big increase in schooling wage premiums in the 1980s emerged, however, when significant upgrading of schooling occurred. One of the most significant general conclusions in these studies, documented in detail by Kevin Murphy and Finis Welch, is that changes in the relative supply of skilled workers—resulting from changes in the schooling of the work force—cannot be the only factor that influenced relative wage patterns in the 1980s. Evidently demand changes were also at work.

The influence of changes in demand on relative wage patterns in the 1980s was apparently linked to changing international trade patterns. The influence of trade on wage trends was reflected by measures of the size and composition of changes in the trade balance, as shown by Murphy and Welch, and by indirect evidence on shifts of production operations abroad, as shown by John Bound and George Johnson. The influence of the pronounced change in trade patterns that emerged in the 1980s, however, is difficult to distinguish from competing explanations, such as a surge in skill demands induced by more rapid technological change. A more definitive judgment about the characteristics of demand changes primarily responsible for the changes in wage patterns in the 1980s, and about the extent to which their effects might be temporary, would probably require more direct measures than were available for these studies.

Workers with more schooling earn higher wages on average than those with less schooling, and widening wage differentials between schooling levels consequently produce increased wage dispersion. The underlying skills valued by employers are closely associated with years of school completed, but workers with comparable years of schooling and work experience do not necessarily have the same marketable skills. If demand for these underlying skills increases, dispersion in wages within schooling and work experience categories can also be expected to increase. Chinhui Juhn, Kevin Murphy, and Brooks Pierce examined the slowdown in convergence of wages of black male workers toward those of white males by taking increased wage dispersion into account in establishing appropriate bench marks for comparisons. Their analysis indicates that wage differences associated with differences in years of schooling account for about half the slowdown in black-white wage convergence in the 1980s. Differences in schooling quality apparently account for a substantial portion—possibly all—of the remaining slowdown in black progress.

Evidence on deficiencies in schooling quality, especially at the elementary and secondary level, received a great deal of public attention in the 1980s. John Bishop's review of evidence from test scores shows a decline in achievement levels during the late 1960s and 1970s, followed by a recovery to earlier levels during the 1980s. The influence on relative wages of differences in years of school completed was much more important than differences in achievement levels that prevailed when workers obtained their schooling. Changes over time in schooling quality seem to have contributed to changes in schooling wage premiums, but schooling quality, as measured by high school achievement tests, is apparently also influenced by changes in the college wage premium. Both achievement levels and years of schooling are endogenous, and they can be expected to adjust in response to changes in wage differentials generated in the labor market.

The pronounced rise in schooling wage premiums in the 1980s, concurrent with a substantial upgrading of schooling levels, is evidence of a strong growth in demand for skilled workers. The high wage premiums for schooling that emerged can be expected to lead to increased investment in schooling and skills. Further upgrading of the schooling and skills of the work force would help to raise average wages and living standards for the work force as a whole, to stabilize or perhaps even to reduce the size of wage differentials between workers with different average schooling and wage levels, and to bring about a resumption of convergence toward average wages for workers in groups with below-average schooling and skills. Improving education and skills would contribute to a more productive work force with smaller disparities in wages and living standards.

The analyses and commentaries in this book were presented at a conference at the American Enterprise Institute, Washington, D.C., November 3, 1989. The conference was organized to promote discussion and better understanding of the pronounced changes in relative wage relationships during the 1980s. The essays were prepared for publication to make them available to a broader audience.

MARVIN H. KOSTERS

Contributors

MARVIN H. KOSTERS is resident scholar and director of economic policy studies at the American Enterprise Institute. He was a senior economist at the President's Council of Economic Advisers and held senior policy positions at the Cost of Living Council and at the White House. Mr. Kosters received a Ph.D. in economics from the University of Chicago.

JOHN H. BISHOP is associate professor of personnel and human resource studies at the Industrial Labor Relations School, Cornell University. He was director of the Center for Research on Youth Employability and associate director for research of the National Center for Research on Vocational Education at Ohio State University. Mr. Bishop received his Ph.D. in economics from the University of Michigan.

JOHN BOUND is assistant professor of economics and faculty member of the Population Studies Center at the University of Michigan. He is a specialist in labor and health economics and is affiliated with the National Bureau of Economic Research. Mr. Bound earned his Ph.D. in economics from Harvard University.

GARY BURTLESS is senior fellow at the Brookings Institution, where he does research on labor markets, income distribution, social insurance, and behavioral effects of taxes and transfers. His books include *A Future of Lousy Jobs? The Changing Structure of Wages* (1990). Mr. Burtless earned a Ph.D. in economics from the Massachusetts Institute of Technology.

GEORGE JOHNSON is professor of economics at the University of Michigan. He has been a visiting professor at Princeton University and the London School of Economics. Mr. Johnson has held positions with the U.S. Department of Labor and the President's Council of Economic Advisers. He is affiliated with the National Bureau of Economic Research. Mr. Johnson earned his Ph.D. from the University of California at Berkeley.

CONTRIBUTORS

CHINHUI JUHN is a Ph.D. candidate at the University of Chicago and a research assistant to Kevin Murphy. Ms. Juhn's research has focused on wage inequality, labor market participation, and employment differences among demographic groups.

LAWRENCE F. KATZ is professor of economics at Harvard University and research associate at the National Bureau of Economic Research. He has studied changes in the structure of wages, unemployment and labor mobility, theories of wage determination, problems of disadvantaged youth, and the impact of international trade and immigration on the labor market. Mr. Katz is an editor of the *Quarterly Journal of Economics*. He earned his Ph.D. from the Massachusetts Institute of Technology.

KEVIN M. MURPHY is professor of business economics and industrial relations at the University of Chicago. His research interests include the effects of demographic trends and international trade on the structure of wages and returns to schooling and skill. Mr. Murphy is research associate at the National Bureau of Economic Research. He earned his Ph.D. from the University of Chicago.

WALTER Y. OI is the Elmer B. Milliman Professor of Economics at the University of Rochester. He has held positions at Northwestern University and the University of Washington. Mr. Oi is a fellow of the Econometric Society and vice president of the Western Economic Association. He earned his Ph.D. in economics from the University of Chicago.

BROOKS PIERCE is assistant professor of economics at Texas A&M University. His research has focused on wage inequality by race, returns to skill, and occupational choice. Mr. Pierce earned his Ph.D. in economics from the University of Chicago.

ALBERT REES is research associate at the Industrial Relations Section, Princeton University. He was president of the Alfred P. Sloan Foundation and professor of economics at Princeton University and the University of Chicago.

SHERWIN ROSEN is the Bergman Professor of Economics and chairman of the Department of Economics at the University of Chicago, where he earned his Ph.D. He is also research associate at the National Bureau of Economic Research and the Hoover Institution, a fellow of American Academy of Arts and Sciences and of the Econometric ety, and an editor of the *Journal of Political Economy*.

FINIS WELCH is visiting professor of economics at Texas A&M University and professor of economics at UCLA. He is chairman of Unicon Research Corporation and president of Welch Associates. He previously directed labor and population studies at the RAND Corporation. Mr. Welch received his Ph.D. from the University of Chicago.

1
Wages and Demographics

Marvin H. Kosters

Trends in wages and living standards and in characteristics of jobs have recently received extensive discussion. Attention has focused particularly on the wage stagnation accompanying strong employment growth, the increased dispersion in wages and incomes, and the real wage losses of young workers with low skill levels. The discussion has been influenced by the slowdown in productivity growth since the early 1970s, which produced slower pay increases than realized earlier.[1]

In contrast, changes in relative wage patterns, particularly relationships between wages and schooling, have received less public attention. This is somewhat surprising in view of the remarkable increase in wage premiums for additional schooling during the 1980s. Although the decline in economic returns to schooling during the 1970s attracted a good deal of attention, labor market specialists have only recently analyzed the much larger subsequent rise in the economic rewards to additional schooling.[2] The marked increase in the attractiveness of schooling as an investment to improve earnings capabilities has apparently not been widely recognized.

This chapter focuses mainly on the rise of economic returns to schooling during the 1980s. Primarily descriptive, the chapter shows how demographic changes in the work force have influenced wage trends and documents the recent rise in the economic rewards for additional schooling. Schooling and work experience changes for both sexes are examined to describe their influence on wage patterns since the early 1970s.

The analysis of hourly wages shows extraordinarily large increases in wage premiums for schooling during the 1980s. Average hourly wages of college-educated males with approximately ten years

I owe thanks to Susan S. Collins, research associate at AEI, for her work in processing the data and to the Alfred P. Sloan Foundation and the U.S. Department of Labor for partial support of the research.

1

of work experience, for example, were about 85 percent higher in 1988 than for high school graduates with comparable work experience, and they were about 60 percent higher for females. The wage premium for college was more than 100 percent larger for men and more than 50 percent higher for women in 1988 than in 1980. Although the sizes of these wage premiums for schooling depend on how they are measured, all measures show increases in wage premiums for schooling far beyond those prevailing in the early 1970s.

The first part of the chapter discusses changes in real wage levels and the influence of changes in demographic composition. The relationship between schooling and wages and between work experience and wages is then examined. The next two sections consider how schooling quality, growth of the labor force, and the pace at which schooling has been upgraded have affected the wage premium for additional education. A discussion of the data appears in an appendix.

Average Real Wages

The slowdown in the growth of labor productivity at least since the early 1970s has been accompanied by slower growth of workers' hourly pay. The increasing proportion of workers' total pay consisting of nonwage benefits paid for directly by employers (mainly health and pension plan costs) has resulted in flat wage and salary growth relative to total compensation. Thus, although real hourly compensation did increase somewhat—by 13 percent from 1973 to 1988 compared with 40 percent over the preceding fifteen years—real wages have increased very little since the early 1970s.

According to the measures developed here, in 1988 real wages for the work force as a whole were roughly comparable to wages in 1973. Real wages generally declined until about 1981 and then recovered during the 1980s. The behavior of the average, of course, reflects changes in the composition of the work force and different rates of change for major demographic components, such as males and females. In addition, changes both in the average and in relative wage relationships depend greatly on how wages are measured.

The two wage measures considered here are the arithmetic mean of hourly earnings and the geometric mean (the antilog of the logarithmic mean). Differences among demographic groups in the shapes of distributions and differences in changes in their shapes have resulted in noticeable differences in comparisons according to the measure used. Because one measure is more appropriate than the other for particular comparisons, it is useful to examine both.

TABLE 1–1

Average Real Wage Levels, Changes in Selected Periods, 1973–1988
(percent change)

	Arithmetic Means			Geometric Means		
	Male	Female	Total	Male	Female	Total
1973–78	−1.6	0.0	−2.0	−1.7	1.0	−1.7
1978–83	0.6	1.3	−1.0	−3.0	−0.3	−3.0
1983–88	8.7	5.3	7.1	3.8	3.9	3.6
1973–80	−4.9	−3.3	−5.7	−4.9	−2.4	−5.3
1980–88	11.8	10.4	10.2	4.1	7.2	4.3
1973–88	6.3	6.7	3.9	−1.0	4.6	−1.3

NOTE: The arithmetic mean estimates from which percentage changes are calculated are weighted average measures of average hourly earnings, with census population weights applied to the sample for which arithmetic means of average hourly earnings are computed. The geometric means for males and females are the antilogs of mean log wages for the samples. The geometric mean for the total is the weighted arithmetic mean using census population weights of the geometric means for both sexes.
SOURCE: Author's calculations.

Comparisons of changes in real wage levels illustrate the importance of differences in how "average" wages are measured. Real wages rose by almost 4 percent from 1973 to 1988, for example, according to the arithmetic mean, compared with a decline of 1.3 percent according to the geometric mean. Comparisons for various subperiods for males and females and for the work force as a whole are shown in table 1–1. Both measures show declines or very small increases for the early part of the period for both sexes and for the total, with all measures showing increases after the beginning of the 1980s. Both measures show stronger wage growth for females than for males for the period as a whole. But because women's wages are lower (only about 64 percent of those for males), the rise in the proportion of female workers, from 39 to 45 percent from 1973 to 1988, produces a total wage growth that is smaller than that for either sex separately.

The difference in the two measures of average real wages is apparently larger for males than for females and larger during the 1980s than during the 1970s. The most striking comparison of the two measures concerns how females have fared relative to males. Geometric means show a rise in women's wages relative to men. Arith-

FIGURE 1–1
Real Hourly Wage–Potential Experience Profiles, 1984–1988 Averages

Real average wage in 1988 dollars

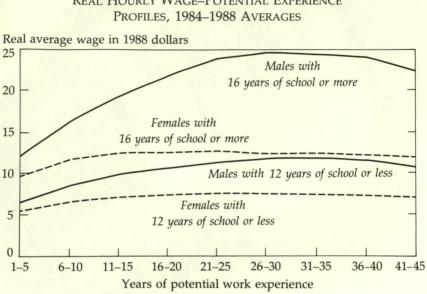

Years of potential work experience

Source: Author's calculations.

metic means, however, show women approximately holding their own relative to men. The contrast is particularly noticeable during the 1980s when arithmetic means show females losing ground relative to men while geometric means show them making substantial relative gains. The gains indicated by the geometric means are consistent with results reported in several other studies.[3]

The Effects of Schooling and Work Experience

Changes in the educational attainment and the work experience of the work force, as well as changes in sex composition, have influenced real wages. As is well known, workers with more schooling on average earn higher wages. Wages also increase for several years as workers accumulate experience, before wages taper off in middle age and then gradually decline. Changing composition of the work force by sex, schooling, and work experience consequently influences real average wage levels.

The influence of potential work experience on wages is illustrated in figure 1–1 for both sexes for two broad schooling classes. In addi-

FIGURE 1–2
REAL AVERAGE HOURLY WAGES,
ACTUAL AND FIXED-WEIGHT INDEX, 1973–1988

Hourly wages in 1988 dollars

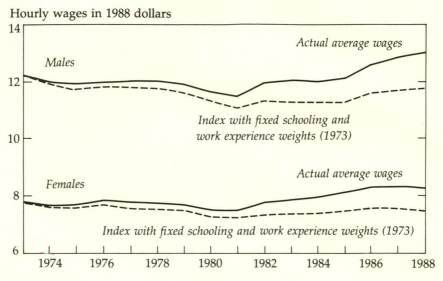

SOURCE: Author's calculations.

tion to the major differences in wages by sex and schooling class, the figure shows the difference in experience profiles between schooling levels. Especially for men, additional work experience contributes more strongly to higher wages for those with more schooling. The difference in the shape of experience profiles is even more pronounced when women are compared with men. Additional potential work experience is associated with much larger increases in wages for men than for women, partly because potential work experience translates more directly into actual work experience for men than for women.[4] Wage-experience profiles for women are very flat after more than about ten years of potential experience. The data charted in figure 1–1, averages for the five years ending in 1988, are intended to illustrate characteristic shapes of wage profiles and differences in wage levels. In view of the marked difference in wage levels and profiles between men and women, trends for men and women are considered separately in most of the subsequent discussion.

Average real hourly wages for males and females are charted in figure 1–2. These data, based on arithmetic means, show the decline in average wages during the 1970s and the subsequent rise during the

5

FIGURE 1–3

MEASURES OF ACTUAL REAL WAGES AND EFFECTS OF
CHANGES IN SCHOOLING AND
WORK EXPERIENCE FOR MALES, RATIOS COMPARED
WITH FIXED-WEIGHT INDEX, 1973–1988

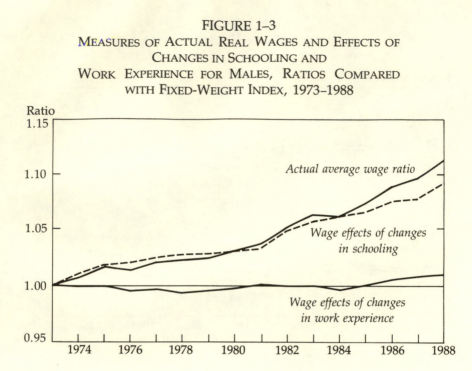

SOURCE: Author's calculations.

1980s. Measures of the trends that real wages would have followed if schooling and work experience patterns had remained unchanged are also charted in the figure. The fixed-weight measures are averages calculated by weighting actual annual real wages earned by workers in each schooling and work experience category by the share of the work force accounted for by each category in 1973. Average real wages, as measured by arithmetic means, rose slightly over the period as a whole. The fixed schooling and work experience measures, however, show an overall decline in real wages, with that decline concentrated in the 1970s.[5] These comparisons illustrate the influence of demographic changes in the work force on wage trends.

To illustrate how changes in schooling and work experience have influenced actual wage trends, figures 1–3 and 1–4 measure their separate effects for males and females, respectively. These wage measures are calculated relative to the level of the fixed-weight index in each year to abstract from changes in real wage levels and focus explicitly on the proportionate contributions of schooling and work experience changes. These charts feature most prominently the con-

6

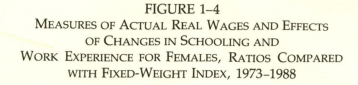

FIGURE 1–4

MEASURES OF ACTUAL REAL WAGES AND EFFECTS
OF CHANGES IN SCHOOLING AND
WORK EXPERIENCE FOR FEMALES, RATIOS COMPARED
WITH FIXED-WEIGHT INDEX, 1973–1988

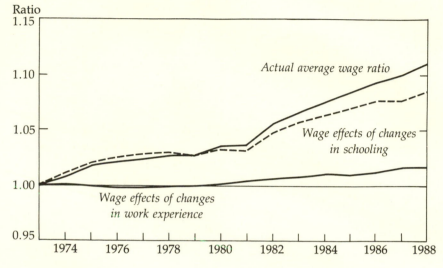

SOURCE: Author's calculations.

tribution made by increases in schooling to actual wage trends. Increased education accounts for most of the divergence between actual
wage trends and the index that holds fixed the schooling and work
experience composition of the labor force.

Changes in the work experience of the labor force produced
different effects on wages in the 1980s from those in the 1970s. The
entry of large numbers of young workers during the 1970s increased
the proportion with little work experience and therefore tended to
produce lower average wages. When the baby-boom contribution to
the labor force began to taper off in the late 1970s and the extraordinarily large numbers of workers who had entered the labor force
earlier accumulated more potential work experience, the earlier effect
that produced lower average wages was reversed. This shift in the
influence of work experience began in the late 1970s, with positive
effects for both men and women by the mid-1980s.

The effects on wages of increased schooling were large because
the increase in schooling levels was substantial and wage differences
derived from more schooling are quite large. From 1973 to 1988 the
fraction of the work force with less than twelve years of schooling

7

declined by about thirteen percentage points for both males and females. The fraction with sixteen years of school or more increased by over seven percentage points for both. The fraction with thirteen to fifteen years of schooling also rose, more for females than for males, while the fraction with a high school education remained roughly unchanged for males and declined slightly for females.

The effects of schooling and work experience separately do not completely account for the difference between the wage index defined by fixed labor force composition and the actual wage trend because of such factors as the interaction between schooling and work experience. So that the effects of schooling could be isolated, for example, they were calculated by keeping work experience distributions within each schooling class fixed at their 1973 pattern for the entire period. As a consequence, the implied work experience distribution for the work force as a whole changes when shifts among schooling classes take place. Likewise, so that the effects of work experience can be isolated, the distribution of schooling within each work experience category was fixed, which permits change in the implied schooling composition of the work force. In addition to these compositional shifts, both the indexes and the actual wage trends are influenced by shifts in relative wages because these relative wage changes are correlated with compositional shifts.

Schooling and Wages

Among the demographic characteristics that influence earning capability, education makes the most systematic and quantitatively important contribution. More education, as measured by years of schooling completed, produces higher wages and earnings for the work force as a whole and within age, sex, and race categories. One of the most remarkable features of wage behavior in the 1980s is the sharp rise in the wage premium paid for workers with higher levels of schooling and thus in the economic return to additional schooling.

Trends in wages by years of schooling are shown in figures 1–5 and 1–6 for males and females, respectively. The rise in the wage premium is shown by the widening gaps between wages at different schooling levels during the 1980s. The measures charted in the figures are arithmetic averages of real wages for each schooling category in each year, relative to the general average for the sixteen-year period. The figures show that the rise in wage premiums for schooling in the 1980s is accounted for by both a decline in real wages for those with a high school education or less and an increase in real wages for those with a college education or more. Real wages of males with a high

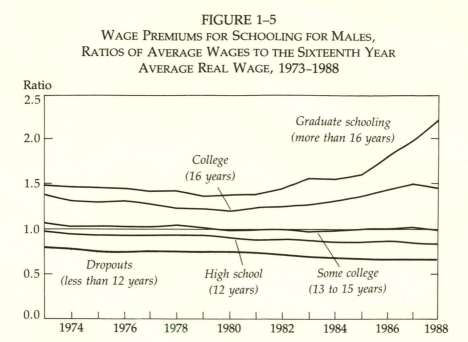

FIGURE 1–5
WAGE PREMIUMS FOR SCHOOLING FOR MALES,
RATIOS OF AVERAGE WAGES TO THE SIXTEENTH YEAR
AVERAGE REAL WAGE, 1973–1988

Ratio

*Graduate schooling
(more than 16 years)*

*College
(16 years)*

*Dropouts
(less than 12 years)*

*High school
(12 years)*

*Some college
(13 to 15 years)*

SOURCE: Author's calculations.

school diploma, for example, declined by 6 percent from 1980 to 1988, but for college graduates wages rose by 20 percent.

The pattern of real wage changes underlying the rise in returns to schooling was somewhat different for males and females. For males, real wages below the college level declined during the period as a whole, although real wages for males with some college stabilized in the 1980s. For females, only high school dropouts experienced a decline in real wages. Thus, while declining real wages for workers with little schooling were a factor at work, especially for males, rising real wages for workers completing college or additional schooling were also important.

The rise in returns to schooling can also be characterized partly as a recovery from an earlier decline in returns to schooling. This is especially apparent for women with both college and graduate schooling, but it is also apparent for men who completed college. Wage premiums for schooling rose during the 1980s, however, to levels that greatly exceeded earlier patterns.

Trends in apparent returns to schooling for dropouts and workers with some college and for those with graduate schooling may be

FIGURE 1–6
Wage Premiums for Schooling for Females, Ratios of Average Wages to the Sixteenth Year Average Real Wage, 1973–1988

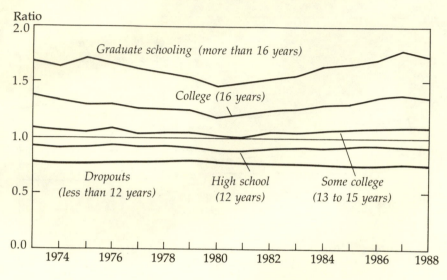

SOURCE: Author's calculations.

affected to some extent by changes in average years of schooling within these broad categories. It is therefore useful to examine the schooling categories for those who completed high school and for those who completed college. The change in the wage premium between these two classes also accounts for much of the change in the spread of wages between all schooling classes.

Table 1–2 shows the size of wage premiums for college relative to high school and changes in premiums over time. Two measures of the wage premiums are presented there, based on arithmetic and geometric means. The measures show important differences for males, especially during the 1980s. Despite the differences in magnitudes, all the measures show a remarkable rise in the college wage premium during the 1980s.

Men who completed college earned wages 43 percent higher than those who completed high school in 1973 (based on arithmetic means). After declining to about 35 percent by 1978, the wage premium more than doubled during the next ten years. During the 1980s

10

TABLE 1–2
College/High School Average Wage Ratios and Changes in Wage Premiums, Selected Periods, 1973–1988

	Arithmetic Means		Geometric Means	
	Males	Females	Males	Females
College/high school average wage ratio				
1973	1.43	1.48	1.37	1.45
1978	1.35	1.35	1.31	1.35
1980	1.39	1.34	1.32	1.32
1983	1.48	1.38	1.40	1.37
1988	1.78	1.51	1.61	1.49
Change in college and high school wage premiums[a]				
1973–78	−7.6	−12.0	−6.8	−10.1
1978–83	12.2	2.9	9.3	1.6
1983–88	30.2	12.3	21.2	12.5
1973–80	−4.3	−14.0	−5.3	−13.0
1980–88	39.1	17.2	28.9	17.1
1973–88	34.8	3.2	23.7	4.1

Note: See note for table 1–1 for explanation of how measures of average wages were calculated. College and high school level workers are workers with sixteen and twelve years of schooling, respectively, and wages for each schooling class are averages across all experience classes. The ratios in the top panel of the table can be read as one plus the percentage wage premium, from which the changes in the premium in the lower panel are calculated.
a. Percentage point change.
Source: Author's calculations.

alone, the wage premium for college rose thirty-eight percentage points according to arithmetic means, and even the geometric means showed a twenty-nine-point rise. The levels of both wage premium measures, 78 and 61 percent, respectively, show unusually large economic returns to college education for males.

The wage premium measures for females were roughly comparable in size to those for males for most of the period, although they fell somewhat more in the first part of the period and rose somewhat less during the 1980s than those for males. According to both measures, the wage premium for college for females rose about seventeen percentage points during the 1980s. Comparisons of these measures suggest that the rise in relative wages of college graduates was accompanied by a greater increase in the proportion of males in the upper part of the distribution than of females.

The measures of returns to schooling reported in table 1–2 are based on averages across all experience categories at each level of education. They consequently reflect changes in experience composition within each schooling category. In addition, they do not take into account changes in the shape of wage profiles across experience categories. In view of the very substantial changes in returns to schooling that occurred, it seems reasonable to expect that relative wage changes might be more pronounced for young workers than for older, more mature workers.

Measures of returns to schooling similar to those for the averages reported in table 1–2 are shown for workers with ten years of potential work experience in table 1–3. These measures for relatively young workers show a much larger swing in returns to schooling for males and a somewhat larger swing for females than those for the work force as a whole. The college wage premium for males with ten years of potential work experience rose fifty-five percentage points by 1988, for example, from its 1980 level of 31 percent, according to arithmetic mean measures. Measures based on geometric means, however, also indicate that returns almost doubled during the 1980s. For females, the rise in the wage premium for college was also somewhat larger for young workers than for older workers. These data not only show that returns to college rose enormously during the 1980s but also suggest that there has been a systematic relationship between changes in returns to schooling and changes in the experience profiles.

To place the size of the change in the wage premium for college in perspective, we should consider how it translates into a rate of return. A simple, shorthand computation of a rate of return to college based only on earnings forgone can be obtained by dividing percentage premiums by four. According to such calculations, implied rates of return to schooling rose during the 1980s from about 8 percent to 20 percent for men and from slightly less than 10 percent to 15 percent for women. These dramatic increases in cross-sectional rates of return for young workers make college an extraordinarily attractive investment.

Work Experience and Wages

Important changes have also occurred in the wage premium for additional work experience, particularly for males but also for females with less than sixteen years of schooling. To illustrate trends in re-

TABLE 1–3

COLLEGE/HIGH SCHOOL AVERAGE WAGE RATIOS FOR WORKERS WITH
TEN YEARS OF WORK EXPERIENCE AND CHANGES IN WAGE PREMIUMS,
SELECTED PERIODS, 1973–1988

	Arithmetic Means		Geometric Means	
	Males	Females	Males	Females
College/high school average wage ratio				
1973	1.49	1.49	1.44	1.51
1978	1.36	1.38	1.34	1.41
1980	1.31	1.37	1.35	1.38
1983	1.44	1.46	1.49	1.47
1988	1.86	1.59	1.69	1.61
Change in college/high school wage premiums[a]				
1973–78	−13.0	−10.7	−9.7	−9.9
1978–83	8.8	7.7	11.0	5.8
1983–88	41.5	13.4	23.9	14.7
1973–80	−17.6	−11.6	−8.5	−12.8
1980–88	54.9	22.0	33.7	23.4
1973–88	37.3	10.4	25.2	10.6

NOTE: The arithmetic means for workers with ten years of potential work experience were calculated as a weighted average of wages of workers with six to ten and those with eleven to fifteen years of work experience. Geometric means are the antilogs of the logarithms of wages predicted by separate logarithmic regressions for each year and schooling class with the equations evaluated at ten years of potential work experience.
a. Percentage point change.
SOURCE: Author's calculations.

turns to work experience, ratios of average wages of workers with six to ten years of work experience relative to wages of workers with twenty-one to thirty years of potential work experience were computed for high school and college graduates for males and females separately. These work experience categories permit comparisons of wages of younger workers with wages of mature workers whose earnings have reached a plateau close to their peak. Measured wage profiles are quite steep during the first few years of work experience, partly because workers typically make major investments by learning through work experience in their initial working years and partly perhaps because job changes after the initial entry into the work force

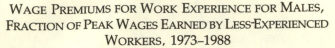

FIGURE 1–7
WAGE PREMIUMS FOR WORK EXPERIENCE FOR MALES,
FRACTION OF PEAK WAGES EARNED BY LESS-EXPERIENCED
WORKERS, 1973–1988

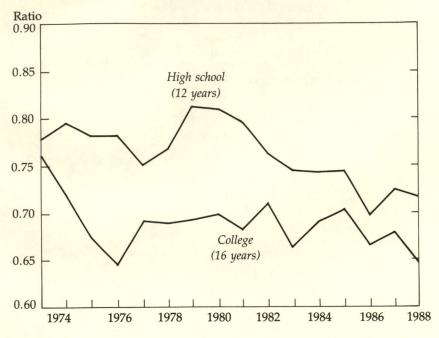

NOTE: Wages of workers with twenty-one to thirty years of potential work experience were used as an estimate of peak wages; less-experienced workers were those with six to ten years of experience.
SOURCE: Author's calculations.

are quite frequent as workers find jobs that interest them and best suit them. Wages of workers with six to ten years of work experience were compared with those of mature workers to examine wage profiles over a period beginning after initial entry and extending to near-peak earning years.

The data for males, charted in figure 1–7, show quite substantial wage premiums for additional work experience. Wages of workers with six to ten years of experience are 70 to 80 percent of the level they reach fifteen to twenty years later for workers with a high school education and generally less than 70 percent for workers with a college degree. Workers with a high school education experienced a downtrend during the 1980s in the fraction of peak wages that young workers receive. Relative wages of male high school graduates de-

FIGURE 1-8
Wage Premiums for Work Experience for Females, Fraction of Peak Wages Earned by Less-Experienced Workers, 1973-1988

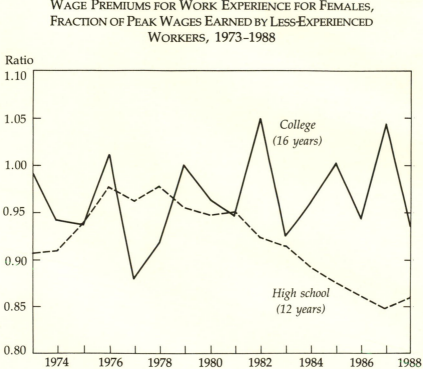

NOTE: Wages of workers with twenty-one to thirty years of potential work experience were used as an estimate of peak wages; less-experienced workers were those with six to ten years of experience.
SOURCE: Author's calculations.

clined during the 1980s, and their relative abundance apparently produced more downward pressure on wages of younger workers than on those of workers with more experience. After a decline in the mid-1970s, the fraction of peak wages that young workers were paid was relatively stable for college graduates. The difference in the trend for young workers with a college degree during the 1980s is consistent with the upturn in the wage premium for college. In view of the dramatic increase in the wage premium for college, however, it is surprising that the wages of relatively young college graduates were not bid up relative to wages of more mature college graduates.

Experience profiles for females (shown in figure 1-8) differ considerably from those for males. In the first place, wage premiums for additional work experience are much smaller than for males (as is clear in figure 1–1). In addition, in contrast to males, wage profiles as work experience is accumulated are steeper for female high school graduates than for those with college degrees, especially in the 1980s. In a comparison of work experience profiles of males and females, it is important to recognize, however, that actual work experience generally conforms much more closely to potential work experience for males than for females. Because females' work lives are often interrupted, their actual work experience generally falls far short of potential experience. Rising participation in the labor force over the years and recent shifts in the occupations chosen by women suggest that the wage profiles of young women now entering the work force may be quite different from those presented here.

Like the experience profiles of males in the 1980s, profiles for females indicate a growing wage premium for increased work experience for those with a high school education. This pattern is consistent with downward pressures on the wages of young high school graduates felt by both males and females in response to the relative scarcity of workers with more schooling. For women with college degrees, however, these cross-sectional data show very little premium for work experience and virtually no trend over the years.

Schooling Quality

The decline in the wage premium for college during the 1970s and its subsequent rise in the 1980s could have resulted from changes in the relative quality of high school and college schooling. If the growing public concern during the 1980s about the quality of elementary and high school education developed in response to actual deterioration, for example, the rising wage premium for college could be simply a consequence of such deterioration. Another possibility is that, given the growing fraction of young people completing at least some college, those completing only high school or less might not be as able as earlier generations of students.[6]

Without quality measures, it is impossible to analyze directly whether changes in the quality of education over time might have contributed to changes in wage premiums for additional schooling. The data might give some insight into the probable contribution of schooling quality to changes in the wage premium, however. Because differences in work experience correspond to differences in the time when schooling was acquired, "vintage" effects may be important, or changes in the wage premium may mainly reflect contemporary labor market forces, irrespective of when schooling was acquired.[7]

The sixteen years of data grouped into five-year experience intervals provide a convenient basis for following cohorts of workers over time, examining changes in wage premiums, and comparing these changes with those for workers with fixed years of work experience. Such comparisons can provide evidence only on the relative quality of college and high school as reflected in the valuation placed on schooling in the labor market, of course, and not on high school or college quality separately. In addition, even if college schooling quality had not changed, such comparisons could provide only crude evidence on possible changes in high school quality.

The data on relative wages are, first of all, estimates subject to considerable statistical "noise." In addition, the slopes of wage-experience profiles can be expected to change as work experience increases, and the slopes of wage-experience profiles for high school and college graduates are somewhat different. Moreover, if younger workers experience changes in relative wages more quickly or strongly, then changes in experience profiles will not be independent of changes in wage premiums for schooling.

Despite these reasons why only rough comparisons are possible, the data can suggest whether changes in college/high school wage premiums seem to be affected primarily by contemporaneous labor market forces or instead whether changes in the quality of schooling might be at work. For each cohort of workers who received their schooling at about the same time, wages can be examined to see how their schooling wage premium changes over time. For workers with a particular length of work experience who received their schooling at different times, the behavior of their schooling wage premium can also be calculated for comparison with changes for workers from fixed schooling cohorts. Data on changes in wage premiums are reported in tables 1–4 and 1–5 for males and females, respectively.

Two somewhat different kinds of comparisons can be considered. First, comparisons of the signs and magnitudes of changes can be made among the three columns of the tables. Changes within each column that are more closely comparable than changes in the data between columns constitute evidence that contemporaneous labor market forces, influencing college wage premiums across vintage and experience classes, are more important than differences between demographic cohorts. Pairwise comparisons of changes in wage premiums for a cohort followed over time with corresponding changes for workers in a given experience class provide a second, somewhat different perspective. The information that such pairwise comparisons can reveal is limited, however, because differences can arise from sources other than vintage effects and the data are too variable to inspire much confidence in the significance of differences.

TABLE 1–4

Changes in Male College/High School Wage Premiums, Selected Schooling Cohorts and Work Experience Categories, 1973–1988

Cohort by Years When Schooling Was Completed (by years of work experience)	Change in College/High School Wage Premiums		
	1973–78	1978–83	1983–88
Schooling completed 1948–52	−1.7	3.7	31.2
(21–25 years' experience)	−7.5	12.2	40.9
Schooling completed 1953–57	−13.0	13.1	12.5
(16–20 years' experience)	−29.0	22.3	15.4
Schooling completed 1958–62	−24.8	28.2	57.6
(11–15 years' experience)	−10.6	0.7	38.8
Schooling completed 1963–67	−0.4	8.1	46.8
(6–10 years' experience)	−12.8	10.0	45.2
Schooling completed 1968–72	−0.8	13.1	22.8
(1–5 years' experience)	−1.1	22.2	20.7
Schooling completed 1973–77	—	10.3	41.9
(1–5 years' experience)	—	22.2	20.7
Schooling completed 1978–82	—	—	33.3
(1–5 years' experience)	—	—	20.7
Average across all experience classes	−4.8	6.0	32.2

NOTE: Wage premiums are computed as the ratio of the arithmetic mean college wage to the high school mean wage. College and high school graduates are workers with sixteen and twelve years of schooling, respectively. Changes in the wage premiums are percentage point changes.
SOURCE: Author's calculations.

The general pattern for comparisons between columns is fairly clear, especially for males. For males wage premiums for college decline for all measures from 1973 to 1978, and they rise strongly from 1983 to 1988. From 1978 to 1983, wage premiums rise modestly, although with considerable variability in the magnitudes. For females, wage premiums for college also declined across the board from 1973 to 1978. Their wage premiums generally rise from 1983 to 1988, particularly for younger workers, and the pattern for 1978 to 1983 is very mixed. The conclusion I draw from these comparisons is

TABLE 1–5

CHANGES IN FEMALE COLLEGE/HIGH SCHOOL WAGE PREMIUMS,
SELECTED SCHOOLING COHORTS AND WORK EXPERIENCE CATEGORIES,
1973–1988

Cohort by Years When Schooling Was Completed (by years of work experience)	Change in College/High School Wage Premiums		
	1973–78	1978–83	1983–88
Schooling completed 1948–52	− 25.2	− 21.0	1.0
(21–25 years' experience)	− 31.4	2.1	10.2
Schooling completed 1953–57	− 15.1	0.4	9.5
(16–20 years' experience)	− 12.1	− 4.7	21.0
Schooling completed 1958–62	− 11.5	− 0.9	− 4.3
(11–15 years' experience)	− 12.6	6.3	8.9
Schooling completed 1963–67	− 1.0	− 3.5	14.0
(6–10 years' experience)	− 8.3	8.0	16.6
Schooling completed 1968–72	− 19.2	13.5	11.2
(1–5 years' experience)	− 12.6	16.2	14.3
Schooling completed 1973–77	—	1.4	14.4
(1–5 years' experience)	—	16.2	14.3
Schooling completed 1978–82	—	—	1.8
(1–5 years' experience)	—	—	14.3
Average across all experience classes	− 14.0	− 0.5	11.1

NOTE: See note for table 1–4 for explanation of wage premium calculations.
SOURCE: Author's calculations.

that contemporaneous forces, with effects felt across cohorts and experience classes, were the dominant influences raising wage premiums for college during the 1980s.

Pairwise comparisons are of some interest even though they are quite inconclusive. The somewhat smaller increases in the college wage premium for males from 1983 to 1988 for the two oldest cohorts than for workers with fixed experience, for example, probably reflect the tendency for wages of college graduates to decline more steeply after their peak earning years. For the youngest groups of workers, in contrast, cohorts are moving up experience profiles that are steeper for workers with college, at the same time as the experience profile for high school graduates is steepening (as shown in figure 1–7). These effects are almost certainly more important than any likely vintage effects.

For women pairwise comparisons generally show smaller increases from 1983 to 1988 in college wage premiums for cohorts than for workers in given experience categories. This is particularly noticeable for the three oldest vintage categories and for the youngest. One possible reason for this pattern is that actual work experience for women increasingly falls short of potential work experience as cohorts are followed over time. Perhaps a more likely explanation, however, is that more recent entrants with college education have acquired training and entered occupations that pay higher wages and that are more similar to those for males. This explanation also accords with the substantial increase in college wage premiums of younger women during the 1980s. If this explanation is correct, it reflects a particular type of increase in relative schooling quality, one that involves a change in the mixture of college training and not necessarily an increase in the quality of specific kinds of college training.

The most reasonable interpretation of these data, I believe, is that changes in wage premiums do not mainly reflect changes in schooling quality. Although the evidence for females suggests that some sort of change in schooling characteristics has been at work, we can be skeptical about whether changes in relative schooling quality are responsible. The data on women do not appear to support claims of a declining quality of high school education, for example, because real wages of workers completing high school have held up better for women than for men. For men, the real wages of high school graduates have declined substantially, and wage premiums have widened more than for women; little evidence thus supports claims of diminished quality of schooling over time. The evidence on changes in the quality of schooling is subject to important qualifications, but the comparisons provide little support for the idea that changing quality of schooling has contributed importantly to changes in college wage premiums. Although changes in relative schooling quality may have occurred, contemporaneous labor market influences on wage premiums for college were the dominant forces during the 1980s.[8]

Schooling and Relative Labor Supply

Years of schooling of the work force have risen over the years, a trend continuing during the 1980s. As a greater proportion of workers has acquired more schooling, the demand for workers with more education has risen. As new entrants with more schooling than those

TABLE 1–6

PROPORTION OF WORK FORCE BY YEARS OF SCHOOLING, SELECTED
PERIODS, 1973–1988

	Years of Schooling for Males		Years of Schooling for Females	
	12 or less	16 or more	12 or less	16 or more
Proportion of Work Force (percent)				
1973	68.2	17.2	73.1	14.1
1978	61.7	21.0	66.9	16.6
1980	60.5	21.3	65.2	16.5
1983	57.3	24.1	61.1	19.4
1988	56.0	24.9	56.5	21.5
Change in Proportion of Work Force (percentage points)				
1973–78	−6.5	3.8	−6.2	2.5
1978–83	−4.4	3.0	−5.8	2.8
1983–88	−1.3	0.8	−4.6	2.1
1973–80	−7.7	4.1	−7.9	2.4
1980–88	−4.5	3.6	−8.7	5.0
1973–88	−12.2	7.7	−16.6	7.4

NOTE: Proportions of the work force with twelve or less years of schooling
and with sixteen or more years of schooling are computed as the ratio of the
number of workers in each of the two broad schooling classes to the total
work force in each year.
SOURCE: Author's calculations.

already there poured into the work force during the 1970s, however,
raising schooling levels sharply, returns to schooling declined. The
subsequent rise in returns to schooling during the 1980s may be
attributable partly to a slowdown in the rise of schooling levels for the
work force as a whole.

As shown by the data in table 1–6, the rise in schooling levels for
men slowed during the 1980s, although the rate of improvement for
women was evidently little changed. These data divide the work
force, taking men and women separately, into two broad schooling
categories—workers with twelve or less years of schooling and those
with sixteen or more. Workers with some college are excluded, and
while this group accounts for a rising share of the work force for both
males and females, the increase is somewhat larger for females.

The proportion of the male work force with twelve or less years schooling has declined, but by progressively smaller amounts. The share of the work force they account for fell by 6.5 percentage points during the first five-year period, for example, by 4.4 percentage points during the middle period, and by 1.3 percentage points during the last five-year period. Correspondingly, the proportion with sixteen or more years of schooling has also increased by somewhat smaller increments, especially during the 1980s—by 3.8, 3.0, and 0.8 percentage points for the three five-year periods. For women, the proportion with twelve or less years of schooling declined at a slightly slower pace during the sixteen-year period, but the proportion with sixteen years of schooling or more increased more rapidly in the latter part of the period. This difference in the pace at which schooling levels were upgraded for men and women corresponds to the wider swing in wage premiums for additional schooling that men have experienced during the 1970s and 1980s.[9]

Changes in the educational attainment of the work force as a whole are, of course, influenced both by the schooling levels of recent entrants and of workers withdrawing from the work force. To determine trends in years of schooling for workers entering the work force and for those departing, I compared data on educational attainment of recent entrants into the work force with data for those near retirement. To characterize recent entrants, I chose those with six to ten years of work experience, and to characterize those near retirement, I chose those with thirty-six to forty years of work experience. I then analyzed changes over time in the proportions with high and low schooling levels.

These measures are most appropriately regarded as indicators of trends in schooling levels for recent entrants and prospective retirees, since they are not direct measures for workers actually entering or retiring. Even if we abstract from temporary withdrawal and reentry into the work force during normal working years, which is particularly important for women, structuring an analysis to measure precisely the schooling levels of additions to and departures from the work force is difficult. Young workers entering the labor force, for example, often combine work with schooling, and sometimes they temporarily interrupt schooling to take a job. For these reasons, I used six to ten years of work experience (instead of one to five years) to obtain a more reliable indicator of schooling levels likely to be relevant for most of these young people's working lives.

Older workers, in contrast, do not uniformly work until they reach a given age, or a specific number of years of experience, and then retire. For older workers I chose thirty-six to forty years of work experience, which for college graduates extends to sixty-three years old. Workers with twelve or less years of schooling are some five years younger at this level of potential work experience. Age at retirement has been declining over the years, and measures of proportions at different levels of schooling could be affected by this trend, particularly if the trend has been systematically different between workers with more or less schooling.[10]

Workers near the beginning and the end of their working lives, represented by these different levels of work experience, will be referred to for brevity as entering and retiring workers. In table 1–7, averages over selected subperiods of proportions of these cohorts with high and low schooling levels are reported. Differences in these averages can be viewed as changes in rates at which workers with different levels of schooling flow into and out of the work force.

The trend toward higher schooling for entering male workers stabilized during the late 1970s, as shown in table 1–7. The average proportion of entering male workers with twelve or less years of schooling was actually slightly higher in the 1980s than during the 1970s, with no further increase in the share with sixteen or more years. This contrasts sharply with the pattern for women. Although the rate at which schooling levels were upgraded for entering female workers apparently slackened in the 1980s, the proportion of women with low schooling was smaller in the 1980s than in the 1970s, and the proportion with college or more schooling was larger.

The declining rates of improvement in schooling levels of entering cohorts need to be compared with rates for workers near retirement to assess the net impact. The schooling composition of retiring workers can be viewed as influencing the demand for replacement of workers with different levels of schooling. Changes in proportions of the work force with high and low schooling levels are larger for retiring workers than for entering workers. For retiring male workers, for example, the fraction with twelve or less years of schooling was more than ten percentage points lower in the 1980s than in the 1970s, and most of the decline took place during the late 1970s. The average share with college level schooling correspondingly rose by almost eight percentage points. In other words, replacement demands rose sharply for college graduates while declining for dropouts and high school graduates. This shift in replacement demands for men, which reflects rapidly rising schooling levels some forty years earlier, came at a time when schooling levels of entry-level male workers were no longer advancing.[11]

The shift in replacement demands for women was much smaller but in the same direction as that for men. The net effect of small advances in schooling for young women and a small shift in replace

TABLE 1–7

Proportion of Entering and Retiring Workers by Years of Schooling, Selected Periods, 1973–1988

	Years of Schooling for Males		Years of Schooling for Females	
	12 or less	16 or more	12 or less	16 or more
Entering Workers [a]				
Average proportion of entering workers (percent)				
1973–78	53.3	25.8	61.6	19.5
1979–83	51.4	27.4	53.3	23.6
1984–88	54.3	26.1	50.5	25.9
1973–80	52.4	26.3	59.5	20.3
1981–88	53.6	26.4	51.5	25.2
Change in proportion of entering workers (percentage points)				
1973–78 to 1974–83	−2.0	1.6	−8.3	4.1
1974–83 to 1984–88	2.9	−1.3	−2.8	2.3
1973–80 to 1981–88	1.2	0.1	−8.0	4.9
Retiring Workers [b]				
Average proportion of retiring workers (percent)				
1973–78	81.7	8.2	81.9	8.3
1979–83	72.8	13.1	79.7	7.5
1984–88	68.5	18.2	77.1	9.5
1973–80	80.0	8.9	81.7	7.7
1981–88	69.6	16.7	77.8	9.1
Change in proportion of retiring workers (percentage points)				
1973–78 to 1974–83	−8.9	4.9	−2.2	−0.8
1974–83 to 1984–88	−4.3	5.1	−2.7	2.1
1973–80 to 1981–88	−10.4	7.8	−3.8	1.4

NOTE: Proportions of workers in each school-experience category are defined as the number of workers in each category divided by the total number of workers for each year.
a. Workers with six to ten years of work experience.
b. Workers with thirty-six to forty years of work experience.
SOURCE: Author's calculations.

ment demand for more educated women is consistent with weaker pressures for increased returns to schooling for women than for men.

This discussion presumes a significant degree of segmentation of the labor market between men and women. Differences between men and women in the size of increases in wage premiums during the 1980s and the wider swing in returns to schooling for males, at a time when males had slowed the upgrading of their schooling levels, are consistent with substantial segmentation. Although distributions of occupational training and choice for men and women have converged a great deal, they still remain substantially different. Thus, it is reasonable to expect some degree of segmentation.

My comparisons of the schooling composition of entering and retiring components of the work force do not take into account the fact that young workers were entering in substantially larger numbers than older workers were retiring. With the rapid expansion of the work force during the past twenty years, young workers were more than twice as numerous as older workers near retirement. As a consequence, the proportion of all workers with a college education continued to rise during the 1980s.

The relative supply of workers with advanced schooling has increased over the years, but the education level of the work force has been upgraded at an uneven pace, with a slowdown beginning in the 1980s. Throughout the past twenty years, as the work force grew rapidly, the schooling level of new entrants was much higher than that of retiring workers. Conditions began changing during the 1980s, however, in three important ways. First, the rate of growth began to taper off as fewer young workers entered a work force that had grown much larger during the 1970s. Second, the schooling composition of new entrants to the work force stabilized, and for males the proportion with a high school education or less even rose slightly. Third, replacement demands for workers with more education began rising because schooling levels of retiring workers were higher. The resulting shift to slower growth in the relative supply of workers with advanced schooling would lead to rising schooling wage premiums unless growth in demand for workers with more schooling also slowed down.

In their extraordinarily systematic and detailed analysis of trends in the age and schooling composition of the work force and in wages, Kevin Murphy and Finis Welch conclude that changes in wage patterns observed in the 1980s cannot be explained by changes in relative supply alone.[12] Thus, changes in demand must also have influenced wage patterns. They analyze the rise in the trade deficit in the 1980s a a possible source of demand change by tracing its differential imp on industries. The evidence they present shows a pattern of implied wage effects on workers in different demographic categories broadly consistent with observed changes in relative wages. John Bound and George Johnson also see international trade as a source of demand change, and they interpret a reduction in blue-collar employment in manufacturing as evidence that production operations were shifted abroad.[13]

Changes in the industry production mixture in the 1980s were accompanied by strong pressures for modernizing production operations. Sources of these pressures included strong competition from international trade and deregulation. Partly because of the higher educational attainment of workers with management responsibilities in the 1980s, they were more likely than their predecessors to respond to these pressures by introducing the dramatically new technology that was available and to make the requisite adjustments in numbers and schooling qualifications of their workers. In 1970, for example, about 25 percent of those in the broad executive, administrative, and managerial occupational categories had four years of college or more. By 1980 the fraction had risen to 40 percent. Both the sophistication of the new production arrangements they developed and the educational qualifications of workers needed to operate them were presumably influenced by the upgraded schooling levels of managerial personnel.

Conclusions

The remarkable increase in wage premiums for schooling in the United States during the 1980s occurred when strong competition from international sources and global links between markets were becoming more apparent. Evidence from several studies suggests that these conditions contributed to a realignment of relative wages in response to worldwide competitive forces. These more competitive conditions seem likely to persist despite possible protectionist policies to contain them, and they can be expected to contribute to maintaining high economic returns to schooling. Even if, for example, growth patterns in industry employment shift in response to restoration of more balanced trade, demands for skills in the industries affected are unlikely to return to earlier levels. Future wage levels and patterns in the U.S. labor market will likely depend more strongly than in the past on the productive capabilities of U.S. workers in a competitive global marketplace.

The pattern of demographic changes in the work force during the ⸱st twenty years *is* broadly consistent with strong demand for improved skills and increased schooling. The extraordinarily large influx of relatively well-educated workers during the 1970s was accompanied by only a small decline in returns to schooling, while the slowdown in the rate at which schooling levels were upgraded during the 1980s produced a pronounced rise in wage premiums for schooling. These trends are consistent with a strong capacity in the economy for making productive use of workers with more schooling and improved skills.

Years of schooling completed can measure only crudely the knowledge and skills acquired. Improving the productivity of schooling can contribute a great deal to raising educational achievement and raising the productive capacity of workers with given levels of schooling. Although most analyses have necessarily been carried out by examining economic rewards for more years of schooling, improving the quality of schooling may be at least as important.

The changes in relative wages occurring when wages generally were stagnant meant that the economic circumstances of workers in some demographic groups improved while others fell behind. The fact that economic circumstances deteriorated for workers with relatively low schooling, who suffered real wage losses, is extremely unfortunate. But it was the inevitable consequence of relative wage adjustments when productivity growth was slow. The most constructive response to these conditions from the point of view of the economy as a whole is to pursue policies that might foster more rapid productivity growth and not to attempt to prevent or reverse the relative wage adjustments directly.

We can reasonably expect the market to adapt in various ways to the relative wage changes that have occurred. If high economic returns to schooling are expected to persist, they will stimulate acquisition of more schooling by young people for whom such investments are most valuable. These incentives produced by the rise in wage premiums for schooling should therefore be viewed as constructive. The decline in real wages of workers with less schooling, in contrast, makes hiring these workers more attractive to employers. The lower wage costs encourage employers to explore ways to structure their production processes to employ workers with less schooling, often after training them if prospects for retaining them are sufficiently favorable to enable employers to recoup such investments. Cross-sectional age-earnings profiles for workers with high school or less have steepened during the 1980s, but whether these workers will move along such steeper profiles or whether instead they will realize more sluggish wage gains will depend on the extent to which they acquire valuable training and skills as a part of their work experience

A variety of policies could be considered to encourage the market to adapt more quickly to changing relative wages and skill demands. To improve employers' incentives to hire and train workers with low schooling levels, for example, management tools such as gradual and delayed vesting of employer contributions to pension plans to encourage retention of workers and thus stimulate more employer training could receive more emphasis. So that young people who would benefit from such investment could acquire a college education, greater efforts could be made to ensure the availability of loans to support additional schooling. To improve incentives for educational achievement while students are in school, it would be constructive to explore acceptable ways of restructuring employment testing to emphasize general educational achievement over the capacity to fill particular, often entry-level, jobs. To make effective use of the skills of older, retired workers, incentives for them to continue working could be improved by removing the implicit tax that arises from the social security retirement test, which is particularly important for those with valuable skills and high earnings. Policy changes along these lines would help to supplement market forces already at work, make more effective use of available labor resources, increase the supply of workers with greater educational achievement and more schooling, and improve the earnings prospects of workers with little education and poorly developed skills.

Appendix—The Data

The data on wages in this chapter were obtained from Current Population Survey tapes for 1973 through 1988. For 1973 through 1978 the data are from the May surveys, and averages from the April, May, and June monthly surveys were used for 1979 through 1988. The wage data are measures of hourly earnings based on data reported for the week preceding the survey. The sample includes only people whose major activity is work (thus excluding those whose primary activity is school) and workers for whom information on usual hourly earnings or on usual hours of work and weekly earnings is available. The size of the annual samples ranges from about 52,000 to 62,000 observations.

Estimates of hourly wages were constructed for five schooling classes as follows: less than twelve years, twelve years, thirteen to fifteen years, sixteen years, and more than sixteen years. Measures of potential work experience were constructed by subtracting from reported age the number of years of reported schooling plus six. Five-

TABLE A–1
PROCEDURE FOR ESTIMATING POTENTIAL WORK EXPERIENCE BASED ON YEARS OF AGE AND SCHOOLING OF WORKERS

Years of Potential Work Experience	Less than 12 Years	12 Years	13–15 Years	16 Years	More than 16 Years
1 to 5 yrs.	18–22	19–23	21–25	23–27	24–28
6 to 10 yrs.	23–27	24–28	26–30	28–32	29–33
•	•				•
•					•
41 to 45 yrs.	58–62	59–63	61–65	63–67	64–68

SOURCE: Author.

year intervals were used to construct nine potential work experience classes.

This approach to calculating potential work experience was employed by Jacob Mincer.[14] Potential work experience categories were defined in relation to age and schooling class as shown in table A–1. The proportion of the work force accounted for by workers in each schooling class is shown for selected years in table A–2.

Estimates of hourly wage rates were constructed for males and females separately for forty-five schooling and work experience combinations for sixteen years. The analysis for the work force was carried out by applying the population weights to the hourly wage estimates derived from the sample.

Measures of average hourly earnings for each worker were obtained as follows. For workers paid by the hour who report usual hourly earnings, this was taken as a measure of their hourly wage. The hourly wage for workers not paid by the hour was computed as the quotient of their weekly earnings and usual hours of work, unless their weekly earnings were at the maximum recorded in the data, the census top-code. This top-code places an upper limit on the amount of weekly earnings reported—$999 per week throughout the period covered here—even though actual weekly earnings may be much higher. Special procedures consequently need to be used to estimate actual weekly earnings in the upper part of the earnings distribution.

For workers not paid by the hour with reported weekly earnings at the census top-code, estimates of weekly earnings were obtained by using Pareto distribution parameters estimated separately by school-

TABLE A–2

SCHOOLING COMPOSITION OF THE WORK FORCE BY SEX, SELECTED
YEARS, 1973–1988

(Percent of work force in each schooling class)

	Less than 12 Years	12 Years	13–15 Years	16 years	More than 16 Years
Males					
1973	29.7	38.6	14.5	9.6	7.6
1978	23.3	38.4	17.2	12.0	9.0
1983	18.7	38.7	18.6	13.6	10.4
1988	16.5	39.5	19.1	14.3	10.6
Females					
1973	24.9	48.2	12.8	9.3	4.8
1978	19.3	47.6	16.5	10.3	6.3
1983	13.8	47.3	19.5	12.0	7.4
1988	11.8	44.7	22.0	13.5	8.0

SOURCE: Author's calculations.

ing class, sex, and year. The resulting estimates of average weekly earnings for workers affected by the top-code were then divided by the average of their weekly hours to obtain an estimate of their average hourly earnings.

Nominal hourly earnings were adjusted for inflation to obtain estimates of real wages by using CPI-U-X1, a measure based on the consumer price index adjusted to take into account the change in measurement of costs of owner-occupied housing introduced in 1983.

A brief discussion of how observations with weekly earnings affected by the top-code were treated here seems worthwhile because various approaches have been used in analyses of earnings trends, and some earnings measures may be sensitive to the treatment of observations affected by top-coding. The Pareto distribution is customarily used to represent the upper tail of the earnings distribution. The mean of that part of the distribution affected by the top-code is estimated as $\alpha/(1-\alpha)$ multiplied by the top-code, where α is the primary parameter describing the Pareto distribution.

One question involves alternative procedures for estimating α; the approach used in this chapter is a modified maximum-likelihood method suggested by Sandra A. West.[15] A second question involves the choice of whether a common estimate of α should be used for different years and demographic groups or whether instead different estimates should be constructed for subgroups with different distributions and among which comparisons are of interest.

In this chapter, separate yearly estimates of α were made for each schooling class for both sexes. This approach has the disadvantage of possibly producing more variability in the estimates of α than if broader groups were used to make the estimates. Constructing separate estimates, however, should help to avoid introducing biases in comparisons between schooling classes that could result from using common estimates when separate estimates would be more appropri-

TABLE A–3

INCIDENCE OF TOP-CODED WEEKLY EARNINGS OBSERVATIONS AND ESTIMATES OF THE PARETO DISTRIBUTION PARAMETER (α), 1973–1988
(percentage of sample observations in schooling category)

	Less than 12 Years	12 Years	13–15 Years	16 Years	More than 16 Years
Proportion with Weekly Earnings at the Census Top-Code by Years of Schooling and Sex					
Men					
1973	0.0	0.1	0.2	0.7	0.9
1978	0.1	0.2	0.7	1.7	3.1
1983	0.3	1.1	2.1	7.6	12.6
1988	1.0	1.9	5.0	16.3	26.4
Women					
1973	0.0	0.0	0.0	0.0	0.3
1978	0.0	0.0	0.0	0.0	0.2
1983	0.1	0.1	0.3	0.4	1.5
1988	0.3	0.3	0.6	2.1	6.4
Estimates of α by Schooling Level and Sex					
Men					
1973	—	3.2	3.1	2.8	3.1
1978	2.6	3.3	2.9	2.8	2.5
1983	2.3	2.9	2.7	2.4	1.9
1988	2.1	2.5	2.1	1.9	1.5
Women					
1973	—	—	—	—	3.3
1978	—	—	—	—	3.7
1983	2.3	3.1	3.4	3.1	3.0
1988	2.0	2.9	3.1	3.0	2.6

SOURCE: Author's calculations.

ate. The rationale for constructing separate estimates is that fractions of workers affected by the top-code differ very substantially over the years and among demographic subgroups of the work force.

Estimates of α constructed from the sample components generally range between 1.5 and 3. The estimates are typically smaller for males than for females, for higher schooling classes, and for more recent years when larger fractions of demographic groups are affected by the top-code. Proportions of totals of sample components affected by the census top-code and estimates of α for selected years are reported in table A–3.

The Payoff to Education in the Labor Market

A Commentary by Gary Burtless

Marvin Kosters's survey of recent wage developments is lucid and illuminating. Briefly, Kosters finds that inflation-adjusted wage rates have shown little trend since 1973—falling through 1981 and then regaining lost ground over the remainder of the 1980s. Women's wages have risen relative to those of men, particularly if we exclude recent trends among the top male earners.

Because women were initially paid less than men, however, and because women's participation in the labor force has risen so much over the past fifteen years, the *general* trend in wages—including the average wage of both men and women—has actually risen more slowly than that of either men or women separately.

Over the past fifteen years the age profile of earnings (or the "potential work experience" profile, as Kosters prefers to call it) has shifted. In particular, the cross-sectional age earnings profile steepened, especially among men, although the trend has also been visible among women with no schooling beyond high school.

The main movement in wages over the past decade and a half, however, has resulted from changes in the return to educational attainment. After a slight decline, the wage premium paid to workers with at least a college degree rose sharply. Figures 1–5 and 1–6 illustrate this vividly—good news indeed for college recruiting officers. Kosters reminds us that the wage pie is not growing: wage earners are just fighting over the size of each slice.

After reading this paper, I felt vindicated in my decision to get a college degree. A male my age who settled for a high school diploma is now earning less than a high school graduate of the same age was earning back in 1972. It is fortunate that not many workers with only a high school diploma will read this chapter, because we might see armed rebellion if word spread that only MBAs, lawyers, and PhDs have enjoyed any significant wage gains over the past fifteen years.

In thinking about reasons for these wage trends, Kosters dismisses one explanation and embraces another. He rejects the idea that quality of education can explain the declining fortunes of high school dropouts and high school graduates. If poor schools explain poor wages, then we should expect that the decline in high school graduates' wages would be concentrated among people who have graduated in the past twenty years or so, when education really deteriorated. Instead, Kosters finds that the relative drop in the earnings of high school graduates is spread across the age spectrum, among those who graduated recently, those who graduated in the distant past (that is, the 1950s), and those who graduated at the peak of American schooling in the 1960s.

A recent conference at Brookings looked at the same question. McKinley Blackburn, David Bloom, and Richard Freeman asked if declining school quality could explain the growing wage premium for college.[1] They found, like Kosters, that the wage gap between high school graduates and college graduates skyrocketed in all age groups. They concluded, however, that the gap widened most among recent high school graduates. Thus, they found some evidence consistent with the proposition that the most recent cohorts have been badly educated. They pointed out, however, that if unskilled workers suffered a loss in wages because of a downturn in demand for their services, then the youngest unskilled workers would probably sustain the largest loss. Older less-educated workers already held jobs when the drop in demand took place. Unlike younger workers, they had benefited from some investment in job-specific skills, making them more difficult for employers to replace. Drawing strong inferences about the quality of schooling from time series data on relative wages is therefore difficult.

Like Blackburn, Bloom, and Freeman, Kosters examines the relative supply of labor in different skill classes. He finds, along with the earlier analysts, that even though the supply of highly educated labor has continued to grow through the 1980s, it grew much more slowly—especially for men—than it did in the 1970s. Table 1–6 presents the general story. Table 1–7 breaks the story into two parts—one about the educational qualifications of workers entering the labor force and the other about the qualifications of retiring workers. Among entering cohorts of men, the proportion of workers with less than a college education has risen slowly, and the proportion of college graduates has held steady or fallen slightly. For women the situation is a little different—average schooling attainment continued to rise in the 1980s, although a bit more slowly than in the 1970s.

The conclusion Kosters draws from this set of facts is convincing.

34

The supply of highly educated workers is growing much more slowly than it did in earlier periods. (Perhaps if he showed trends in schooling attainment over the 1950s and 1960s this point would be even more convincing.) Because the wage premium for college education has exploded, we can infer that the demand for labor has continued a shift toward better-educated and more highly skilled workers. The supply of highly skilled workers more than kept pace with demand through the 1970s, when the wage premium for schooling shrank slightly. But the anemic growth of a highly skilled labor supply in the 1980s led to a sharp rise in the premium for education and skill.

Since this is exactly the conclusion drawn by Blackburn, Bloom, and Freeman, I cannot quarrel with the author's reasoning. But I would like to draw attention to some of the limitations in the data used in the chapter to show how the Kosters's findings are linked to those of other recent analysts who focus on annual earnings rather than on hourly wage rates.

First, Kosters works under a handicap imposed by the unfortunate data processing procedures of the Census Bureau. Weekly earnings reported to the census taker are truncated at $999, amounting to a bit less than $52,000 a year. The effects of the truncation, shown in note 5, mean that a substantial fraction of workers—especially well-educated workers—is top-coded toward the end of the period under analysis. The top-code procedure affects the author's tabulations differentially over time, possibly influencing the conclusions he draws.

By way of comparison, the annual earnings data in the March CPS survey are truncated at $99,999 a year—about twice the weekly earnings truncation point. Among men, only about 1 to 1½ percent earn more than that; among women, less than 1 percent earn more. The effect of earnings truncation is thus much smaller in the case of annual earnings data.

Kosters is forced to infer the distribution of earnings above $999 a week by Pareto extrapolation. The accuracy of this procedure is suspect. Like Kosters, I have used the Pareto distribution to make inferences about the distribution of earnings above the top-coded value. I checked my inferences against reported earnings in an untruncated data source, the Statistics of Income (SOI) file prepared from individual 1040 forms by the Internal Revenue Service. Comparison of the CPS and SOI files shows a close correspondence between the distributions of people with annual earnings from $10,000 to 99,998 per year, although there may be too few people on the March CPS with earnings above $100,000.

In spite of this correspondence, no estimate of the Pareto distribution I was able to obtain using the CPS data yielded an accurate extrapolation of average annual earnings above $99,999 in the SOI data set. I have read the Bureau of Labor Statistics (BLS) report cited by Kosters, and I used the BLS extrapolation method as well as two or three other methods proposed in the literature. I cannot agree with the BLS author that the Pareto distribution yields an accurate prediction of earnings above the top code. I should remind readers, however, that the BLS and Kosters are using the Pareto extrapolation procedure to infer average weekly wages rather than average annual earnings above the top code. Perhaps the extrapolation problem is less severe for weekly wages than for annual earnings. Nonetheless, I am a little skeptical of the author's estimates, particularly for well-educated males.

Second, Kosters may understate the gains made by the well-off. His estimates show us the changing returns to schooling and experience, assuming that weekly hours and employment remain essentially constant. If weekly hours or employment of the college educated have risen in comparison with those of the less well educated, the trends he shows underestimate the gains in earnings and living standards enjoyed by the well-off. Three of the papers at the recent Brookings conference showed that hours and employment gains have indeed taken place.

Let me mention a few statistics. Among twenty-five- to sixty-four-year-old men, the unemployment rate (measured in March of each year) rose between 1973 and 1988. Among men with less than a high school education, unemployment was 4.4 percent in March 1974, 7.4 percent in March 1980, and 9.2 percent in March 1988. Among men with just a high school diploma, the rates were 2.7 percent, 4.7 percent, and 5.4 percent, respectively, in the three years. But among men with at least a college degree, the rates were virtually unchanged over the period: 1.4 percent in 1974, 1.5 percent in 1980, and 1.5 percent in 1988. If we consider employment-to-population ratios, the relative fortunes of the less skilled appear to have deteriorated even faster, because workers with limited education are more likely to be outside of the labor force in a given month than are workers with a college degree.

What do the author's results imply? By focusing on hourly wages, he may understate the decline in earnings and living standards suffered by the less educated. In the May CPS, men who are unemployed or out of the labor force in the reference week are not even represented in the statistics. But many of them are represented in the March data on annual earnings. Indeed, both Robert Moffitt and I, in separate studies, find that part of the rise in the inequality of annual earnings is attributable to the rising inequality in wage rates, as

Kosters finds, but that an important part can also be attributed to the rising correlation between low wage rates and low weekly hours and the rising correlation between low wage rates and low annual weeks at work. People with limited education and skills have not only suffered losses in the purchasing power of their hourly wages but also are now less likely to work full-time hours or fifty-two weeks a year. The rise in the return to schooling may thus be even greater than Kosters suggests.

Kosters appears to accept calmly the sagging fortunes of less-skilled workers—fortunes that were none too healthy in the early 1980s. While he notes that the real earnings losses suffered by the less skilled are "extremely unfortunate," he also describes this as an "inevitable consequence" of changes in market-determined relative wages when productivity growth is slow. According to Alexander Pope, "What is, is right." We see in the conclusion to this chapter a less extreme variant of Pope's maxim: "What is market determined, is right."

While this formulation is popular among some economists, I do not accept it. The United States is only one among many industrialized countries that permit market-determined wages largely to determine the pretax distribution of income. Few if any of the other advanced capitalist societies accept quite the range of wages tolerated in the United States, however. Workers in countries like Japan and Sweden, where there is far less inequality in wages and earnings, manage to enjoy a tolerable standard of living—and one that is improving at faster rate than workers in this country have witnessed for nearly two decades.

Given the growing disparity in wages produced by the market, one would hardly expect the government, through changes in the tax and transfer system, to make a bad situation even worse. In analyzing the effects of tax and transfer reforms on the labor supply during the 1980s, I recently calculated the marginal and average tax burdens on single-worker families who received 50 percent, 100 percent, and 200 percent of median family income. (Median family income for a four-person family was about $39,000 in 1988.) Since the beginning of the 1980s, combined marginal tax rates have fallen 7 percent for earners receiving half the median income, have fallen 25 percent for earners receiving the median income, and have fallen 35 percent for earners receiving twice the median income. Average tax rates *rose* 3 percent in the lowest income group while falling 12 percent and 20 percent, respectively, in the next two income groups.

Even if economists can be complacent about the changing relative rewards handed out in the U.S. labor market, none of us should deceive ourselves that public policy has been particularly benign over the 1980s. An unprecedented surge in pretax wage differentials to the advantage of the college-educated and highly skilled has been reinforced by a dazzling set of reforms in the tax code. By coincidence, perhaps, these reforms have tended to benefit the well-heeled and college-educated at the expense of the less well-off. As I mentioned earlier, it is probably a good thing that only the college-educated will read this book.

2
The Role of
International Trade in
Wage Differentials
Kevin M. Murphy and Finis Welch

Better-educated workers earn more than less-educated workers, on average. With exceptions for the last few years before retirement, older workers earn more than younger workers. Men earn more than women. The literature that studies these relationships has rationalized or explained them as though relative wages either remain constant or vary within limited ranges. It is also true that blacks earn less than whites, but the convergence toward equality is so well documented that few view the discrepancy as fixed. Instead it is often characterized as diminishing. Although these are the commonly understood features of the wage structure, there is a substantial literature that examines changes and their causes.

Richard Freeman's work on the declining value of a college education has been widely cited.[1] Concentrating on the early 1970s, he noted a collapse for younger white men in the traditional differential according to which college graduates earned half again more than high school graduates. During this period numbers of college graduates grew faster than education-intensive industries could absorb them. Using data from the Current Population Surveys (CPS), we find that between 1963 and 1971 college graduates in their first five years out of school earned from 34 to 46 percent more than high school graduates in their first five years. In 1971 the differential was 37 percent and, as observed by Freeman, it had fallen to 28 percent by 1974. The differential continued to narrow to 22 percent in 1976, and it increased marginally to 25 percent in 1979.

Similarly, the incomes of young men fell relative to those of older men. For example, in the late 1960s college graduates with thirty years of experience earned roughly 75 percent more than new entrants, and by the mid-1970s the differential had increased to 100 percent.

Changes in relative wages between groups classified by experience have been attributed to changes in the age composition of the labor force. The cohort size or baby boom literature includes the work of Freeman, Finis Welch, Mark C. Berger, and more recently Kevin Murphy, Mark Plant, and Welch.[2]

Most of us know that women earn 59 percent as much as men. Causes underlying this amazing constant are the subject of a vast literature dealing with male-female differentials in the quality and continuity of work careers and, among college graduates, with differences in fields of concentration. Two important papers, one by June O'Neill and one by James P. Smith and Michael Ward, argue that the constancy is a product of two opposing trends.[3] Recent cohorts of women are more likely than earlier ones to maintain more or less continuous work careers. Increasing participation for recent cohorts coincides with increasing participation for earlier cohorts, who are either joining the labor force for the first time or are returning after lengthy interruptions. Increased job experience for increasing numbers of continuous participants is offset by increased numbers with little previous experience. Both O'Neill and Smith and Ward argue that if participation rates remain as high as they are now or continue to rise, the first trend must eventually dominate the second. Smith and Ward project that the female-male wage ratio will increase to 0.76 by the turn of the century as experience-related skill differentials erode. Our data show that between 1963 and 1979 the female-male wage ratio for whites fluctuated between 0.55 and 0.59.

No wage history has been more closely examined than black-white differentials, and all who have examined the data are aware of the remarkable convergence toward equality. Unlike the previous examples of relative wages, which are often described as though they show only minor perturbations, black-white comparisons reflect smooth trends.[4] Black men earned about 60 percent as much as white men in the early 1960s, for example, and their relative wage increased to 72 percent by the late 1970s. The picture for women is more dramatic: in the early 1960s black women earned 70 percent as much as white women, and by 1979 black women earned 95 percent as much as white women.

The controversy surrounding the black-white literature is concerned with alternative interpretations of causes for convergence. Freeman and, earlier, Wayne Vroman have argued that the dominant force has been the antidiscrimination legislation of the 1960s, reinforced by affirmative action requirements.[5] Alternatively Smith and Welch maintain that affirmative action has played a minor role.[6] Convergence in skill levels and its source, convergence in quantity and quality of schooling, are cited as the primary factors.

The wage ratios described thus far refer to the period before 1980. Since then many of the traditional relationships have changed. Qualitative orderings are as they always have been, but changes in magnitudes exceed anything we have seen in equivalent intervals of time. Unlike the preceding period, wages for black men did not increase relative to wages for white men in the 1980s. The same is true for women: convergence toward equality between 1963 and 1979 contrasts starkly with an increasing black-white differential during the 1980s. Although wages for white women remained stable relative to wages for white men until the late 1970s, they showed pronounced growth during the 1980s. Comparing the relative wage for black women to that for white men we find a continued increase in the 1980s but at a reduced rate.

Comparisons between school completion levels show educational wage differentials increasing during the 1980s to levels higher than anything seen before. For men in their first five years since leaving school, the 1980s reversed the narrowing differentials of the 1970s. When emphasis shifts from schooling to potential work experience, we find a pronounced acceleration in the wage differential between peak earners twenty-six to thirty-five years out of school and new entrants among high school graduates, but for college graduates we find the opposite. The peak earner–new entrant differential narrowed slightly during the 1980s.

The section entitled "Wages from 1963 to 1986 and Patterns of Industrial Employment" describes wage patterns during that period and proposes a unifying explanation. We note that a shift in wage structures that uniformly increases skill-related wage differentials explains many of the changes observed during the 1980s, but there are prominent exceptions. An increased skill premium is therefore rejected as the sole explanation. A more likely explanation would focus on shifting structures of product demand. After describing changes in relative wages we characterize similarities (between groups defined by race, sex, potential work experience, and education) in industrial employment patterns. If the story is one of shifting product demand structures, effects on wages should be linked to differences in factor intensities between industries. Groups whose wages are similarly affected should be those with the most congruent industrial employment patterns. The congruence calculations show that sex and education are important in identifying differences in industrial employment distributions, but race and potential work experience are not important.[7]

Ordinarily one expects that patterns of industrial demand will shift only gradually. Explanations that link observed changes in wage structures to industrial shifts only redirect attention, unless causes of

41

rapid shifts can be identified. In an admittedly speculative foray we suggest that changing patterns of international trade are a possible explanation. In 1979 exports amounted to 11.2 percent of gross national product. By 1986 they had fallen slightly, to 10.1 percent. In 1979, international trade was effectively balanced, exports exceeded imports by 1 percent. This minor surplus quickly eroded so that in 1986, imports exceeded exports by 40 percent. Although the durable goods share of exports remained constant during this period, their share of imports increased from one-third to one-half. Growth in the trade deficit in durable goods accounted for 80 percent of the total growth in all trade deficits between 1979 and 1986.

The section entitled "International Trade and Labor Demand" illustrates the effects of changes in balanced and unbalanced trade on the demographic distribution of labor demand. The key parameters are changes in the industrial structure of demand associated with shifts in the level and the balance of trade, together with variations in factor intensities between industries. We use a highly aggregated industrial structure with only four parts to match statistics provided in the *Economic Report of the President*.[8] The traded goods sector has three parts: durables, nondurables, and services. The residual and largest part consists of industries whose products are not traded. A few simplifying assumptions permit us to map shifts in trade patterns into shifts in labor demand for various demographic groups.

We summarize results of our earlier paper, "The Structure of Wages"[9] which examined relative wages for white men distinguished by age and schooling, and which showed that changes between 1963 and 1979 can be adequately explained by a model that ignores demand shifts. With labor designated by 160 skill classes (4 education levels × 40 experience levels), the own-wage-own labor quantity covariance structure is negative-definite, up to allowances for measurement error. Although this demonstration does not prove that demand shifts are unimportant, it does show that the data are *consistent* with an ordinary production structure with diminishing marginal properties and stable demand.

When observations are extended to the period after 1979, the tests applied to the 1963–1979 data reject stable demand. A statistically significant element reflects a positive correlation between relative wages and relative labor quantities. This earlier work and the data we describe in it provide what we believe is overwhelming evidence that demand has changed in ways favorable to the most skilled.

We noted in "Structure of Wages" that our approximate demand shift calculations are highly correlated with the evolving pattern of trade deficits in durable goods. This relationship not only holds for the 1980s, when the data are strongly trended, it also helps explain earlier wrinkles otherwise appearing to be wage fluctuations, not related supply shifts.

The calculations in the section "International Trade" suggest that growth in trade deficits during the 1980s coupled with shifts in the industrial composition of net imports results in significant predictions of changes in the industrial structure of employment demand that effectively agree with observed changes in industrial employment patterns.

The industry-specific calculations compute shifts in labor demand using industrial employment distributions for groups specified on the basis of sex, race, and education. Qualitative predictions from calculations based on changes in trade agree with qualitative predictions when observed changes are substituted for the trade calculations. Although observed changes predict larger dispersion in relative demand shifts than are predicted by the trade calculations, the magnitudes are surprisingly similar. Moreover, wage changes parallel the demand shift calculations.

Changes in relative wages during the 1980s are so extreme that alternative explanations ought to be explored. Wage determination has always been an important subject of research, and in light of the recent evidence we expect the level of research activity to increase. The evolving pattern of international trade is perhaps a primary cause of recent wage changes. While there is room for supplemental explanations—we have not examined changes within industry, and the industrial composition effects we have examined cannot tell much about changes in relative wages between experience groups—we think it would be a mistake to ignore trade in subsequent research. To the extent that trade deficits are transitory, wage shifts may also be transitory. This is something the data will quickly test.

Wages from 1963 to 1968 and Patterns of Industrial Employment

The primary data come from the March income supplements to the Current Population Surveys, 1964–1987. The March CPS collects wage and salary earnings in the year preceding each survey, so wages refer to 1963–1986.[10] Wage calculations are for aggregates based on age, race, gender, and schooling from the 704,000 black and white individuals described in the twenty-four surveys who are reported as having completed more than seven years of schooling. The schooling partition refers to eight to eleven, twelve, thirteen to fifteen, sixteen, and seventeen or more years completed. Age is mapped into potential work experience as age minus eighteen, nineteen, twenty, or twenty-

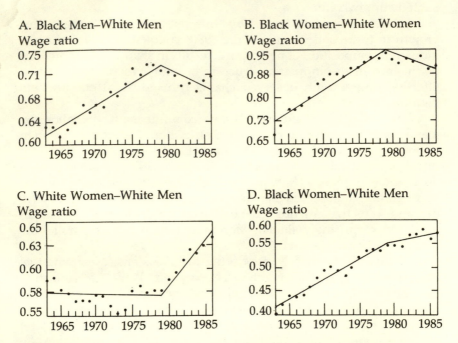

FIGURE 2–1
RELATIVE WAGES BY RACE AND SEX, 1963–1986

A. Black Men–White Men
Wage ratio

B. Black Women–White Women
Wage ratio

C. White Women–White Men
Wage ratio

D. Black Women–White Men
Wage ratio

SOURCE: Authors' calculations based on March *Current Population Survey*, 1964–1986.

two years, as the level of schooling is eight to eleven, twelve, thirteen to fifteen, or sixteen or more years, respectively. Observations are restricted to one to forty years of (potential) experience.

For each race × sex partition in each year we have 200 (= 5 × 40) schooling-by-experience cells. Average weekly wage is first computed for each cell as aggregate wages and salaries divided by total weeks worked. Next, a fixed schooling × experience distribution is constructed as the mean over the full twenty-four-year period. Except as noted, the ratios of average wages we report refer to fixed-weight averages of cell means. By using the fixed weights we avoid confounding wage changes with shifts in the weights used to construct averages.

Figure 2–1 displays 1963–1986 wage ratios between black and white men, black and white women, white women and men, and black women and white men. The small *o*'s identify the observed values. To direct attention to changes in the 1980s, observed wage ratios are regressed on a simple linear trend that is allowed to change its slope for observations after 1979. Fitted values of trend predictions are displayed by the line with the kink in 1979.

The first thing to notice is that the trends toward equality in black-white wage ratios before 1979 vanish thereafter when members of the same sex are compared, in panels A and B. When black women are compared with white men in panel D, the trend continues, but the rate of increase observed before 1979 is reduced thereafter.

To anyone concerned about inequality between the races this is a disappointing and perhaps surprising development. Not so for those concerned about inequality between women and men; earnings of women rise relative to men after 1979, and every observation after 1979 exceeds each observation before. In the period after 1979 only one year shows a ratio that failed to increase.

Because scaling is used in the figures the increase should not be exaggerated. Between 1979 and 1986 average weekly earnings for white women as a fraction of the average for white men increased from 0.58 to 0.63, an increase in the relative wage of about 10 percent. Even so, a rapid increase of this magnitude is not predicted in the Smith-Ward projections that allow for relatively slow growth in women's work experience.

The numbers in figure 2-1 refer to ratios of averages that do not correct for differences in age distributions or levels of schooling between groups. Figure 2-2 examines changes among white men classified by schooling and potential work experience.[11] As in figure 2-1, the o's refer to observed values, and the line traces fitted values from a linear trend splined at 1979. Panel A of figure 2-2 refers to men with one to five years of experience and presents average earnings of college graduates relative to high school graduates.

Reductions between 1971 and 1979 are as described in the introduction. Between 1979 and 1986 the college–high school differential grows from 25 percent to 65 percent. The 1986 value exceeds any calculation we have seen for earlier periods.

Panel B of figure 2-2 also gives earnings of college graduates relative to high school graduates. Cross-sectional wage profiles consistently show that wages are lowest for new entrants. They increase with work experience, rapidly at first and then at a decreasing rate until they reach a maximum about thirty years after leaving school. The decline after thirty years is minor. Potential experience in panel B is restricted to the twenty-six to thirty-five-year interval, that of the peak earners. The trend after 1979 is less pronounced than the one for new entrants, but the college–high school differential is greater in 1986 than at any time in the earlier period.

Panels C and D of figure 2-2 contrast peak earners with twenty-

FIGURE 2–2
Relative Wages by Education and Experience, 1963–1986

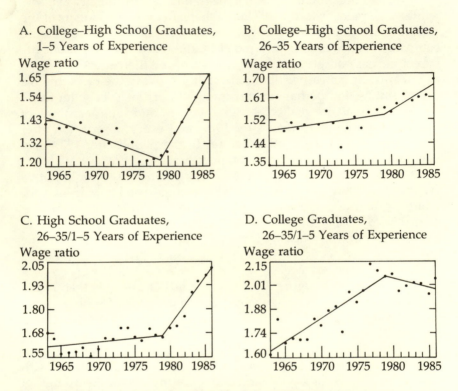

A. College–High School Graduates, 1–5 Years of Experience

B. College–High School Graduates, 26–35 Years of Experience

C. High School Graduates, 26–35/1–5 Years of Experience

D. College Graduates, 26–35/1–5 Years of Experience

Source: Authors' calculations based on March *Current Population Survey*, 1964–1986.

six to thirty-five years of experience against new entrants with one to five years. Panel C refers to high school graduates, and panel D to college graduates. Among high school graduates, earnings of older workers increase sharply relative to new entrants after 1979. In 1979 the wage ratio is 1.65; it grows to 2.01 in 1986.

The pattern for college graduates is different, however. Although earnings at profile peaks increase relative to earnings at labor force entry in the period before 1979, they do not increase in the 1980s.

The data in figures 2–1 and 2–2 are listed in appendix tables 2–11 and 2–12. In reviewing these figures it is clear that the period after 1979 is unlike the period before. The stylized facts describing race and sex differentials no longer hold. Similarly, schooling and experience differentials are not what they have been. There have obviously been fundamental changes in the structure of compensation. Our objective

46

TABLE 2–1

SIGN PATTERNS AND AVERAGE VALUES OF WAGE CHANGE–POPULATION CHANGE INTERPRODUCTS FOR SELECTED INTERVALS, 1963–1985

Interval	1963–65	1966–69	1970–73	1974–77	1978–81	1982–85
A. Number of negative interproducts/number of pairs of years in interval						
1963–65	1/3					
1966–69	4/12	2/6				
1970–73	8/12	13/16	6/6			
1974–77	9/12	16/16	16/16	5/16		
1978–81	12/12	16/16	16/16	15/16	3/6	
1982–85	0/12	9/16	9/16	4/6	0/16	3/6
B. Average value of interproducts in interval relative to the average (absolute value) for all 253 comparisons						
1963–65	0.039					
1966–69	0.120	0.093				
1970–73	−0.208	−0.447	−0.262			
1974–77	−1.057	−1.819	−0.893	−0.216		
1978–81	−0.978	−2.596	−1.814	−0.434	0.003	
1982–85	2.897	0.047	−0.270	0.519	0.866	−0.031

SOURCE: Authors' calculations based on March annual demographic surveys, Current Population Surveys.

is to draw attention to these changes and to speculate about their underlying causes.

In particular we want to know if the compensation changes could have resulted from a fixed structure of labor demand alongside a changing age and educational mix of workers, or if demand must have changed also. If demand has changed, we want to know something about the nature and the source of change. The basic demographic and skill factors that we call the supply changes refer to the job market arrival of the post–World War II baby boom cohorts and the subsequent decline in the number of young workers as birth rates fell after the 1957 peak. The supply factors also include a rise in average levels of education, an increased labor market participation for women, and narrowing differentials between school completion levels for blacks and for whites.

Simple inspection suggests that changes in supply cannot be the only source of observed changes in compensation. As a general rule, if demand were constant we would expect to see wages fall in ranges

TABLE 2–2

DECOMPOSITION OF CHANGES IN BLACK-WHITE RATIO OF AVERAGE
WEEKLY WAGES, SELECTED PERIODS, 1963–1986
(in percent changes)

Period	Within Class	Skill Convergence	Skill Prices	Total
		Panel A		
1963–72	7.2	1.3	1.3	9.8
1972–79	4.0	3.9	0.6	8.5
1979–86	0.8	1.7	−1.9	0.6
1963–86	12.0	6.9	−0.1	18.9
		Panel B		
1963–72	3.6	2.7	3.5	9.8
1972–79	−1.3	8.2	1.5	8.5
1979–86	2.2	3.6	−5.2	0.6
1963–86	4.6	14.5	−0.2	18.9

a. Figures represent observed values of R_1, R_2, and R_3.
b. R_1 includes only parts orthogonal to R_2, and R_3. Parts of R_1 correlated with R_2 and R_3 are included in skill convergence and skill price effects, respectively.
SOURCE: See source for table 2–1.

of the wage structure where populations of workers were increasing most rapidly. Average levels of education, for example, have increased throughout the period of our observations. If demand were stable, then, we would expect to observe narrowing wage differentials between those with different levels of schooling. As the number of young workers increases relative to older workers, we would similarly expect to observe relative wages of young workers to fall if demand were stable. The patterns in figure 2–2 show what might be expected from a hypothesis of stable demand during the 1970s; education-based wage differentials narrowed and age-based differentials widened.

The 1980s appear to contradict the stable demand hypothesis, however. Education-related wage differentials expanded even though average schooling levels increased. Age related wage differentials continued to increase among high school graduates even though the crest of the baby boom passed and average ages increased.

In "The Structure of Wages,"[12] which concentrates on white men, we suggest a rigorous test of stable demand. We note that if white men are viewed as a separate series of productive inputs where wages are their marginal products and the production relation is concave, then for two periods designated by the subscripts 0 and 1 it must be true that

$$(W_1 - W_0)'(N_1 - N_0) \le 0 \qquad (2\text{-}1)$$

provided demand is stable. In equation (2-1), W refers to a (160) vector of average wages for men specified by education (four levels) and age (forty single-year cells for each level of schooling), and N is the associated vector of population counts.

Table 2-1 lists summaries of signs for the interproducts defined in equation (2-1) for the period 1963–1985. The full period is divided into a starting period of three years followed by five subperiods of four years each. Measured wages and survey estimates of population counts are subject to errors. Where the time span between two observations is short, measurement errors may swamp the observations of wage and population differentials, and it is perhaps not surprising that so many of the products described along the main diagonal of table 2-1 are positive.

Ignoring the main diagonal, we see that between 1966 and 1981 ninety-six comparisons between pairs of years (the joint wages × population movement defined in equation (2-1)) are negative ninety-two times. The implication is that during this period, in principle, changes in the structure of wages can be described *as though* demand were stable. The signs shown when we compare the opening period (1963 to 1965) and the most recent period (1982 to 1985) to other years generally do not conform with stable demand.

If we go one step further and assume that demand is linear, then stable demand implies that up to measurement error the wages × population covariance matrix is negative definite. If the data are restricted to the period before 1980 we cannot reject stable demand. For the full period, including the 1980s, the stable demand hypothesis is rejected.

This result is unsurprising given the wage changes summarized in figure 2-2 and the observation that both average worker ages (years of labor market experience) and average education levels increased during the 1980s. It seems obvious that the skill composition of demand must have shifted in a manner generally favorable to the most skilled.

Rising skill premiums help explain some of the observations in figure 2-1. Consider as an example panel A, tracing the average wage of black men as a fraction of the average wage of white men. Although the data in figure 2-1 (and figure 2-2) refer to fixed-weight averages, it is useful to think of the averages using shifting weights for purposes of decomposing trends. Define the ratio of mean wages in year t as

$$R_t = \Sigma_i S_{bit} W_{bit} / \Sigma_i S_{wit} W_{wit} \qquad (2\text{--}2)$$

where the subscripts b and w refer to black and white, respectively. The index i refers to an experience $\times$ schooling cell and takes 200 values. Average wages within cells are W, and the fraction of the year's total observations occurring in the cell is S.

Using logarithmic (base e) changes as approximations of proportional changes, the wage of black men relative to the wage of white men increased 18.3 percent between 1963 and 1979. Between 1979 and 1986 it increased by 0.6 percent.

Because black men have lower average schooling levels than white men, the post-1979 growth in wage premiums associated with extra schooling was reflected in lowered average wages for blacks relative to whites. To identify this effect, we have partitioned the wage ratio into the product of three terms:

$$R_{1t} = \Sigma S_{bi.} W_{bit} / \Sigma S_{bi.} W_{wit} \qquad (2\text{--}2a)$$
$$R_{2t} = (\Sigma S_{bit} / \Sigma S_{bi.} W_{bit}) / (\Sigma S_{wit} W_{wit} / \Sigma S_{wi.} W_{wit}) \qquad (2\text{--}2b)$$
$$R_{3t} = \Sigma S_{bi.} W_{wit} / \Sigma S_{wi.} W_{wit} \qquad (2\text{--}2c)$$

where all sums are over the experience $\times$ schooling index, i, and the fixed weights used to construct the ratios in figure 2–1 are $S_{ki.} = \Sigma_t S_{kit} / 24$ ($k = b$ or w).

The first term measures relative wages in a fixed-experience $\times$ schooling distribution, adjusted to the mean distribution of black men. We refer to growth in R_1 as relative wage growth within experience $\times$ schooling levels. The second term, R_2, gives a measure of the relative importance of differences between period t distributions and average distributions over the schooling and age index i. Growth in R_2 indexes growth in relative wages due to skill convergence (experience and schooling). The third term, R_3, indexes the effect, valued at current wages for whites, of differences in average skill distributions. Changes in this ratio summarize changes in the relative wage as wages vary over the skill index, caused by differences in 1963–1986 average experience by schooling levels. We refer to changes in this term as the skill-price effect.

Note that the product of the first and third terms measures the black-white wage ratio using the fixed-weight distributions. It is these numbers that are traced in panel A of figure 2–1.

Panel A of table 2–2 summarizes fractional changes in the black-white wage ratio for the full period and for three subperiods using the logarithmic approximation and the decomposition defined in equation (2–2). The year-specific detail for the data that are summarized in table 2–2 are listed in the appendix as appendix table 2–13 for panel A and appendix table 2–14 for panel B. Notice in panel A of table 2–2 that the skill-convergence effect, omitted in panel A of figure 2–1, implies 6.9 percent growth in relative wages of black men over the full period.

The most important point of table 2–2 is that the effect of increasing skill premiums in the 1980s has lowered relative wages for blacks, while in earlier periods changing skill premiums favored the skills of blacks relative to whites. Wage convergence within experience × schooling classes was slower in the 1980s than in earlier periods, but it remained positive. The partitions R_1, R_2, and R_3 index skill on the basis of age and schooling only. Skill differences between blacks and whites of the same age and schooling caused by differences in the quantity and quality of experience are part of the R_1 construct in panel A.

Over the full period the black-white wage ratio had an average level of 0.69, but the corresponding average for the between-age and schooling-class component, R_3, is 0.89. It is easy to verify from the definition of R_2 that its mean is 1.00, so it is clear that the mean value of the within-class wage ratio is less than one. It is, in fact, 0.77. The presumption that the black-white wage differential within age and schooling classes refers at least in part to something other than discrimination is supported by the observation that among members of the same race, 70 to 75 percent of wage variation is within age and schooling class.

Panel A of table 2–2 shows decompositions of growth in the black-white wage ratio corresponding to alternative definitions of R_1, R_2, and R_3. Under the alternative, we regressed R_1 on R_2 and R_3 (in full logarithmic form) to partition R_1 into three parts, one correlated with R_2 (convergence in skill levels), another correlated with R_3 (skill-price effects), and a remainder that is orthogonal to R_2 and R_3. In panel A, the part of R_1 that is correlated with R_2 and R_3 is added to them. The thesis is that if there are skill differences between blacks and whites within age and schooling classes and if skill convergence is occurring between classes (R_2 is increasing), then the part of R_1 that is correlated with R_2 refers to skill convergence as well, and the part of R_1 that is correlated with R_3 refers to changing skill prices.[13] Similarly, only the part of R_1 that is not correlated with R_2 and R_3 is left in R_1 under the alternative in panel B. According to this rotation, estimated effects of skill convergence on black-white wage growth swamps the other components of change over the full period. The rotation emphasizes the role of skill prices in the 1980s, however. The estimate in panel B is that if skill prices had remained constant during the 1980s, growth in the black-white wage ratio in the seven years between 1979 and 1986 would have matched growth between 1963 and 1973 (ten years) and would have been only slightly lower than that of the previous seven years, 1972 to 1979.

While the growth in education and work experience premiums in the 1980s helps explain the divergence from trends in the black-white wage comparisons shown in figure 2–1, it cannot explain the trend for wages of white women relative to wages of white men. Although men and women have similar age distributions and similar average levels of schooling, schooling distributions are less disperse for white women than for white men. Women are more likely to complete high school but less likely to graduate from college. Because the wage differentials between college and high school graduates exceed the differentials between high school graduates and dropouts, the wage effects of differences in schooling distributions favor white men. Similarly, women of the same age and education level as men have worked fewer years on average; in other words, they have less experience. Thus, on average white women are less skilled than white men. Rising skill premiums during the 1980s should have lowered wages of white women relative to men, but they did not.

A simple shift toward skill in the structure of demand might be attributed to broadly based technological change that induces substitution toward the most skilled. While there is evidence of shifts toward skill in panels A, B, and C in figure 2–2, and while such shifts appear to contribute to understanding departures from trends in the black-white comparisons of figure 2–1, increased skill premiums cannot be the only source of change.

Panel D in figure 2–2 shows that among college graduates relative earnings of less experienced men have increased. Panel C of figure 2–1 shows increasing relative earnings of white women. Both are inconsistent with increasing skill premiums.

Even if all the changes in relative wages could be attributed to growth in skill premiums, still the source of the growth would be an open question. But because growth in skill premiums cannot be the only explanation for observed changes, the question is refocused. We do not believe that simple technological shifts with substitution counterparts provide adequate answers. Something else must be involved.

Let us consider changes in the composition of product demand as an alternative. The empirical work on industry-of-employment uses a two-digit taxonomy of forty-five industries that parallels the 1970 census definitions. We are unable to map the first four surveys into these aggregates, and they are dropped.[14] Because relative demand increases in industries with growing employment shares, the demographic structure of labor demand is related to group differences in industrial employment distributions.

Table 2–3 lists distributions among eleven industrial aggregates in the first four years of the data, 1967 to 1970, for people whose potential work experience ranges between twenty-six and thirty-five years. For the most recent period, 1983 to 1986, reference is to those with one to ten years of potential experience. Since the periods are sixteen years apart and potential experience differs by twenty-five years, the comparison spans forty-one years between graduation dates for the cohorts considered. The data are divided between high school and college graduates, for black and white men and women.

The table illustrates several phenomena. Most notable is the decline in employment by educational institutions among college graduates. For black women, 78.8 percent of the reference cohort of 1967 to 1970 were employed in education. This number dropped to 22.8 percent for new entrants from 1983 to 1986. The second most prominent feature of the table is that among college graduates the employment distributions from 1983 to 1986 are much more similar for the four groups than they were from 1967 to 1970, or than they were for high school graduates in either period. It is also clear that employment in the aggregate of finance, insurance, real estate, and professional services has expanded hugely for college graduates. Employment in wholesale and retail trade has also increased.

Inspection of the table shows that industrial employment distributions differ sharply between high school and college graduates and among the four demographic groups.

We presume that labor groups similarly affected by changing patterns of industrial production should show the most similar industrial distributions of employment. To this end we constructed reference distributions over the forty-five industries using the 1967–1986 averages of the year-specific distributions for each group. There are four demographic classes (black, white, men, and women), five schooling levels, and five levels of potential work experience for a total of 100 groups. Similarity of employment distributions is measured by a congruence index.

The index is restricted to pairwise comparison between groups designated as 1 and 2. Let n_{1k} represent the fraction of group 1 employed in industry k. Within industry k, let p_{2k} represent the fraction of groups 1 and 2 combined that belongs to group 2. The index is $\Sigma_k n_{1k} p_{2k} / \bar{p}_2$, where $\bar{p}_2$ corresponds to the composite proportion of the two groups that belongs to the second. It corresponds to the mean proportion of group 1's co-workers who are members of

TABLE 2-3

INDUSTRIAL DISTRIBUTIONS OF EMPLOYMENT BY RACE AND SEX FOR COLLEGE AND HIGH SCHOOL GRADUATES, 1967–1970 AND 1983–1986

Industry	Black men				Black women			
	High School		College		High School		College	
	1967–70	1983–86	1967–70	1983–86	1967–70	1983–86	1967–70	1983–86
Wholesale, retail trade	10.5	21.2	4.1	12.1	11.7	18.2	1.9	8.8
Construction	4.1	7.3	1.4	3.5	0.0	1.0	0.0	0.4
Manufacturing durables, mining	23.9	13.7	5.4	11.0	5.5	9.9	1.0	5.1
Manufacturing nondurables	8.1	17.8	4.1	5.1	12.0	12.7	1.9	5.3
Transportation, communication, public utilities	14.8	8.3	4.1	10.7	1.0	5.9	1.0	6.4
Business, repair services, entertainment, recreation	2.3	6.2	1.4	4.8	1.6	3.5	0.0	4.7
Finance, insurance, real estate, professional services	1.9	4.1	1.4	14.2	3.9	10.9	1.9	14.1
Hospitals, medical	3.6	6.2	4.1	8.8	24.4	16.4	5.8	10.8
Welfare, religious	3.6	6.2	14.9	4.6	20.5	7.4	1.0	8.6
Education	6.5	3.7	36.5	13.7	7.1	3.8	78.8	22.8
Governments	20.3	5.3	23.0	11.5	12.3	10.4	6.7	13.1
Total	100.0	100.0	100.0	100.0	100.0	100.0	100.0	100.0

	White men				White women			
Wholesale, retail trade	15.2	26.3	9.7	14.2	20.5	26.2	3.5	9.0
Construction	7.4	13.9	3.8	3.2	1.3	1.4	0.5	0.6
Manufacturing durables, mining	25.8	19.1	17.7	14.5	12.8	9.5	1.8	5.7
Manufacturing nondurables	13.8	14.5	13.3	8.7	14.1	10.3	3.1	6.1
Transportation, communication, public utilities	12.8	7.8	3.8	5.9	5.3	4.5	1.2	4.1
Business, repair services, entertainment, recreation	3.2	7.1	3.3	6.8	2.5	5.1	0.3	6.1
Finance, insurance, real estate, professional services	4.6	3.0	11.0	17.8	12.1	18.1	3.9	15.2
Hospitals, medical	1.3	1.7	3.3	6.5	12.1	11.9	8.5	18.1
Welfare, religious	1.8	2.6	4.3	4.1	3.9	6.7	3.2	4.9
Education	1.9	0.9	18.4	10.6	6.5	2.0	68.9	24.2
Governments	12.3	3.1	11.4	7.8	8.9	4.4	5.0	5.8
Total	100.0	100.0	100.0	100.0	100.0	100.0	100.0	100.0

NOTE: The 1967–1970 data refer to employees twenty-six to thirty-five years after completing school. The 1983–1986 data refer to employees one to ten years after school. In this, college graduates include all with sixteen or more years of schooling.
SOURCE: See source for table 2–1.

TABLE 2–4

COMPOSITE INDUSTRY ASSOCIATION INDEXES
BY RACE AND SEX, 1967–1986 AVERAGES

	White Men	Black Men	White Women	Black Women
A. All education and experience levels				
White men	0.869	0.888	0.725	0.765
Black men		0.884	0.746	0.706
White women			0.845	0.833
Black women				0.836
B. Equal education and experience				
White men	1.000	0.979	0.778	0.824
Black men		1.000	0.862	0.741
White women			1.000	0.958
Black women				1.000
C. Equal education, all experience levels				
White men	0.977	0.961	0.780	0.797
Black men		0.959	0.847	0.754
White women			0.984	0.947
Black women				0.962
D. Equal experience, all education levels				
White men	0.828	0.899	0.726	0.777
Black men		0.857	0.745	0.699
White women			0.786	0.835
Black women				0.794

SOURCE: See source for table 2–1.

group 2, divided by the aggregate proportion of workers who are members of group 2; this measure of congruence is symmetric and is bounded by zero and one. The index is zero when the two employment distributions are mutually exclusive. It is one when they are identical. This index, familiar to students of school desegregation, was introduced by James S. Coleman to measure the extent of integration among schools in a district.[15]

With 100 groups there are a total of 4,950 pairwise comparisons for the industry congruence index. Table 2–4 gives reference averages of the industry congruence computed in different ways.[16] Section A gives averages over all schooling and experience groups between specified race-sex pairs.

TABLE 2–5

AVERAGE INDUSTRY ASSOCIATION INDEXES
BY EDUCATION FOR WHITE MEN

| | Years of School Completed | | | | |
Education	8–11	12	13–15	16	17+
8–11	0.975	0.954	0.887	0.762	0.516
12		0.974	0.954	0.834	0.601
13–15			0.979	0.899	0.649
16				0.986	0.865
17+					0.976

SOURCE: See source for table 2–1.

It is clear that sex segregates industrial–employment distributions more than race, and that age and education result in sharper distinctions between distributions for women than for men.

Section B contrasts distributions among the four race-sex groups, giving average association indexes when comparisons are restricted to the twenty-five cases for which education and experience levels are equal. Again, sex is a more important distinction than race. The same result occurs in sections C and D.

In section C, comparisons are restricted to those with equal levels of schooling, but averages extend to all experience levels. Section D shows the opposite; comparisons are restricted to equal experience levels, and averages include all education levels.

By comparing B, C, and D, we see that the constraint of equal experience is unimportant, but the constraint regarding education is important. The association indexes capture what is easily seen in the previous table: industrial employment distributions are distinguished by education as well as by sex.

While the comparisons in table 2–4 may be informative about general industrial congruence, they cannot directly inform us about the issue concerning the relation between the wage changes observed in figures 2–1 and 2–2 and the question of possible linkages to shifts in industrial demand. As background for calculations that follow, table 2–5 presents industry association indexes averaged over experience levels for white men classified by education. It is clear from the diagonal dominance shown in this matrix that differences in education sharply differentiate industrial employment distributions.

Recall from figure 2–2 that in the period since 1979 wages for college graduates increased relative to those for high school graduates, and the change is more pronounced among the youngest workers. Recall also that figure 2–2 refers to white men only. Table 2–6 lists average industry association indexes between white men classified by education and each of the three other groups: black men, black women, and white women.

The top panel considers white men at all experience levels and compares them with all others, undifferentiated by schooling and experience. While the indexes describing congruence of industrial employment patterns with white men are higher for black men than for black or white women, the congruence declines as education levels increase for white men. This may be the result of lower schooling levels for black men, but it shows one important thing: if the structure of industrial demand were to shift to the relative advantage of the most highly educated white men, it would shift to the disadvantage of black men. The point illustrated in table 2–2 carries through industrial intermediation.

The opposition pattern holds for black women. As schooling levels of white men increase, industrial employment patterns show more congruence between white men and black women. The pattern is not strong, however. The index for those with sixteen years of schooling exceeds the one for high school graduates only by .029, and the one for men with advanced degrees is slightly below the one for high school graduates. A shift in the industrial structure of product demand favoring the most educated white men would favor black women as well. The education relation is sharper for comparisons with white women. The employment distributions of white women and highly educated white men are the most congruent.

The second panel of table 2–6 is restricted to white men in their first ten years out of school. (Recall that the sharpest post-1979 changes in figure 2–2 are for the college–high school differential among the youngest workers.) Reference to high school graduates is to those with twelve years of schooling, and the category of college graduates signifies those with at least sixteen years of schooling. These findings are more dramatic than the ones in the top panel. In comparison to high school graduates, young white men who are college graduates are much more likely to work with white women, somewhat more likely to work with black women, and less likely to work with black men. The post-1979 trends in wages shown in figures 2–1 and 2–2 coupled with the congruence indexes of table 2–6 suggest that patterns of change are broadly consistent with what might be caused by changes in industrial structures of product demand.

Shifts that favor white women will on average also favor black women relative to black men (see table 2–4), and they will favor more-

TABLE 2-6

INDUSTRIAL EMPLOYMENT CONGRUENCE BETWEEN WHITE MEN
CLASSIFIED BY EDUCATION AND OTHER GROUPS NOT DIFFERENTIATED
BY EDUCATION

White Men	Black Men	Black Women	White Women
	All experience and schooling levels		
All experience levels and schooling, in years			
8–11	0.910	0.676	0.625
12	0.958	0.790	0.703
13–15	0.929	0.763	0.736
16	0.890	0.819	0.818
17+	0.712	0.779	0.781
Experience 1–10 years and schooling, in years			
12	0.941	0.752	0.669
16+	0.813	0.841	0.821

NOTE: Numbers are average association indexes.
SOURCE: See source for table 2-1.

educated relative to less-educated white men. Conversely, shifts that favor the most educated white men will also be relatively favorable to women, particularly white women. In the next section we examine changing patterns of international trade as a possible source of product-demand shifts.

International Trade and Labor Demand

The following trade data, taken from the 1988 *Economic Report of the President*, lists values of imports and exports for three industrial aggregates: durable goods, nondurables, and services.[17] We aggregated the CPS employment data into three groups in an attempt to match the trade aggregates. A residual fourth group represents nontraded goods. Our mapping of traded durables combines the ordinary definition and the two-digit mining industry; for nondurables we add agriculture, forestry, and fisheries to the regular definition; and traded services include finance, insurance, and real estate, as well as brokerage, legal, and accounting.

Table 2-7 gives 1967–1986 average employment shares for vari-

TABLE 2-7

AVERAGE EMPLOYMENT SHARES IN TRADED GOODS AND SERVICES AND
NONTRADED GOODS FOR ALTERNATIVE POPULATION GROUPS

Group	Nontraded Goods	Durable Goods	Nondurable Goods	Traded Services
All	62.1	18.2	12.2	7.5
Education				
8–11	53.7	25.1	19.1	2.1
12	59.6	19.9	13.1	7.5
13–15	65.0	16.0	9.2	9.8
16+	71.8	11.2	7.5	9.6
Race and sex				
White men	59.3	22.7	12.8	5.2
Black men	61.1	21.2	14.2	3.5
White women	65.9	11.1	11.0	12.0
Black women	73.2	8.7	11.1	7.0
Sex and education				
Men				
8–11	53.4	28.1	16.9	1.6
12	58.0	25.0	14.1	3.0
13–15	62.0	20.7	10.6	6.6
16+	64.9	15.2	9.3	10.7
Women				
8–11	54.2	18.3	24.2	3.3
12	61.8	12.6	11.6	14.0
13–15	69.9	8.2	6.7	15.2
16+	85.5	3.3	3.8	7.3

SOURCE: See source for table 2–1.

ous groups corresponding to the four-industry taxonomy. The top
panel divides the population by school completion levels and shows
that on average the fraction of workers employed in industries producing traded goods falls as schooling levels increase. The bottom
panel, distinguishing according to sex as well as education, shows
that this effect is much stronger for women than for men. Among
high school dropouts, about the same proportions of men and
women (53.4 and 54.2 percent, respectively) are employed in non-
trade sectors; among college graduates, 64.9 percent of men are employed in the nontraded goods sector, but the corresponding number
for women is 85.5 percent.

Our primary concern is determining whether changing trade

patterns coincide with the wage changes we have seen. Because international trade accounts for a relatively small share of total production and consumption (11–14 percent in the 1980s), we might expect at first blush that trade is an unlikely source of important shifts in labor demand. To obtain order-of-magnitude estimates of what trade effects might be, we provide a straightforward model that identifies essential parameters.

We begin with the key assumption that the industrial structure of product demand is fixed. Demand, $D (P, M)$, depends on prices, P, and aggregate expenditure, M, where D and P are $(K \times 1)$ vectors corresponding to the K industries. We assume J labor classes. In this structure of production nonlabor inputs are assumed to be supplied at fixed prices, and production is subject to constant returns.

Let demand for labor group j in industry k be represented by

$$n_{jk} = (\partial c_k / \partial w_j) \cdot Y_k \qquad (2\text{--}4)$$

where c_k is unit cost in K, Y_k is production in k, and w_j is the wage of group j. Summing over industries gives

$$N_j = \Sigma_k (\partial c_k / \partial w_j) Y_k \qquad (2\text{--}5)$$

The model is one period in which domestic consumption equals domestic production plus net imports, and reference prices are unitary; for example,

$$D(P,M) = Y + I \qquad (2\text{--}6)$$

where Y and I refer to production and I to net imports, and both are of dimension $(K \times 1)$. Differentiate (2–6) to obtain

$$D_p dP + D_m dM = dY + dI \qquad (2\text{--}7)$$

where dY is the change in domestic output and dI is the change in net imports.

Since input prices determine output prices

$$dP = C_w dW \qquad (2\text{--}8)$$

where C_w is the $(K \times J)$ matrix of derivatives of unit costs with respect to wages, W. In this notation, equation (2–6) is written as

$$N = C'_w Y \qquad (2\text{--}9)$$

which after differentiating yields

$$dN = C'_w dY + C_{ww} dW \cdot \qquad (2\text{--}10)$$

where dN is the $(J \times 1)$ vector of employment changes. C_{ww} is a $(J \times J)$ matrix that corresponds to a production-weighted average of the Hessians of the unit-cost functions for the K industries and is negative semidefinite.

Substitute (2–8) into (2–7) and rewrite the result as

$$dY = D_p C_w dW + D_m dM - dI \qquad (2\text{--}7')$$

and substitute this result for dY in (2–10) as

$$dN + C'_w dI - C'_w d_m dM = (C_{ww} + C'_w D_p C_w) dW \qquad (2\text{--}11)$$

61

Equation (2–11), therefore, gives a mapping of labor demand shifts due to changes in net imports and changes in domestic spending into equivalent units of employment change, dN. The translation of demand shifts from labor quantities to wages is given by the aggregate substitution matrix $(C_{ww} + C'_w D_p C_w)$, which is negative semidefinite. Because the substitution matrix is negative, we reverse signs on equation (2–11) in discussing effects of changing trade patterns on labor demand, and thus a supply increase $-dN_j < 0$ reduces wages. For purposes of computing trade effects we assume $dM = -\Sigma dI_K$. This corresponds to our single period model in which trade deficits increase spending by the full amount of the deficit, and trade surpluses drop current spending below GNP by the full amount of the surplus.

Trade has a composition effect $-C'_w dI$, in which increasing net imports reduce employment demand in importing industries, and it has a scale effect $C'_w D_p \Sigma_k I_K$, in which increases in import deficits increase demand due to the effect of increasing aggregate spending.

Since we have no industry-specific detail concerning scale or income effects, we assume that $(\partial D_k / \partial M) Y_k / Y = 1$ for all k where Y is GNP and Y_k/Y is industry k's share of GNP. The assumption is that scale effects are industry-neutral. This simplification gives the full effect of changes in international trade expressed as a fraction of labor group j's total employment as

$$dN_j/N_j = \Sigma_k(N_{jk}/N_j)(\Delta I/Y - dI_k/Y_k) \tag{2–12}$$

where $\Delta I = \Sigma_k dI_k$ is aggregate net imports (the trade deficit).

The expression, $\Delta I/Y - dI_k/Y_k$, estimates the change in labor demand in industry k. Weighted by GNP shares, Y_k/Y, this change sums zero across industries, so it measures relative shifts only. Table 2–8 gives the $\Delta I/Y - dI_k/Y_k$ series for trade changes between 1979 and 1986, alongside observed changes in employment shares by industry.

An example of these calculations is the increased trade deficit of 4.1 percent of GNP between 1979 and 1986. Since the nontraded goods sector by definition has no imports, the prediction from the scale neutrality assumption is that, wages constant, employment shares in this sector would increase by 4.1 percent. The trade deficit is especially notable for durable goods. As a fraction of domestic production of durables it increased by 18.8 percent during this period. The presumed reduction in labor demand from import substitution is offset by the scale effect of 4.1 percent, yielding a net reduction in demand of 14.7 percent. The fact that the observed increase in service industries exceeds the prediction by so much is perhaps not surprising, given the strong trend in services and the crudeness of our approximation in matching Census industrial categories with the

TABLE 2–8

PREDICTED VERSUS OBSERVED CHANGES IN INDUSTRY EMPLOYMENT
SHARES CORRESPONDING TO OBSERVED CHANGES IN TRADE PATTERNS,
1979–1986
(percent)

Industry	Predicted	Observed
Durable goods	−14.7	−17.1
Nondurable goods	−1.8	−8.8
Traded services	1.4	18.7
Nontraded goods	4.1	4.3

SOURCE: See source for table 2–1.

TABLE 2–9

DISTRIBUTIONS OF SCHOOL COMPLETION LEVELS BY SEX AND RACE,
1963–1986
(percent)

Group	8–11	12	13–15	16+	Total
White men	17.7	41.1	17.7	23.5	100.0
Black men	31.2	41.7	15.8	11.2	100.0
White women	12.9	49.5	17.9	19.7	100.0
Black women	22.1	44.6	18.0	15.3	100.0

SOURCE: See source for table 2–1.

trade classification. Even so, we think there is notable agreement in the two columns of table 2–8.

According to the evidence of congruence in employment distributions among industries shown in table 2–4, race and potential work experience are not important in distinguishing employment patterns, but sex and education are important. The mapping that we use from industrial to group-specific shifts in demand therefore distinguishes groups on the basis of sex and education only. Reference distributions for this purpose are given in table 2–9. They represent averages for the full period, 1963–1986.

Our calculations of demand-shifts within race and sex groups mix the data in table 2–8 with the industry employment distributions within sex and education classes (the bottom panel of table 2–7) and the marginal school completion distributions given in table 2–9. The main results, the calculation of relative demand shifts for groups

63

TABLE 2–10
CHANGES IN RELATIVE LABOR DEMAND PREDICTED BY CHANGES IN INTERNATIONAL TRADE, THE INDUSTRIAL DISTRIBUTION OF EMPLOYMENT, AND RELATIVE WAGES, 1979–1986
(percent)

Group	Trade Effect	Industrial Composition Effect	Observed Wages
		Men	
All	−0.80	−1.36	−3.43
Race			
White	−0.77	−1.31	−3.25
Black	−1.13	−2.00	−5.67
Education			
8–11	−1.97	−3.56	−10.21
12	−1.25	−2.32	−7.85
13–15	−0.36	−0.46	−0.33
16+	0.66	1.50	7.80
		Women	
All	1.35	2.31	5.81
Race			
White	1.38	2.36	6.22
Black	1.13	1.87	2.64
Education			
8–11	−0.60	−2.18	−0.80
12	0.91	2.21	4.03
13–15	1.99	3.97	8.47
16+	3.31	4.29	12.70
		Men and women	
Education			
8–11	−1.55	−3.14	−7.33
12	−0.36	−0.45	−2.96
13–15	0.53	1.21	2.98
16+	1.54	2.43	9.43

SOURCE: See source for table 2–1.

defined in various ways, follow equation (2–12) and are listed in table 2–10.

The first column of table 2–10, trade effects, follows equation (2–12) precisely. The second column, industry employment effects, substitutes observed values from table 2–8 of dN_k/N_k for the trade effect calculation, $\Delta I/Y - dI_k/Y_k$ in equation (2–12). The third column, actual wage change, refers to the difference in (log) wages between 1979 and 1986, when each wage is expressed relative to the year-specific fixed-weight mean.

Each of the numbers in the first two columns of table 2–10 refers to an average of four numbers, given in table 2–8; the only difference between them derives from differences in employment distributions between industries, that is, industrial differences in factor intensities. In principle there is no reason for the wage and labor demand calculations in table 2–10 to agree as closely as they do. The mapping between them is given by the substitution matrix defined in equation (2–11), and it does not follow necessarily that the group that experiences the largest proportional change in demand, expressed in units of employment, will experience the largest change in relative wage.

Compare the numbers in the first two columns of table 2–10 and note that for every designation the ordering of change is the same. Trade effects predict that employment demand increases for women relative to men, for whites relative to blacks, and for better-educated relative to less-educated workers. Qualitative predictions using observed changes in industrial employment patterns are identical in these dimensions. The main distinction between them is that variation is more extreme when observed changes are used' than when trade calculations are used for predictions, but they are of the same order of magnitude. Since we began by describing relative wage changes during the 1980s, it is not necessary to repeat them; the qualitative differentials match the trade calculations.

APPENDIX TABLE 2–11

RELATIVE WAGES BY RACE AND SEX, 1963–1986
(percent)

Year	Black Men– White Men	Black Women– White Women	White Women– White Men	Black Women– White Men
1963	0.63	0.68	0.59	0.40
1964	0.63	0.71	0.59	0.42
1965	0.61	0.76	0.58	0.44
1966	0.63	0.76	0.57	0.44
1967	0.64	0.78	0.56	0.44
1968	0.66	0.81	0.57	0.46
1969	0.65	0.85	0.56	0.48
1970	0.66	0.86	0.57	0.49
1971	0.66	0.88	0.57	0.50
1972	0.68	0.88	0.56	0.49
1973	0.68	0.87	0.55	0.48
1974	0.70	0.90	0.56	0.50
1975	0.72	0.90	0.58	0.52
1976	0.71	0.92	0.58	0.53
1977	0.73	0.93	0.57	0.54
1978	0.73	0.93	0.58	0.54
1979	0.72	0.95	0.58	0.55
1980	0.72	0.93	0.59	0.55
1981	0.71	0.91	0.59	0.54
1982	0.69	0.93	0.61	0.57
1983	0.70	0.92	0.62	0.57
1984	0.68	0.94	0.61	0.58
1985	0.70	0.90	0.62	0.56
1986	0.71	0.91	0.63	0.57

SOURCE: Data from figure 2–1.

APPENDIX TABLE 2–12
RELATIVE WAGES BY EDUCATION AND EXPERIENCE, 1963–1986

Year	a College– High School, 1–5 Years of Experience	b College– High School, 26–35 Years of Experience	c High School, 26–35/1–5 Years of Experience	d College, 26–35/1–5 Years of Experience
1963	1.41	1.35	1.68	1.61
1964	1.46	1.60	1.64	1.81
1965	1.39	1.48	1.57	1.67
1966	1.39	1.51	1.57	1.70
1967	1.39	1.49	1.58	1.70
1968	1.42	1.51	1.60	1.70
1969	1.37	1.60	1.55	1.82
1970	1.34	1.50	1.59	1.78
1971	1.37	1.55	1.65	1.86
1972	1.31	1.51	1.64	1.89
1973	1.38	1.42	1.70	1.74
1974	1.28	1.49	1.70	1.98
1975	1.32	1.53	1.65	1.92
1976	1.22	1.49	1.63	1.98
1977	1.23	1.55	1.69	2.14
1978	1.24	1.56	1.66	2.10
1979	1.25	1.57	1.65	2.07
1980	1.27	1.55	1.70	2.08
1981	1.36	1.58	1.71	1.98
1982	1.41	1.62	1.75	2.01
1983	1.48	1.59	1.88	2.03
1984	1.54	1.60	1.94	2.02
1985	1.62	1.61	1.96	1.96
1986	1.65	1.68	2.01	2.05

SOURCE: Data from figure 2–2.

APPENDIX TABLE 2–13

DECOMPOSITION OF BLACK-WHITE RATIO OF AVERAGE WEEKLY WAGES AS SUMMARIZED IN TABLE 2–2, PANEL A, 1963–1986

Year	Skill within (R_1)	Skill Convergence (R_2)	Prices (R_3)	Total
1963	0.716	0.974	0.879	0.613
1964	0.709	1.004	0.887	0.632
1965	0.693	0.981	0.886	0.601
1966	0.715	0.970	0.874	0.697
1967	0.727	0.962	0.876	0.613
1968	0.748	0.984	0.885	0.652
1969	0.737	0.981	0.885	0.640
1970	0.754	0.972	0.882	0.647
1971	0.748	0.988	0.882	0.652
1972	0.769	0.987	0.891	0.676
1973	0.765	0.993	0.885	0.673
1974	0.788	0.990	0.886	0.691
1975	0.817	1.005	0.883	0.725
1976	0.799	1.024	0.891	0.729
1977	0.816	1.018	0.892	0.741
1978	0.812	1.033	0.894	0.750
1979	0.801	1.026	0.96	0.736
1980	0.799	1.034	0.896	0.740
1981	0.796	1.027	0.893	0.730
1982	0.786	1.048	0.881	0.726
1983	0.790	1.050	0.883	0.732
1984	0.776	1.053	0.881	0.720
1985	0.799	1.048	0.879	0.736
1986	0.807	1.044	0.879	0.740

SOURCE: See source for table 2–1.

APPENDIX TABLE 2–14

Decomposition of Black-White Ratio of Average Weekly Wages as Summarized in Table 2–2, Panel B, 1963–1986

| Year | (R_1) | Alternate Definitions R_2 and R_3 Include Parts Correlated with R_1 | | Total |
		(R_2)	(R_3)	
1963	0.923	0.947	0.702	0.613
1964	0.871	1.009	0.719	0.632
1965	0.876	0.960	0.716	0.601
1966	0.936	0.938	0.691	0.607
1967	0.956	0.922	0.695	0.613
1968	0.944	0.966	0.715	0.652
1969	0.933	0.960	0.714	0.640
1970	0.969	0.943	0.708	0.647
1971	0.946	0.975	0.707	0.652
1972	0.956	0.973	0.727	0.676
1973	0.955	0.986	0.715	0.673
1974	0.986	0.979	0.716	0.691
1975	1.011	1.011	0.709	0.725
1976	0.952	1.051	0.728	0.729
1977	0.978	1.039	0.729	0.741
1978	0.953	1.071	0.735	0.750
1979	0.944	1.056	0.738	0.736
1980	0.934	1.073	0.738	0.740
1981	0.941	1.058	0.733	0.730
1982	0.933	1.103	0.705	0.726
1983	0.931	1.108	0.710	0.732
1984	0.915	1.115	0.706	0.720
1985	0.953	1.103	0.701	0.736
1986	0.966	1.095	0.701	0.740

Note: Following a regression of $(\log)R_1$ on $(\log)R_2$ and $(\log)R_3$, the alternative values are computed as: $R_1 = (exp)$(regression intercept plus residual). $R_2 = (exp)R_2$ $(1 + $ regression coefficient for $R_2)$. $R_3 = (exp)R_3(1 + $ regression coefficient for $R_3)$.
Source: See source for table 2–1.

The Changing Structure
of Relative Wages

A Commentary by Walter Y. Oi

Kevin Murphy and Finis Welch summarize the CPS data on average weekly earnings, which is their measure of wages for the period 1963–1986. Some of the perplexing patterns exhibited by the time series data include the following:

- The black-white wage ratio for men was converging toward unity through 1979, but the gap remained stable through the 1980s.
- The gender wage ratio began to climb in 1975 and accelerated in the 1980s.
- The wage ratio of college to high-school graduates declined through the 1970s, reached a trough, and then climbed from 1.35 in 1979 to 1.80 in 1986.
- The returns to work experience climbed from a wage ratio of 1.76 in 1979 (high-school graduate with thirty years of experience in relation to those with three years of experience) to 2.14 in 1986.

This chapter carefully describes these changes in the relative wage structure where the structure is defined by gender, race, schooling, and age. The authors advance the conjectural hypothesis that these changes could have been caused by presumably exogenous changes in the pattern of international trade.

Interrelated Markets for Factors

The authors embrace a background model in which wages and employment are jointly determined by a system of demand and supply functions in a manner analogous to the M. Ishaq Nadiri and Sherwin Rosen model.[1] Black male college graduates with five years of potential work experience represent one factor, while white female college dropouts with fifteen years of work experience constitute another factor. Individuals in one of their groups are presumably homogeneous and interchangeable but differ from persons in another group.

70

No attempt is made to ascertain whether the individuals within a group are alike or if these groups represent truly different factors.

The Baby Boom

Earlier Finis Welch used a market model to analyze the effect of cohort size on relative wages.[2] Assume that there are only two kinds of labor, young and old. Given a stable system of demand equations and exogenously determined supplies, an increase in the relative supply of young workers has to reduce their relative wage. This model can be expanded to a labor market with J types of labor, where individuals within a type are homogeneous but differ across types. If $\{W_1, N_1\}$ and $\{W_0, N_0\}$ denote the J element vectors of wages and employments in periods 1 and 0, and if the relative demand structure is stable, then the vector product of wage and employment changes should be negative; that is $(W_1-W_0)'(N_1-N_0) < 0$. When these calculations were carried out for four subperiods, 1963–1966, 1967–1970, 1971–1980, 1981–1986, the vector products were generally negative for the first three periods. The data were thus consistent with a supply-driven explanation for changes in relative wages. This is, however, not so for the last period.

The Trade-driven Demand Shifters

The change in the wage structure is explained in chapter 2 by first establishing the fact that industrial affiliation is related to differences in skill mix. This fact is established by calculating indexes of congruence showing that the industrial distribution of forty-five–fifty-four-year-old male college graduates is, for example, significantly different from that of thirty-five–forty-four-year-old black female high-school dropouts. These results presented in their table 2–5 suggest that the industrial distributions of various types of labor (defined by gender, race, schooling, and experience) were reasonably stable over the four periods identified in this study. The demand for labor of type j in industry k, n_{jk}, is obtained in their equation (2–4) by differentiating the unit cost function, $c_k(w_1, w_2, \ldots w_j)$, with respect to the jth wage rate.

$$n_{jk} = - \left(\frac{\partial c_k}{\partial w_j} \right) y_k$$

$$(2\text{–}13)$$

Employment was aggregated into $K=4$ industries: durables, nondurables including agriculture, traded services, and nontraded goods a services. The fraction employed in the three traded sectors was lo for more highly educated groups, the effect being stronger for men. The product demand vector for these four sectors is presumed to depend on a price vector P and gross domestic income M; $D = D(P,M)$. The $(K·1)$ vector of price changes is determined by the $(J·1)$ vector of wage-rate changes, dW, via the $(K·J)$ matrix of derivatives of the unit cost functions, C_w, which, in equilibrium, is equal to the input to output ratios, $v_{jk} = (n_{jk}/y_k)$.

$$dP = C_w dW \qquad (2\text{--}14)$$

A bit of algebra leads to a mapping of the changes in employment demands, dN, the vector of net import demands dI, the change in domestic spending dM, and the wage rate changes dW, which is given by their equation (2–11):

$$dN + C_w'dI - C_w'D_m dM = (C_{ww} + C_w'D_p)dW \qquad (2\text{--}11)$$

where $\{D_p, D_m\}$ are derivatives of the product demand vector, and C_{ww} is what they call a $(J·J)$ matrix of the second derivatives of the unit cost functions (weighted by outputs y_k), which has to be negative definite for stability of factor demand functions. The last step assumes that the change in domestic spending, dM, is the negative of the trade deficit, $dM = -\Sigma dI_k$. They further assume that the income elasticities of demand for the $K = 4$ products in their model are equal to unity. In this way changes in the size of the trade deficit, dI, are supposed to generate differential rates of change in demands for the J labor types.

My comments on this model begin with the observation that the wage rate w_j is assumed to be the same for all individuals in the jth labor group, irrespective of their industrial affiliation or hours worked per week. The data contradict this assumption. Further, at the two-digit level we have observed significant changes in average weekly hours, especially in retail trade. Product prices are determined in their equation (2–8) by wages alone and are thus independent of changes in the prices of nonlabor inputs or by the extent of import penetration into that product market.[3] The income elasticities of demand for the $K = 4$ broad product groups surely differ from unity. The authors try to link employment shifts to the relative size of the trade deficit in table 2–7. The relation between the trade deficit and employment shifts are at best suggestive. Indeed one can point to factors other than dI (such as technological advances), which could serve as labor demand shifters. If skill mixes are sector specific, then sectoral shifts in demands that took place before 1981 should have generated changes in the wage structure.

Human Capital and Within-Group Homogeneity

related factor markets model invokes a tacit assumption of homogeneity not only among individuals at a given time but also across cohorts over time. All white fifty–fifty-four-year-old male high-school dropouts in the 1971 CPS survey are assumed to be alike, and each is presumed to be a twin for a person with these characteristics in the 1982 CPS. This is consistent with a simple Mincer human capital model in which the log of the wage rate W^* is a function of years of education E, experience X, and its square.

$$W^* = a_o + a_1 E + b_1 X - b_2 X^2 + \text{error}$$

Schooling is a proxy for general human capital, while X and X^2 are the proxies for on-the-job training. Individuals with the same values for E and X presumably have the same stocks of human capital and hence realize the same expected wages. Schools clearly differ in the amount of human capital they provide, but these differences are caught in the error term. John Bishop, another contributor to this volume, questioned the maintained assumption that the quality of schooling has remained stable over time.[4] I suspect that the average quality of terminal high school graduates has declined because of the increasing fraction who hold general equivalence degrees (GEDs) as opposed to diplomas. Attrition rates in military training courses indicate that those who hold diplomas do better than those with GEDs. This development could explain part of the decline in the relative earnings of terminal high school graduates.

Potential experience measured by $X = (\text{age} - \text{schooling} - 6)$ overstates actual years of work experience.[5] The ratio of actual to potential work experience, A/X, is related to age, gender, and education being higher for men and for younger and more educated workers. Several economists, including June O'Neill, James Smith, and Michael Ward, have argued that the upward trend in the gender wage ratio is caused in part by an increase in (A/X) for female workers.[6]

The use of average weekly earnings as a measure of the wage fails to control for the length of the work week, which is getting shorter, especially for women.[7] Even if wages are determined by stocks of general and firm-specific human capital, changes in the quality of schooling or in the ratio of actual to potential experience could affect the observed structure of wages classified by gender, education, and age.

Job Mobility and a Duality Hypothesis

Jacob Mincer and Yoshio Higuchi have extended the human capital model to incorporate what they call a duality hypothesis.[8] In addition to schooling E and years of general (actual) work experience A, they include years of firm-specific job tenure J in the wage equation. Persons in industries enjoying rapid rates of technical change ge more training, which supports a steeper wage-tenure profile. Tur over rates in these industries fall, and employees of a given age possess larger stocks of firm-specific human capital in these technologically progressive industries. The Mincer-Higuchi study suggests that three-digit industries should be aggregated by rates of technical progress rather than by net import demand effects to study changes in relative wages.

Firm Size and Wages

Henry L. Moore, Richard Lester, and Wesley Mellow have shown that wages are higher in larger firms.[9] At least three reasons can be advanced for this correlation.

- Monitoring costs are apparently related to the number of employees and not to their quality. Large firms confronting higher unit monitoring costs have a stronger incentive to demand more productive employees. In this way they can minimize the sum of monitoring and labor costs for a given labor input measured in efficiency units.
- Large firms establish more rigid and disciplined work settings for which they have to pay a compensating difference.
- Employees in large firms often have to supply more work effort, which raises labor productivity. Higher customer arrival rates at larger retail stores lead to the economies of massed reserves wherein clerks are idle a smaller fraction of each hour. As a consequence they are more productive and can command higher wages. Indeed labor productivity and wages are both positively related to firm size in most industries.

If the distribution of employees across size categories has changed for the labor groups identified in this study, it could explain part of the changing wage structure. The ratio of fringe benefits to wages varies across groups (it is positively related to schooling and age and is higher for men) and has exhibited an upward secular trend through 1980. Other things equal, better benefits should be associated with lower wages. If the benefits-to-wages ratio exhibited a sharper decline for skilled workers in the 1980s, it implies a rise in their relative wages.

Endogenous Labor Supply

In this chapter the supply of labor in each group-year cell is assumed to be exogenously determined. The labor force participation rate (LFPR) and educational attainment are surely endogenous depending on wages and nonwage incomes. Over the past twenty-five years the LFPR of married women, especially of those with infants under one year of age, has sharply increased, while that of older men has declined. These patterns can largely be explained as responses to changing incentives. The relative wages of women workers climbed, and labor market discrimination against married women fell. Donald Parsons and Jonathan Leonard independently advanced the hypothesis that the social security disability insurance program was responsible for the decline in the LFPR of older men.[10] The incidence of work disability is more heavily concentrated among less-educated men and blacks. The individuals who withdrew from the labor force probably came from the left tail of the earnings distribution. The truncated mean earnings of the remaining employees in the low education and black cells should have increased during the 1970s, when the SSDI program was expanding. The cutback in the SSDI program in the 1980s should have resulted in a reversal depressing the earnings of these unskilled men. These supply shifters in the 1980s, which are consequences of changes in labor market regulations, have to be included alongside the demand shifters in an interrelated factor markets model.

Marital Status

The growing instability of the family must surely affect the labor market behavior of individuals. A marriage dummy in a wage equation almost always has a positive coefficient for men but has an uncertain sign for women.[11] In the past 25 years the proportion of men who are married has steadily declined, but I do not know how marital status has changed across the schooling and age groups studied in chapter 2. Marital status is another determinant of wages that could be controlled to examine the changing wage structure.

Miscellany

Seven or eight years ago, Finis Welch and James Smith presented a paper documenting the fact that a growing fraction of respondents to the CPS were refusing to disclose their earnings.[12] I presume that the sample for this paper was limited to individuals who voluntarily supplied earnings data. The suspicion is that nondisclosures are more likely among individuals with high earnings. It would be interesting to look at the fraction of nondisclosures over time in the various schooling and age groups.

Since the turn of the century, we have observed a steady grow in the share of employees in white-collar jobs.[13] Additionally the fraction who are paid by the hour is declining. The proportion of individuals in each cell, defined by gender, race, schooling, and age, who are (1) holding white-collar jobs or (2) paid by the hour has undoubtedly followed different time paths over the twenty-four years covered in the Murphy-Welch study. I would like to see how the wage structure has changed for white- versus blue-collar workers and for salaried versus hourly employees.

The international trade demand shifters offer one of several possible explanations for the observed changes in the structure of relative wages. I, however, am skeptical about whether the changing trade pattern is the single most important factor.

3
Wages in the United States during the 1980s and Beyond

John Bound and George Johnson

Two stylized facts characterize the movement of wages in the United States during the past decade. First, the average level of real wages has been essentially stagnant. Table 3–1 shows that the change in the logarithm of average hourly earnings of private nonagricultural workers from 1979 to 1987 was .072 less than the change in the logarithm of the consumer price index, an annual growth rate of −0.8 percent. The series on average hourly compensation for the nonfarm business sector, which applies to all employees and includes fringe benefits, grew at an annual real rate of 0.3 percent.

The real rate of growth of average aggregate wages was approximately the same for the 1973 to 1979 period (−0.8 percent for average hourly earnings and +0.4 percent for compensation); in this respect the 1980s was a continuation of the post-1973 period. These numbers represent a distinct and startling break from the economic history of the United States since the early 1800s. From 1947 to 1973, the average hourly earnings and compensation series grew at real annual rates of 1.9 and 2.6 percent, respectively, and average real hourly earnings in manufacturing grew by 1.6 percent between 1909 and 1947.

Thus, extrapolating the trend in real wages beyond 1973, we can conclude that the average real wage failed to grow at its past rate of approximately 2 percent per year. This means that the real wage rate in 1987 was $\exp(-.02 \cdot 14) = .756$ of the value that might have been expected in 1973, or about one-third higher than it has turned out to be. Further, there are no signals that the real wage is reverting to its previous trend.

The second stylized fact—or set of facts—concerns the structure of wages. During the 1980s there was a large increase in the pecuniary returns to schooling, a modest increase in the wages of older workers relative to younger workers—especially for those with less than a

TABLE 3–1

CHANGES IN SELECTED WAGES LEVELS AND IN THE CONSUMER PRICE
INDEX, 1947–1987

Period	Private Nonagricultural	Nonfarm Business	CPS	Weights	CPI
1947–1965	.777	.859	—	—	.345
1965–1973	.408	.516	—	—	.343
1973–1979	.446	.513	.466	.035	.492
1979–1987	.376	.465	.418	.023	.448

SOURCE: Authors.

college education, and a substantial reduction in the gender differential.

Table 3–2 shows the proportional increases in estimated wage rates between 1973 and 1979 and between 1973 and 1987 for thirty-two demographic groups from Current Population Survey (CPS) data stratified by sex, potential labor market experience ($<$ ten, ten–nineteen, twenty–twenty-nine, and thirty $+$), and educational attainment ($<$ twelve, twelve, thirteen–fifteen, and sixteen $+$) evaluated at experience equal to five, fifteen, twenty-five, and thirty-five years and at education equal to eight, twelve, fourteen, and sixteen years.[1] A convenient way to summarize what happened to the wage structure in the 1970s and 1980s is to regress the estimated logarithm of the wage for each group on a set of dummy variables, education equal to eight, fourteen, and sixteen years (ED_8, etc.); experience equal to fifteen, twenty-five, and thirty-five years (X_{15}, etc.); sex equal to woman (WOM); and the interaction between woman and the experience variables ($WOM \cdot X_{15}$, etc.). These results are shown in table 3–3. The estimated *ceteris paribus* logarithmic differential between college and high school graduates is the coefficient on ED_{16}, and this fell from .346 to .285 from 1973 to 1979, and then rose to .390 from 1979 to 1987. This means that the college–high school relative wage, which is equal to the exponentiated value of the coefficient on ED_{16}, fell from 1.41 to 1.33 and then rose to 1.48. The estimated ratio of the wages of high school graduates to those of elementary school graduates, the exponentiated value of the negative of the coefficient on ED_8, also increased during the 1980s, from 1.24 to 1.35.

The wages of older workers relative to younger workers also increased during the 1980s—although a glance at table 3–2 shows that

TABLE 3–2
Logarithmic Changes in Estimated Wages by Sex, Potential Experience, and Education, 1973–1979 and 1979–1987, and Labor Weights, 1973, 1979, and 1987

Years of Experience	Years of Education	Education Weight (dW)		Labor Weight (φ)		
		1973–1979	1979–1987	1973	1979	1987
		Men				
5	8	.420	.166	.030	.023	.015
	12	.421	.256	.085	.078	.062
	14	.431	.326	.041	.043	.035
	16	.361	.429	.033	.048	.041
15	8	.469	.206	.039	.021	.018
	12	.426	.298	.066	.056	.064
	14	.403	.347	.023	.030	.037
	16	.345	.393	.021	.036	.050
25	8	.373	.283	.043	.024	.014
	12	.423	.372	.048	.040	.043
	14	.449	.442	.015	.022	.026
	16	.353	.423	.015	.022	.026
35	8	.445	.339	.089	.053	.030
	12	.473	.379	.053	.051	.042
	14	.513	.406	.013	.015	.015
	16	.412	.479	.009	.015	.016
		Women				
5	8	.529	.293	.016	.012	.008
	12	.440	.362	.072	.070	.057
	14	.333	.424	.027	.038	.040
	16	.395	.518	.012	.036	.041
15	8	.484	.333	.018	.013	.011
	12	.443	.449	.039	.050	.058
	14	.410	.505	.010	.019	.033
	16	.375	.509	.003	.017	.035
25	8	.531	.361	.025	.016	.012
	12	.465	.443	.041	.038	.049
	14	.466	.547	.007	.012	.020
	16	.520	.505	.003	.011	.018
35	8	.512	.351	.049	.030	.019
	12	.481	.466	.046	.048	.046
	14	.462	.501	.008	.012	.014
	16	.440	.512	.003	.008	.009

Source: Authors.

TABLE 3–3

DETERMINANTS OF ESTIMATED LOG WAGES BY LABOR TYPE,
1973, 1979, AND 1987

Variable	1973	1979	1987
Const.	1.265	1.694	1.972
ED_e	−.230	−.219	−.302
ED_{14}	.138	.120	.181
ED_{16}	.346	.285	.390
X_{15}	.299	.302	.316
X_{25}	.391	.372	.457
X_{35}	.380	.403	.506
WOM	−.245	−.239	−.137
WOM•X_{15}	−.198	−.177	−.131
WOM•X_{25}	−.306	−.239	−.256
WOM•X_{35}	−.274	−.247	−.284

SOURCE: Authors.

this result applied only to those with less than a college education. The wages of male high school dropouts with thirty-five years of experience (age fifty-one), for example, relative to that of similarly educated males with five years of experience (age twenty-one) increased by 19 percent.

The third major fact about wage structure changes during the 1980s is that the relative wages of women increased by about ten percentage points relative to those of men. There was a slight decrease in the gender differential during the 1970s—primarily at the two higher experience levels. During the 1980s, however, the average gender differential fell from .306 to .188 (women's average wage disadvantage was reduced from 26 percent to 17 percent).

These large changes in the structure of wages took place when the average real wage level was essentially stagnant. The average change in logarithmic wages across all groups from 1979 to 1987 was .418 (see table 3–1), three percentage points less than the change in the price level. Since the relative wages of some labor types (the more educated, the older, and the women) increased, the real wage rates of other labor types decreased. To take the most extreme example, a male high school dropout with five years of labor market experience in 1987 earned $\exp(.166-.448) = .754$ as much as did his equivalent in 1979, who earned only .931 as much as his equivalent did in 1973.

The major purpose of this chapter is to explore *why* the wage structure changed so dramatically over the past decade. We highlighted the first stylized fact—the stagnation or slight decline in the average real wage level—to show that the redistribution of earnings that has been occurring in the United States has been in a "zero per capita sum" environment. Some groups gained at the expense of other groups rather than receiving a disproportionate share of the growth dividend.

Another reason for pointing out the two stylized facts at the outset is our original suspicion that the dramatic cessation of real wage growth and the equally dramatic shifts in relative wage rates might share a common source. The disappearance of real wage growth, however, commenced in 1973, and the widening of the wage structure (narrowing with respect to the gender differential) began in the 1980s. Further, the usual suspects in the explanation of the first phenomenon—a cessation of technical change that increases total factor productivity, a reduction in capital per worker brought on by higher real interest rates, and an overall reduction in labor quality because of a reduction in the quality of schooling or worker motivation—appear not to be relevant in the explanation of changes in the structure of wages.

The remainder of this chapter is addressed to the problem of determining why the wage structure in the United States during the 1980s changed the way it did. In the next section we lay out a fairly comprehensive set of explanations and attempt—as best we can—to evaluate the relative merits of each of them.

Explaining the Change in the Wage Structure

We can identify seven alternative explanations of the dramatic changes in the wage structure in the United States during the 1980s. Some of these can be tested in a fairly straightforward way; the tests of some of the others are rather elusive.

Internal Relative Supply Changes. An obvious first candidate to explain relative wage changes is a change in the structure of relative supply. For illustrative purposes it is useful to consider a model with two types of labor, type 1 and type 2. The labor supply explanation, which is shown geometrically in figure 3–1, posits that there is an exogenous increase in the supply of type 1 relative to type 2 workers, $(N_1/N_2)_s$, such that, with a stable relative demand function, $(N_1/N_2)_d$, the wages of type 1 workers are reduced relative to those of type 2 workers.

Any meaningful disaggregation of aggregate labor input would specify many more than two labor types. Our manipulation of the

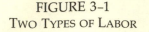

FIGURE 3–1
TWO TYPES OF LABOR

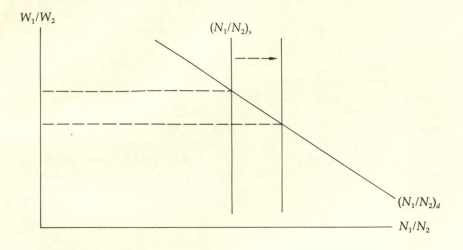

SOURCE: Authors.

CPS data sets yielded thirty-two types (four educational categories, four experience groups, and two sexes). Now make the following two assumptions: (i) the aggregate flow of labor services in the economy is generated by a constant elasticity of substitution production function in these thirty-two labor types, and (ii) this production function did not shift between 1979 and 1987. It then follows that the proportional change in the wage rate of group i workers between 1979 and 1987 is given by

$$d(\ln W_1) = C - (1/\sigma)d(\ln N_1) \qquad (3\text{–}1)$$

where C is a constant reflecting inflation and real wage growth over the interval of time, $d(\ln N_1)$ is the proportional change in the employment of type 1 labor, and σ is the elasticity of intrafactor substitution. In other words, if we plotted percentage wage increases over this interval against percentage employment increases, we would expect to find a negative slope (with an absolute slope of less than 1, for, following Hamermesh, $\sigma > 1$).[2]

The trouble with this as an explanation of the wage structure change phenomena of the 1980s is that it does not work. A glance at table 3–2 reveals that the labor types that had the highest wage changes from 1979 to 1987 also had the largest increase in relative supply (the biggest increase in labor weights, the ϕs). In fact, a regression (weighted by the square root of ϕ_{79}) of the annualized rate

82

TABLE 3–4
Weighted Estimates of the Inverse of the Elasticity of Intrafactor Substitution, 1973–1979 and 1979–1987

Variable	1973–1979	1979–1987	Fixed Effect Unadjusted	Adjusted
Constant	.072 (.001)	.048 (.002)	−.027 (.002)	−.025 (.002)
G_N	−.050 (.020)	.174 (.041)	−.144 (.033)	−.126 (.031)
Unskilled	—	—	—	−.020 (.073)

Note: Estimated standard errors are in parentheses.
Source: Authors.

of growth of wages during the 1979–1987 interval on the annualized rate of growth of relative employment (G_N), which is reported in table 3–4, yields an estimated coefficient of +.174. This is consistent with an elasticity of intrafactor substitution of *minus* 5.7, which is, of course, nonsense.

Our assumption of the generation of the labor aggregate by a CES production function is obviously only an approximation, but it is difficult to conceive of any pattern of intrafactor cross-elasticities of complementarity (which, by the CES, are all assumed to equal $1/\sigma$) that would generate the wage structure changes that were observed in the 1980s. Indeed, in the most detailed study of intrafactor substitution of which we are aware, Kevin Murphy and Finis Welch conclude that the system of labor demand equations was not stable during the 1980s.[3]

This leads to the conclusion—as it led Murphy and Welch—that the relative labor demand function must have shifted during the 1980s.[4] In other terms, some variable or variables have been left out of equation (3–1), and it or they both had a positive influence on demand and hence on wages, and are positively correlated with relative supply changes $[d(\ln N_1)]$.

Immigration. Before giving up on supply shifts as a cause of the wage structure developments of the 1980s, we should consider the large flows of illegal immigrants into the United States during the past decade. The conventional wisdom on the labor market impact of this immigration is that it has not had much effect.[5] Most of the evidence on which this wisdom is based, however, is cross-sectional. Given a high rate of internal labor mobility, we might expect that the true effects of immigration on the wages of lower-skilled domestic workers would be understated by a comparison of what happened to relative wages in obvious receiving areas (like Tucson) and in other areas (like Minneapolis).[6]

Consider the following illustrative computation. Assume first that undocumented immigrants are directly competitive with younger workers (less than twenty years of potential labor market experience) who have not completed high school. Employment of the domestic population in this category, denoted by N_{ud}, was 0.069 of total Current Population Survey employment in 1979 and fell to .053 in 1987. The logarithmic difference between the average wages of unskilled and skilled workers (all other labor types) changed by $-.159$ between 1979 and 1987, that is, $d(\ln(W_u/W_s)) = -.159$.

Total "unskilled" employment, N_u, equals N_{ud} plus the total number of employed undocumented immigrants, M, and total "skilled" employment equals N_s. If the relative demand for skilled and unskilled labor had remained stable during this period, it would have been true that

$$d(\ln(N_u/N_s)) =$$
$$(dN_{ud} + dM)/(N_{ud} + M) = \qquad (3\text{--}2)$$
$$-d(\ln N_s) - \sigma d(\ln(W_u/W_s))$$

N_{ad} equaled 6.82 million in 1979; dN_{ud} was -0.88 million between 1979 and 1987; and $d(\ln N_s)$ was .146 over the period. Assuming that the value of M in 1979 was 2.0 million, the change in M (in millions of immigrants) necessary to yield the observed change in relative wages is

$$dM = 0.88 + 8.82(.146 + .159\sigma) \qquad (3\text{--}3)$$

For values of σ of 1.5, 3.0, and 4.5, the number of additional immigrants that would have yielded the observed changes in relative wages is 4.3 million, 6.4 million, and 8.5 million.

Although there is no reliable way to be sure about the effect of immigration, the preceding calculation suggests that at least some and perhaps a large part of the huge decline in the relative wages of the least skilled segment of the labor market may have resulted from illegal immigration.

Product Demand Shifts. Because the distribution of employment by age, education, and sex differs substantially across industries, the position of the demand function by labor type depends upon the composition of product demand. Accordingly, shifts in product demand—brought about by changes in tastes or by changes in the

FIGURE 3-2
Increased Relative Wages of Highly Educated Labor, 1980s

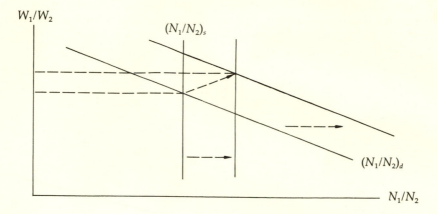

W_1/W_2

$(N_1/N_2)_s$

$(N_1/N_2)_d$

N_1/N_2

Source: Authors.

degree of foreign penetration of markets—can cause shifts in the relative labor demand function that, in addition to the effects of relative supply changes, can alter the wage structure. A possible explanation of the increase in the relative wages of highly educated labor during the 1980s in the face of a large increase in its relative supply is illustrated in figure 3-2. Defining N_1 as the employment level of more highly educated workers, changes in the composition of product demand (for example, the decline in manufacturing and the growth of professional services) caused the relative demand curve to shift to the right more than did the relative supply curve. Thus we observed an increase in W_1/W_2 associated with an increase in N_1/N_2— hence the "perverse" estimate of the elasticity of intrafactor substitution.

To give a flavor of what is involved in testing the hypothesis that shifts in the composition of product demand are responsible for the observed changes in the relative wage structure, consider a simple model. There are two types of labor, as expressed by the equation $i = 1$ and 2, that are employed in two industries, as expressed by the equation $j = a$ and b. The production function for each industry is Cobb-Douglas with a share coefficient for labor type equal to α_j, or

$$Q_j = N_{1j}^{\alpha j} N_{2j}^{1-\alpha j} \qquad (3\text{--}4)$$

The relative demand for the two products is given simply by

$$(Q_a/Q_b) = \Theta p^{-1} \qquad (3\text{--}5)$$

where p is the price of good a relative to good b and Θ is a product

85

demand shift variable (an x percent increase in Θ causes the relative demand for good a to increase by x percent while p is held constant). Wage rates are assumed to be equal in both industries for each type of labor, and this implies that the two wage rates (relative to the price of good b) are given by

$$W_1 = \alpha_a P Q_a / N_{1a} = \alpha_b Q_b / N_{1b}$$
$$W_2 = (1 - \alpha_a) P Q_a / N_{2a} = (1 - \alpha_b) Q_b / N_{2b} \qquad (3\text{--}6)$$

Finally, the (inelastically supplied) aggregate supply of each of the two labor types is employed in the two industries: that is, $N_1 = N_{1a} + N_{1b}$.

It is straightforward to solve this model for the relative wage of the two types of labor. This is

$$W_1 / W_2 = [(\alpha_b + \alpha_a \Theta)/(1 - \alpha_b + (1 - \alpha_a)\Theta)] (N_1/N_2)^{-1} \qquad (3\text{--}7)$$

If the production functions in the two industries are identical ($\alpha_a = \alpha_b = \alpha$), Θ cancels out of equation (3–7), and the relative wages of the two labor types are a function only of their relative supply. In the extreme, if all 1s work in industry a and all 2s in b ($\alpha_a = 1$ and $\alpha_b = 0$), the expression within brackets in equation (3–7) reduces to Θ, in which case a *ceteris paribus* x percent change in the relative demand for good a causes W_1/W_2 to change by x percent.

How important were product demand shifts in the changes in the wage structure observed during the 1980s? Murphy and Welch argue that this was the major determinant of the shifts.[7] In an earlier paper we expressed skepticism of product demand shifts as a causative factor. Using a more general approach than the above simple model (seventeen rather than two industries and the thirty-two labor types discussed in the opening section; a CES production function—with the same σ but different share parameters—and a single relative price elasticity of product demand), we find that the net effect of product demand changes between 1979 and 1987 was essentially neutral with respect to education, age, and sex. While it was true that some important employers of male blue-collar labor (for example, manufacturing and utilities) declined during this period, some important employers of male and female white-collar labor (for example, education and public administration) also declined. If one confines the analysis to the private sector, the changes in the implied labor demand shift parameters are in the correct direction, but their magnitude falls far short of that necessary to shift the demand functions far enough to yield positive relative wage increases for those groups that in fact enjoyed them.

Given the stringency of the assumptions that had to be made in order to derive the above-mentioned indexes, the product demand shift hypothesis has not been decisively refuted. It could be that a finer level of aggregation of industries and skills, or a more complex production function, would yield more favorable evidence. At this point, however, evidence in favor of the hypothesis is, at best, weak.

Changes in the Incidence and Level of Rents. A popular analysis of the reasons for the decline in the relative wages of relatively low-educated men is that the "good jobs" are disappearing and being replaced by "bad jobs."[8] What is generally meant by good in the context of blue-collar employment is a unionized job, and it is indeed true that during the past decade the fraction of workers represented by trade unions has declined. Indeed, this is a continuation of a trend from 1955. As shown in table 3–5, the fraction of all nonagricultural workers between the ages of eighteen and sixty-four who were members of trade unions fell from .27 in 1973 to .23 in 1979 and then to .15 in 1987.

Given this basic stylized fact, it is at least a possibility that some of the wage structure developments of the 1980s that we are seeking to explain are related to the decline of unionization in the United States. Under what conditions would a decline in unionization of a subset of the work force lead to a reduction in the average wage of that subset relative to the rest of the work force?

To answer this, we first note that the average logarithmic wage differential between labor types i and k is given by

$$D_{ik} = (y_{in} - y_{kn}) + (\mu_i U_i - \mu_k U_k) \qquad (3\text{–}8)$$

Where y_{in} is the average (logarithmic) nonunion wage of type i workers, μ_i is the proportionate wage advantage of union members, and U_i is the fraction of type i labor represented by trade unionism. It then follows that the change in the differential between these two labor types over some time interval is

$$dD_{ik} = (dy_{in} - dy_{kn}) + (\mu_i dU_i - \mu_k dU_k)$$
$$+ (U_i d\mu_i - U_k d\mu_k) \qquad (3\text{–}9)$$

Holding constant the other factors that can affect relative nonunion wages (changes in relative supply and shifts in demand), nonunion wages can be affected by changes in the extent of unionization and the union-nonunion wage differential if unions and management do not bargain over employment as well as wages. As an approximation, if the relative wage elasticity of labor demand is unity, changes in the Us and μs will have offsetting effects on nonunion wage rates such that D_{ii} is constant. With a unit labor demand elasticity, for example, an increase in μ_i will raise the wages of type i union workers, but the reduction in the wages of type i nonunion workers will exactly offset the increase in union wages. (If the wage elasticity is greater (less) than one, the average wage will fall (rise) with increases in μ_i or U_i.

TABLE 3–5
PROPORTION OF WORKERS UNIONIZED (U_i) AND ESTIMATED
LOGARITHMIC UNION-NONUNION WAGE DIFFERENTIAL (μ_i) BY
EDUCATION, EXPERIENCE, AND SEX, 1973, 1979, AND 1987

Years of Experience	Years of Education	U_i			μ_i		
		1973	1979	1987	1973	1979	1987
			Men				
<10	8	.25	.16	.09	.32	.22	.24
	12	.36	.31	.15	.29	.28	.31
	14	.25	.26	.15	.24	.21	.17
	16	.07	.10	.05	.00	.03	.15
10–19	<12	.37	.32	.12	.29	.35	.31
	12	.44	.43	.27	.14	.17	.27
	13–15	.25	.27	.21	.11	.10	.16
	16+	.05	.12	.06	−.16	.18	−.01
20–29	<12	.46	.45	.30	.27	.27	.24
	12	.42	.43	.38	.11	.14	.27
	13–15	.20	.28	.38	.05	.03	.09
	16+	.06	.08	.07	−.26	−.10	−.08
30+	<12	.48	.48	.33	.27	.25	.36
	12	.42	.40	.39	.10	.08	.12
	13–15	.27	.29	.23	.00	−.02	−.01
	16+	.13	.12	.12	.26	−.34	.09
			Women				
<10	<12	.15	.12	.03	.16	.20	−.06
	12	.14	.12	.07	.16	.19	.29
	13–15	.10	.10	.04	.15	.17	.05
	16+	.07	.10	.04	.14	.18	.10
10–19	<12	.20	.17	.10	.21	.20	.31
	12	.13	.15	.10	.18	.18	.19
	13–15	.12	.11	.10	.13	.10	.24
	16+	.08	.11	.06	−.18	−.04	−.03
20–29	<12	.27	.25	.13	.26	.12	.19
	12	.15	.16	.10	.16	.21	.24
	13–15	.09	.13	.06	.07	−.11	.40
	16+	.06	.08	.09	.06	.31	.09
30+	<12	.23	.26	.18	.26	.24	.19
	12	.16	.18	.12	.06	.13	.25
	13–15	.07	.08	.14	.11	−.11	.03
	16+	.09	—	.02	.24	.00	.57

TABLE 3–5 *(Continued)*

Years of Experience	Years of Education	U_i			μ_i		
		1973	1979	1987	1973	1979	1987
			All Levels				
Both sexes		.27	.23	.15	.17	.15	.18
Men		.34	.30	.21	.18	.15	.18
Women		.16	.14	.09	.16	.15	.19
			$ED\leq12$				
Both sexes		.31	.29	.19	.20	.20	.25
Men		.41	.38	.27	.22	.21	.27
Women		.17	.17	.10	.18	.18	.23

SOURCE: Authors.

The above point is illustrated geometrically in figure 3–3. Initially all workers of a particular type receive the same wage rate in industries A and B. Then industry A is organized by a trade union causing the wage in that industry to increase. Those workers in A who are displaced are forced to take employment in B, which drives down W_b. Whether the new average value of the wage for all workers of this type is greater, the same, or less than its initial value depends on the slopes of the demand curves in the two industries. The average wage will rise only if both are relatively steep; that is, the elasticities are less than one.

In order for a change in the relative extent of unionism or in the relative effects of unionism to have an unambiguous effect in D_{ik}, one must assume that unions and management bargain (Pareto optimally) over both wages and employment. (In terms of the above geometric example, N_a would be more or less unchanged as a result of the initial increase in W_a.) There are theoretical reasons for making this assumption, but the empirical evidence is, at best, quite weak. Instead, unions and management appear to bargain over various aspects of work rules. This leads to the conclusion that the absolute elasticity of labor demand in the union sector is smaller than it would be solely on technological grounds, but is still positive.[9]

With available data we can make estimates of the average union-nonunion logarithmic wage diffential for each labor type, m_i. This is done by regressing the logarithm of the hourly wage (y) for each observation within each type on a one-zero union membership vari-

FIGURE 3–3
Effects of Rise in Wage of Industry A

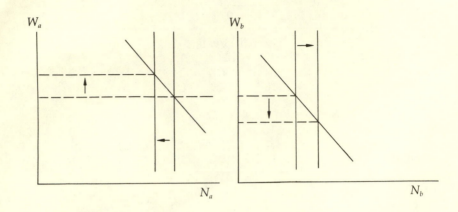

SOURCE: Authors.

able (U) and a set of observable control variables (X, including the same variables used to derive group averages in the opening section). The resultant regression model is

$$y = m_i U + \alpha_i X + e \qquad (3\text{--}10)$$

where e is the statistical error term. The estimated values of the m_is for the thirty-two labor types in our data in 1973, 1979, and 1987 as reported in table 3–5. The weighted (by the ϕs in table 3–1) averages of the estimated union effects across all thirty-two groups are .17 for 1973, .15 for 1979, and .18 for 1987.

A major problem with these estimates is that most of them are subject to an upward or downward bias. The m_is are generally higher for less-educated workers and, indeed, are often negative for workers with some or all of a college education. It has long been hypothesized that employers who are forced to pay higher than market wages for blue-collar workers will set hiring standards that will, in turn, yield work forces that are above average in terms of unobserved productivity-enhancing characteristics. So, the estimated m_i is greater than the true union effect μ_i for these groups. Conversely, the relatively small number of college graduates who are represented by trade unions are likely to be subject to the opposite selection bias; that is, they are lower with respect to unobserved characteristics than those who are not union members. (Professors at Cisco Kid State College, for example, are more likely to be represented by a trade union than professors •t, say, the University of Chicago; the former are not going anywhere in their careers, whereas the latter benefit from a market determination of their compensation.)

Available techniques can adjust for this selection bias, but they have not proved to yield robust estimates of μ. The estimates of the μ_is in table 3–5 are probably upward biased for labor types with low education and downward biased for those with high education. It is also not clear how much of the increase in the average value of m from 1979 to 1987 reflects an increase in μ as opposed to an increase in the average quality of union workers associated with the large reduction in the extent of union representation.

Among male workers with twelve or fewer years of schooling—the groups for which unionism in the United States is most important—the reduction in the extent of union organization between 1979 and 1987 is greater for younger workers and for high school dropouts than for older workers and high school graduates. For a μ of .15 (Lewis's preferred estimate)[10] for all groups, the amount of the 1979 to 1987 college–high school differential change "explained" by the change in relative union representation (assuming no effect on nonunion wage rates) is as follows: X_5, .017 of a total change of .173; X_{15}, .015 of .095; X_{25}, .006 of .050; and X_{35}, .002 of .100. The equivalent estimates of the contribution of the change in union representation on the differential between male high school graduates and dropouts is X_5, $-.014$ of .90; X_{15}, .006 of .092; X_{25}, .015 of .089; and X_{35}, .021 of .060.

Despite the questionable assumption of no effect of the deunionization on the nonunion wage rate, these effects are a relatively small fraction of the total changes. Moreover we observe roughly the same changes in educational differentials for women as for men. Since unionism is historically much less important for women than for men, it seems that the erosion of union representation was not a major cause of the changes in the wage structure during the 1980s.

Another source of rents that clearly changed during the 1980s is the federal minimum wage, and this has been identified as a potential cause of some of the observed changes in the wage structure.[11] Since the minimum had not changed from $3.35 since 1981, its real value has fallen (by 26 percent from 1981 to 1987) as has its value relative to other wages (by 24 percent relative to average hourly earnings in manufacturing over this period). Indeed, in large sections of the country the $3.35 minimum wage is well below the market wage for teenage entry labor and might as well be set at its 1938 value ($0.25).

Since minimum wage legislation does not apply to all jobs relevant to low-wage sectors (for example, lawn mowing, babysitting, and dope running), analysis of its effect on the average wage of affected groups is in principle similar to that of the effect of a change in the union-nonunion differential—except there is no even theoretical reason for supposing that the relevant demand elasticities are close to zero. A significant increase in the federal minimum wage would raise the wages of those in the covered sector and lower those in the uncovered sector, yielding an ambiguous effect on the *average* wage of affected labor types.

Changes in Labor Quality. One of the more difficult possible explanations of the observed changes in the structure of wages is that the relative unobserved quality of different labor types changed. The first application of this hypothesis is to the male-female differential. The major source of the differential is that, on average, women have much less actual labor market experience, relative to potential, than do men. Because of long-term increases in labor force participation rates of women, this gap is beginning to diminish. Based on data up to 1980 and extrapolation of relative experience levels, Smith and Ward predicted that the average gender differential would decline by at least fifteen percentage points between 1980 and 2000.[12] Our estimates suggest that the differential declined by almost twelve percentage points between 1979 and 1987. Thus either the experience gap between the sexes is falling faster than Smith and Ward expected or something else is going on.

A hint in favor of the latter explanation is contained in table 3–6. The last column of the table shows the estimated change in the logarithmic differential by education and potential experience from 1979 to 1987. The estimated slope of the logarithmic wage–experience profile for males with 5 to 15 years of experience is about .03 (the coefficient on X_{15} in table 3–3 divided by 10). To the extent that the decrease in the gender differential was caused by an increase in average actual labor market experience of women, one can calculate how much actual labor market experience would have to have changed for each education-experience category. Given that each year of actual labor market experience increases wages by 3 percent, actual experience of those women with 5 years of potential experience must have increased by 2.4 to 3.7 years. At potential experience equal to 15 years, actual experience must have increased by 3.5 to 4.7 years. These seem like much larger increases in actual experience than are likely during this 8-year period. Indeed, in a study of trends in the gender differential between 1976 and 1985 using the Panel Study of Income Dynamics (PSID), a data set that contains information on

TABLE 3–6

ESTIMATED LOGARITHMIC MALE-FEMALE DIFFERENTIAL BY YEARS OF
EDUCATION AND POTENTIAL EXPERIENCE, 1973, 1979, AND 1987

Years of Experience	Years of Education	Differential			Change from 1979 to 1987
		1973	1979	1987	
5	8	.364	.255	.129	−.126
	12	.262	.253	.147	−.106
	14	.129	.227	.129	−.098
	16	.252	.219	.140	−.079
15	8	.473	.457	.330	−.127
	12	.441	.424	.272	−.152
	14	.380	.372	.215	−.157
	16	.439	.409	.294	−.115
25	8	.615	.466	.378	−.088
	12	.505	.463	.393	−.070
	14	.482	.464	.360	−.104
	16	.712	.545	.463	−.082
35	8	.556	.489	.477	−.012
	12	.484	.476	.388	−.088
	14	.432	.482	.388	−.094
	16	.542	.514	.481	−.033

SOURCE: Authors.

actual experience, Wellington found a small contribution of the decline in the actual experience gap to the decline in the wage differential.

Another possible change in relative labor quality could have arisen because of differential changes in the average (unmeasured) ability and motivation of different labor groups. For example, for those with education less than high school and potential experience less than ten years the fraction of employment fell from 3.5 percent to 2.3 percent between 1979 and 1983. Quite possibly the average value of the unobserved variables' innate ability and motivation was much lower for this group in 1983 than in 1979 because of a change in the rules by which educational selection was determined. Similarly women who entered the labor force between 1977 and 1987 (that is, those whose potential experience level equaled zero at some point in that interval) may have had, on average, different expectations con cerning their lifetime attachment to the labor force than women who entered the labor force between 1969 and 1979. If this were true, their behavior—and, perhaps more important, the expectation on the part of employers concerning their behavior—would have resulted in higher wage rates relative to men in the 1980s than in the 1970s.

Bishop recently argued that a cause of the overall productivity slowdown (and hence of the initial stylized fact cited in this chapter) is the observed decline in average test scores of the working population, with education constant.[13] Such a decline would be relevant to the explanation of the increase in wage differentials by education if it could be shown that the relative cognitive ability of more educated workers relative to less educated workers increased during the 1980s. (Bishop does not go into this.) The observed increase in the slope of the age-earnings profile could be caused in part by a decline in the test scores of those entering the labor market starting in the late 1960s, which, indeed, Bishop does report.

Technological Change. Another possible explanation of the wage structure changes during the 1980s is that the aggregate production function of the labor aggregate shifted because of changes in technology. A systematic change in the relative productivity of different labor types may have favored those with certain characteristics, such as high levels of education and experience. The impetus for this could have been the widespread adoption of computer technology in a major segment of the U.S. economy.

To examine this possibility more closely, suppose that the production function generating aggregate labor input (L) is given by

$$L = [\sum_m \delta_m \, (b_m N_m)^{\,(\sigma-1)/\sigma}]^{\,\sigma/(1-\sigma)} \tag{3–11}$$

where b_i is a technological parameter relating to the productivity of labor type i, δ_i is an unchanging share parameter, and σ is, as before, the elasticity of intrafactor substitution. The aggregate production function for the economy is

$$Y = Kf(L/K) \tag{3–12}$$

where Y is real GNP and K is the capital stock. The marginal physical product of labor input is $MP_L = f'(L/K)$, which declines with increases in the labor-capital ratio L/K (that is, $f'' < 0$). The marginal physical product of capital in the United States is in equilibrium equal to real user cost (z), which we assume for our purposes to be exogenous. Thus $z = f(L/K) - (L/K)f'(L/K)$; in the long run the stock of capital will adjust such that the capital market is in equilibrium. In particular, assuming that the aggregate production function is linear homogeneous, the proportional change in the capital stock is given by

$$d(\ln K) = d(\ln L) - (\sigma_2/\alpha)d(\ln z) \qquad (3\text{--}13)$$

where σ_1 is the elasticity of capital-labor substitution and α is labor's share of output. The proportional change in the marginal product of the labor aggregate is then

$$d(\ln MP_L) = -[(1-\alpha)/\alpha)\ (d(\ln L) - d(\ln K))]$$
$$= -((1-\alpha)/\alpha)d(\ln z) \qquad (3\text{--}14)$$

The marginal product of the labor aggregate is in the long run affected only by the real cost of capital.

The real marginal product of the i_{th} labor type is equal to the marginal product of the labor aggregate times the derivative of L with respect to N_i. Assuming that the real wage of each labor type equals its marginal product, we have

$$W_i = MP_L\delta_i b_i\ (L/b_i N_i)^{1/\sigma} \qquad (3\text{--}15)$$

This implies that the proportional change in the real wage of labor type i is equal to

$$d(\ln W_i) = -[(1-\alpha)/\alpha]d(\ln z) + (1-1/\sigma)d(\ln b_i)$$
$$- (1/\sigma)d(\ln N_i) + (1/\sigma)_m\Sigma\beta_m\ [d(\ln b_m) + d(\ln N_m)] \qquad (3\text{--}16)$$

where β_m is the share of labor type m in the labor aggregate.

If the changes in the individual labor type productivity parameters (the b_is) are identical across all labor types, equation (3–16) reduces to equation (3–1) for all terms except those involving $d(\ln N_i)$, which are the same for all types and can thus be represented by the constant C. If, however, the changes in the technological parameters varied across groups and happened to be correlated with changes in employment, the estimated coefficient on $d(\ln N_i)$ would be biased given $\sigma > 1$.

Assume for the moment that changes in production technology during the 1979–1987 interval increased the relative demand for more-educated, older, and female workers—the groups whose relative supplies increased. Then the wage rates of these groups would have risen faster than if technological change had been neutral regarding labor type. If the magnitude and distribution of this technological change were sufficiently great, the wages of the groups that grew relatively rapidly might rise (along the lines of the two-factor example in figure 3–2). Indeed the estimated coefficient on the change in employment for the 1979–1987 interval was seen to be positive.

Now suppose that this technological change was similar in both magnitude and incidence across labor types in the 1973–1979 interval. Subtracting the annual value of equation (3–16) in the 1973–1979 interval from that for the 1979–1987 interval, one eliminates $d(\ln b_i)$

from the right-hand side. This suggests an estimation equation of the form

$$d(\ln W_i)_2 - d(\ln W_i)_1$$
$$= C' - (1/\sigma)[d(\ln N_i)_2 - d(\ln N_i)_1]e' \qquad (3\text{-}17)$$

where the 1 and 2 subscripts refer to the 1973 to 1979 and 1979 to 1987 intervals, respectively. The disturbance term e' is now purged of the hypothesized positive correlation with the independent variable.

The estimated parameters of this fixed effects model are reported in the third column of table 3–4. The estimated inverse of the elasticity of substitution is $-.144$, which, although implying an overly high σ of 6.9, is not totally implausible given the stringent assumptions necessary to estimate it—specifically that technological change had exactly the same form in the two periods and that the labor aggregate is generated by a CES function. The adjusted version of the model, reported in the last column of table 3–4, adds a dummy variable for high school dropouts in the two lower-experience categories to account for the possible effect of undocumented immigration during the 1979–1987 interval. The estimated coefficient implies that the wages of younger high school dropouts grew at an annual rate of 2 percent lower in the 1980s than they "should" have.

These results do not represent a smoking gun that *proves* the technological change explanation rather than the other explanations. Secular changes in relative labor quality, for example, the hypothesis that women are gradually behaving more like men about the labor market (or *vice versa*) would also be represented by changes in the distribution of the b_is. Indeed an alternative story concerning the decline in the gender gap is that the discrimination coefficient for women has been diminishing since the early 1970s; this, following Arrow-Becker,[14] leads again to the same prediction. Secular changes in the distribution of product demand could also have had an effect similar to what we have hypothesized as changes in technology—although this explanation can be tested directly.

This particular skilled labor augmenting technological change, which we have hypothesized, is only one component of general technical change and is probably not responsible for the stagnation of average real wages in the United States. Thus $d(\ln b_i)$ can be considered equal to a constant term, reflecting improvements in technique that are neutral with respect to labor type, plus the deviation of the value for type i from the average increase. If the general rate of introduction of new techniques, the improvement of infrastructure, and the like decline, this constant will fall, and real wages will not grow as quickly. Bishop's finding of a general decline in test scores implies a negative value of the constant during the period of decline.[15] Our hypothesized shift in technology in favor of certain labor types deals with the second term.

Outsourcing. Another possible explanation for the observed changes in the wage structure is the growth in the practice by U.S. manufacturing industries of purchasing intermediate goods from foreign suppliers. The automobile industry, for example, has allegedly retained most of its highly educated engineering and marketing departments and its largely female clerical staff, but it has shifted much of its production, involving largely males with relatively low educational attainment, to Mexico, Korea, and such. If this phenomenon were of sufficiently large magnitude, it would lower the wages of relatively low educated workers both directly, through a reduction in rents, and indirectly, through market forces.

The importance of this during the 1980s is shown by changes in the employment distributions in manufacturing between 1979 and 1987. Table 3–7 shows the fraction of the thirty-two labor groups that were employed in 1979 and 1987 in both durable and nondurable manufacturing and in an aggregate of three industries: construction, public utilities, and transportation. The share of total employment in manufacturing fell from 28.1 to 22.4 percent over the interval; the odds of any worker being employed in manufacturing versus all other industries fell from $.281/(1 - .281) = .391 \approx 2$ to 5 in 1979 to $.289 \approx 2$ to 7. In 1987, looking at the shares of total employment in the manufacturing for individual groups, say the s_is, for the two years, largest absolute declines obviously occurred for younger, less-educated workers of both sexes. Since employment in either durable or nondurable goods manufacturing has a strong positive *ceteris paribus* effect on wage rates, for whatever reason, the reduction in the size of the manufacturing sector lowered the wages of younger, less educated workers (by roughly 2 percent).[16]

The outsourcing hypothesis suggests that the reduction in employment in manufacturing will be *proportionally* larger for workers engaged in direct production activities. The expected change in s_i over the interval would be greater the higher its 1979 value (since the weighted average share fell). To test the hypothesis of a relative decline in blue-collar employment, we regressed the change in the log odds of being employed in manufacturing, $y_i = \ln[s_i'/(1 - s_i')] - \ln[s_i/(1 - s_i)]$, where s_i' and s_i are the values of the fraction in manufacturing in 1987 and 1979, on a dummy variable for women, years of schooling (ED_i, taking the values of 8, 12, 14, and 16), years of

TABLE 3–7

PROPORTION OF EMPLOYMENT BY EDUCATION, EXPERIENCE, AND SEX IN
MANUFACTURING AND IN CONSTRUCTION, PUBLIC UTILITIES, AND
TRANSPORTATION, 1979 AND 1987

		Manufacturing		Construction, Public Utilities, and Transportation	
Experience	Education	1979	1987	1979	1987
			Men		
<10	<12	.37	.27	.24	.26
	12	.35	.25	.23	.23
	13–15	.27	.19	.19	.18
	16+	.20	.21	.09	.11
10–19	<12	.43	.34	.25	.29
	12	.39	.33	.26	.25
	13–15	.31	.19	.20	.21
	16+	.24	.22	.09	.11
20–29	<12	.43	.37	.27	.28
	12	.38	.36	.25	.26
	13–15	.30	.30	.19	.20
	16+	.27	.24	.07	.09
30+	<12	.42	.37	.25	.26
	12	.37	.33	.21	.24
	13–15	.33	.30	.19	.17
	16+	.28	.26	.09	.09
			Women		
<10	<12	.38	.23	.03	.03
	12	.21	.15	.06	.05
	13–15	.13	.11	.07	.06
	16+	.07	.11	.04	.05
10–19	<12	.45	.36	.03	.04
	12	.23	.21	.08	.07
	13–15	.14	.12	.08	.07
	16+	.06	.07	.03	.04
20–29	<12	.42	.35	.03	.03
	12	.20	.19	.08	.07
	13–15	.14	.12	.06	.07
	16+	.05	.06	.02	.03

TABLE 3–7 *(Continued)*

Experience	Education	Manufacturing		Construction, Public Utilities, and Transportation	
		1979	1987	1979	1987
30+	<12	.38	.36	.03	.02
	12	.20	.19	.23	.23
	13–15	.14	.12	.19	.18
	16+	.06	.07	.09	.11
All		.28	.22	.15	.14

SOURCE: Authors.

experience (X_i, taking the values 5, 15, 25, and 35), and the interaction between ED_i and X_i. The results, with estimated standard errors in parentheses, are

$$y_i = -1.52 + .143 \, WOM_i + .109 \, ED_i$$
$$(.28) \quad (.063) \quad\quad\quad (.022)$$

$$+ .034 \, X_i - .00220 \, ED_i {\cdot} X_i \qquad\qquad (3\text{–}18)$$
$$(.012) \quad\quad (.00095)$$

This implies that the relative reduction in manufacturing employment was greater for less-educated and younger workers but that the net effect of both education and experience is roughly zero at high levels of both variables.

This is consistent with the outsourcing hypothesis with the addition of an inverse seniority layoff assumption. Many manufacturing firms reduced blue-collar employment relative to white-collar employment during the 1980s as they shifted part of their production abroad. With seniority provisions, a disproportionate fraction of the remaining blue-collar workers were older. Further, there was relatively little hiring of new labor force entrants who have zero to nine years of experience with low education. Women's representation in manufacturing increased relative to men's in part because a larger fraction of jobs held by women were in clerical activities rather than in production.

A problem with this evidence in favor of the outsourcing hypothesis is its consistency with a technological change explanation. The relative loss in employment of less educated workers in manufacturing might have resulted from change in production technology that was unfavorable to them, for example, the adoption of robotic technology. Then, as blue-collar work forces were reduced, more senior, that is, older blue-collar workers, were retained while younger workers were laid off and not hired. A suggestive but inconclusive test between these alternative explanations is to look at what happened to the share of the total employment of each labor type in selected other industries. A set of industries that is important to blue-collar workers (in terms of representation and *ceteris paribus* wages that are roughly equal to those in manufacturing) includes construction, public utilities, and transportation. Unlike manufacturing, however, the output of these industries is (largely) nontradeable. Thus, if (a) the outsourcing phenomenon is responsible for the decline in relative employment and (b) technological shifts are similar in the two sets of industries, we would not expect to observe the same change in relative employment patterns in construction, etc., as in manufacturing.

The last two columns of table 3–7 reveal that there was no pattern of change in the s_is as in manufacturing. Indeed all the estimated coefficients in a set of regressions similar to equation (3–18) were insignificant. If assumption b—that the nature of technological change in the two sets of industries was similar—is correct, then the outsourcing explanation is preferred to the technological change explanation discussed earlier. In the context of an aggregate production function, a more or less constant rate of shifting of production facilities abroad would be represented in lower values of the proportionate change in b_i for groups at the low end of the educational spectrum than at the high end. If this phenomenon had been proceeding at roughly equal rates in the 1970s and 1980s, the procedure involved in equation (3–17) is differencing out the differential effects of outsourcing rather than rates of technological change.

Some of the positive coefficient on the women dummy variable in equation (3–18) may reflect a change in women's choices concerning type of employment. Notice in table 3–7 that the fraction of women college graduates who were employed in manufacturing increased from 1979 to 1987 for all four experience groups. This probably reflects a gradual expansion of the range of jobs that are open to women (and that they tend to choose) more than the effects of increased outsourcing or technological change. To the extent that women are becoming more like men in the labor market, at least in higher educational levels, the working assumption used at many stages in this chapter—that the labor aggregate can be represented by a CES production function—is shaky. More important for the questions on the floor, a large share of the observed decline in the gender differential results from women increasingly working in jobs that were held solely or primarily by men.

Implications for the Future

Having examined several alternative (though not necessarily mutually exclusive) explanations concerning the three stylized facts about changes in the U.S. wage structure during the 1980s, we ought to be able to say what will likely happen in the 1990s. Will the observed (a) increase in the return to education, (b) increase in the relative wages of older relative to younger workers, and (c) decrease in the gender differential continue, stop, or turn around toward 1979 levels?

Although we think we have learned something from the exercise to explain the changes, the honest answer to the above question is "it depends." First, consider the increase in the earnings of college graduates relative to high school graduates. We are fairly confident, on the basis of a plethora of past studies[17] and even the results in this chapter, that W_{co}/W_{hs}, suitably adjusted for other things, will reflect the shift in the relative demand function for college graduates to the right and the rightward shift in the relative supply function. We have identified some potential reasons—nonneutral technological and outsourcing being the most compelling—for the rightward shift in the demand function during the 1980s. If these continue into the 1990s, the relative demand function will continue its rightward course. In addition, if the public sector is expanded to its 1979 levels—and there are many reasons for supposing that this may happen—there will be a further shift to the right in the relative demand for college graduates (a Murphy-Welch effect), for the public sector is much more skill-intensive than the private sector.

The 1970 Welch model provides insight into the continuation of college labor augmenting technological change into the 1990s.[18] The relative productivity advantage of highly educated labor is positively related to the rate at which techniques of production are changing—educated workers being quicker to learn new methods. While the major changes in techniques during the 1980s were related to the widespread adoption of computer technology across most industries, the crucial issue in the 1990s concerns whether new computer technology will be as difficult as in the 1980s. Once a firm adapts it accounting functions to Lotus 1-2-3, for example, it could turn over most of the work to clerks who had only a high school degree; during the adoption period in the 1980s, the firm had to employ a lot of well

TABLE 3–8

FRACTION OF EIGHTEEN- TO NINETEEN-YEAR-OLDS ENROLLED IN
COLLEGE, BY SEX, OCTOBER 1963–OCTOBER 1988

Year	Men	Women
1963	.344	.233
1964	.356	.264
1965	.401	.303
1966	.425	.306
1967	.412	.333
1968	.433	.331
1969	.440	.340
1970	.402	.346
1971	.412	.344
1972	.376	.343
1973	.348	.311
1974	.334	.330
1975	.367	.367
1976	.351	.369
1977	.352	.362
1978	.350	.361
1979	.330	.359
1980	.343	.376
1981	.363	.387
1982	.347	.382
1983	.346	.406
1984	.374	.398
1985	.380	.427
1986	.401	.428
1987	.419	.429
1988	.372	.456

SOURCE: CPS Series P-20. Adjustment made by authors to numbers after 1986 to retain comparability.

educated, thus expensive, workers. If the new computer technology of the 1990s does not change the basic techniques (that is, if the firm does not have to redesign a system), it will not need to hire additional highly educated workers.

Adjustment of the future relative supply of college graduates is slow. Because the fraction of eighteen- to nineteen-year-olds enrolled in college during the late 1980s (see table 3–8) appears to be about 15 percent higher than in the late 1970s, the relative supply of college graduates will increase gradually in the 1990s. Further, the social rate of return to an investment in a four-year college degree for males increased from 5.1 percent in 1979 to 8.4 percent in 1987 (given that the resource cost of each year of schooling equals the average undergraduate tuition at a private university, that the real level and structure of earnings remain constant over the worklife expectancy of a high school graduate, and that each worker spends 2,000 hours per year at work). The private rate of return has probably also increased by this magnitude, for the decrease in the progressivity of the federal tax structure has at least offset the rise in relative tuition costs. How much further enrollment rates will increase is an open question. These rates do not seem to have responded to the increased profitability of college degrees as much as they have responded to the Vietnam War.

According to the results in this chapter, the differential between high school graduates and dropouts depends on the extent of continuing technological change and an acceleration of outsourcing, as well as on the rate of illegal immigration in the 1990s. There is not much that we can say about the first sets of factors, but an abatement of the outflow of workers from Latin America seems highly unlikely in the foreseeable future.

The age differential in wages should fall on the basis of demographic trends into the next century. Most of the decline in the relative wages of younger workers was centered on those with less than a college education, and the factors that affect the educational differential are probably all relevant for the determination of the old-young differential during the 1990s. Much of the labor market adjustment in the less skilled segment of the work force apparently concerns workers with less than a college education and with less than twenty years of labor market experience. Accordingly, in ten years those workers with less than thirty years of experience will earn relatively low wages, unless there is some sort of unexpected recovery.

Finally, women, especially those with high levels of education, have improved at a rapid rate, more than a percent per year relative to men, according to the CPS data. All the factors for which there seems to be favorable evidence—technological change, outsourcing, trends in educational attainment, and changes in unobserved relative labor quality—have worked positively for women relative to men. This appears especially true for younger women. The decline in the gender differential is likely to continue through the 1990s.

A Reinterpretation of the Role of Relative Supply Shifts

A Commentary by Lawrence F. Katz

John Bound and George Johnson have written a highly informative chapter that documents major changes in the structure of wages in the United States in the 1980s. It provides a reasonably evenhanded discussion of alternative explanations for these changes. They examine three aspects of the changes in the wage structure during the 1980s: (1) rising education differentials, (2) expanding experience differentials, and (3) narrowing male-female differentials. A fourth major change that is not documented by Bound and Johnson but is of great importance for assessing alternative explanations, is the expansion of earnings inequality within education-experience-gender groups during the 1980s.[1] Bound and Johnson concluded that relative supply changes are not a major part of the explanation for recent changes in the wage structure and that the relative labor demand function must have shifted substantially in the 1980s. They pointed to nonneutral technological change and outsourcing as potential causes that drive forces behind relative demand shifts.

In this comment I discuss three issues related to the Bound and Johnson analysis. First, I show that if one looks at a longer period, one concludes that relative supply shifts are important in explaining wage structure changes in the 1980s. In particular, since reconciling secular increases in wage inequality over the last twenty years clearly requires relative demand growth favoring more-skilled and more-educated workers, it is more fruitful to focus on changes in the rate of growth of relative supplies between periods than on changes in the levels of relative supplies. Second, I examine how immigration affects young, less-educated workers in the 1980s. Third, I discuss the potential usefulness of comparing changes in the wage structure across countries for understanding explanations for changes in the U.S. wage structure.

While I strongly agree that relative demand shifts are crucial to understanding rising inequality in the 1980s, Bound and Johnson have been too quick to dismiss the role of relative supply changes, especially for changes in education differentials. A longer-term perspective on the changes in the structure of wages over the past twenty-five years suggests that differences in movements in relative wages in the 1960s, 1970s, and 1980s may be strongly related to relative supply changes. In particular, a reformulated supply-and-demand explanation that postulates smooth trend shifts in relative demand in favor of more-educated and more-skilled workers since the early 1960s combined with observed fluctuations in the rate of growth in relative supply goes quite far toward explaining observed movements in education differentials. In particular, Lawrence Katz and Kevin Murphy found that education differentials expanded moderately in the 1960s, declined in the 1970s, and expanded dramatically in the 1980s, while the rate of growth of the relative supply of college graduates was moderate from 1963 to 1971 (2.4 percent a year), more rapid from 1971 to 1979 (3.0 percent a year), and slowest in the 1980s (1.9 percent a year).[2] Furthermore, earnings inequality within gender-education-experience groups expanded as rapidly in the 1970s as in the 1980s.[3]

These observations suggest that relative demand shifts favoring the more educated and more skilled were as important in the 1970s as in the 1980s but that the rapid growth of college graduates in the 1970s more than offset the demand shift leading to narrowing education differentials. At the same time the deceleration in the rate of growth of college graduates implied that similar demand shifts translated into rising educational wage premiums in the 1980s. Estimates of within- and between-industry demand shifts indicate little or no acceleration in the 1980s.[4] Based on this, a reinterpretation of the Bound and Johnson demand-shift story is possible: rising inequality since the early 1970s is driven by relative demand shifts, but the differences in the 1970s and the 1980s depend substantially on differences in relative supply shifts.

The observed decline in the real and absolute earnings of young, less-educated workers appears too large for this combination of smooth demand growth and supply shifts to be the entire explanation. This suggests a demand acceleration in the 1980s (possibly outsourcing or trade shifts) or unmeasured supply shifts. Bound and Johnson made an interesting point concerning the potential role of illegal immigration as an unmeasured supply shift that could help explain the tremendous decline in the real and relative economic position of young, less-educated workers in the 1980s. If illegal immigrants are good substitutes for young, less-educated workers, then a major expansion in illegal immigrants not picked up by the CPS could help explain the observed changes. The problem with this explanation is that the magnitudes of increases in unmeasured illegals postulated by Bound and Johnson are far greater than the most reasonable estimates of increase in undocumented immigrants.[5] Yet, documented and undocumented immigration has become an increasingly important source of less-educated labor in the United States. George Borjas, Richard Freeman, and Lawrence Katz found that the legal and illegal immigrant share of the supply of high school dropouts in the United States increased from 17 percent in 1975 to 31 percent in 1985 and that the implicit supply of high school dropouts embodied in net imports to manufacturing increased from 1.5 percent to 12 percent over this same period.[6] This suggests that an increase in the supply of less-educated workers from abroad embodied in imports and in immigrants may be part of the story for the extremely poor labor market performance of less-educated, young American in the 1980s.

International differences in changes in wage structure help shed light on U.S. explanations. Japan did not have similar changes,[7] while the United Kingdom did.[8] Japan had a trade surplus, stable manufacturing employment, a more rapidly aging society, continuing expansion of college education, and little outsourcing; young, less-educated workers did relatively well in the 1980s. The United Kingdom had a major collapse of manufacturing employment, more severe than the United States. Further international comparisons would be quite useful.

4

Accounting for the Slowdown in Black-White Wage Convergence

Chinhui Juhn, Kevin M. Murphy, and Brooks Pierce

In 1963 the average black male worker earned about 63 percent as much per week as the average white male worker. By the late 1970s the weekly wage differential between black and white men had decreased by about one third, and black men earned about 75 percent as much as their white counterparts. Based on these numbers, wages for black men increased 1.1 percent faster per year than wages for whites from 1963 through 1979. This rapid convergence toward equality is well known and is actually a continuation of past trends of wage convergence dating back to at least 1940.[1]

The recent evidence on wage convergence is strikingly different. During the early 1980s relative wages for black men actually declined slightly and only recently have recovered to the levels of the late 1970s. The decade and a half of rapid wage convergence from 1963 through 1979 has been followed by a slight divergence in black-white wages. At best there has been no improvement in the relative earnings of black men over the past decade. The changes are equally dramatic for newly entering cohorts of blacks. Among workers with fewer than ten years of experience, blacks earned about 68 percent as much as whites in 1963. This fraction increased to about 80 percent by 1980 and has actually declined to about 78 percent in recent years. As in the calculation for workers of all experience levels, a period of rapid wage convergence has been followed by a period of wage divergence or at best no progress.

One popular explanation is that antidiscrimination and affirmative action policies have slowed in the 1980s. Another possible explanation points to the business cycle and the recession of 1982, which may have more adversely affected black workers. The business cycle explanation at least does not seem to be supported by the data. The slowdown in black progress continued through the 1980s long after the recovery from the recession. An alternative explanation we consider in this chapter is that the slowdown in black-white convergence reflects a more general trend of growing wage inequality affecting all workers—black and white alike.

Recent growth in wage inequality has been dramatic. Since 1979, for example, the earnings differential between workers with a college degree and those with a high school degree has increased by about 30 percent, and the college–high school wage differential for younger workers has approximately doubled.[2] During this period the wage differential between high school graduates with twenty-six to thirty-five years of experience and young high school graduates has increased by about 50 percent.[3] Such dramatic swings in relative wages have not been limited to differentials between groups. Even within education and experience groups, workers at the 90th percentile of the earnings distribution have gained about 30 percent relative to workers at the 10th percentile.[4] Thus the recent period—particularly the 1980s—is characterized by growing wage inequality, both within and between education and experience groups. The evidence suggests a demand change in favor of better-educated and better-skilled workers as a partial explanation for the relative wage changes. Insofar as black workers are behind in education and the attainment of other market skills, these demand changes will slow their progress relative to whites.

Our goal in this chapter is to account for the slowdown in black-white wage convergence within the broader context of the wage structure changes described above. We would like in particular to distinguish the part of the slowdown caused by changes in skill prices (such as returns to education) from the component caused by factors that are black-specific (such as changes in the impact of discrimination, affirmative action, and black-white skill convergence).

The standard approach for this type of analysis has been to "correct" the black-white wage differential for observable differences between blacks and whites. This allows the analyst to identify the effects of changes in the observable differences between blacks and whites (skill convergence), as well as changes in the black-white differential caused by changes in the relative wages of observable groups (price effects). The residual is typically attributed to convergence in unmeasured dimensions of skill or to changes in discrimination (changes in the relative prices paid to whites and blacks for the same skills). This approach ignores completely the effect of changes in prices of unmeasured skills. Given the large changes in wage inequality for whites that we observe even when we control for education and experience effects, such a neutrality assumption seems particularly inappropriate over the span of our data.

When relative wages among whites are not stable, measuring black-white wage convergence is somewhat problematic. One must select a particular group of whites as a yardstick for black economic progress. The standard regression approach assumes that whites with the same observable characteristics are the appropriate benchmark. When part of the gap between wages for whites and for blacks is caused by differences in unobserved skills, due to differences in schooling quality for example, whites with the same number of years of schooling are not the appropriate benchmark. More appropriately, whites and blacks with the same "effective" years of schooling could be compared. When relative wages across schooling levels are constant, this change in reference would make no difference for calculating black-white convergence. When the returns to education have increased significantly as they have in recent years, however, such a change can have an enormous effect on convergence calculations.

This chapter is organized as follows. First we describe the data used in our analysis. Next we describe black-white wage convergence over the past twenty-five years, identify the recent slowdown, and outline the changes in education, occupation, and inequality differentials observed over the sample period. We then describe basic techniques and our statistical framework and present several descriptions of the slowdown based on alternative empirical implementations of these techniques. The final section summarizes our results and suggests avenues for future research.

The Data

The data we use in this analysis come from twenty-five consecutive annual March current population surveys, from 1964 through 1988. Our wage data come from the annual demographic supplement and refer to earnings and weeks worked in the previous calendar year, thus covering 1963 through 1987. From the survey we included all white and black men who worked at least one week, usually worked full-time, participated in the labor force for at least thirty-nine weeks, and met several other sample inclusion criteria. The conclusions drawn in this chapter are relatively insensitive to these sample inclusion criteria.

For purposes of analysis we measure the average weekly wage as annual wage and salary earnings divided by the number of weeks worked by the individual. The earnings data are deflated by the personal consumption expenditure deflator from the national income

FIGURE 4–1
BLACK-WHITE WEEKLY WAGE DIFFERENTIAL, 1963–1987

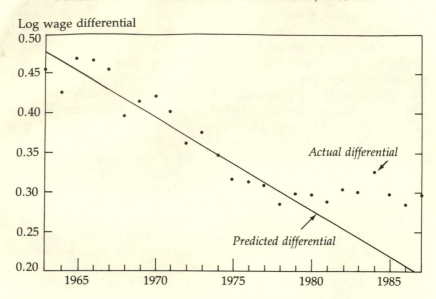

NOTE: The actual log wage differential is the average log wage for whites minus the average log wage for blacks. See the text for the construction of the wage measures. The predicted differential is a linear trend based on the 1963–1979 data; hence the 1980–1987 predicted differentials represent extrapolations of what the differential would have been, had the 1963–1979 wage convergence continued in the 1980s.
SOURCE: Authors' calculations.

and product accounts. Throughout this chapter we refer to the natural logarithm of the deflated average weekly wage as the wage.[5] In describing black-white wage convergence we organize the data around years of potential work experience, where potential experience is defined as the minimum of age minus education minus seven and age minus seventeen.

The Slowdown in Black-White Wage Convergence

Figure 4–1 shows the unadjusted or raw difference between wages for whites and blacks, across all experience levels, from 1963 through 1987. The figure also shows a trend line, estimated from a regression of the wage differentials on a constant term and a linear time trend using data from 1963 through 1979. As the figure illustrates, the black-white differential declined from about .45 in the mid-1960s to about .30 by 1979. In contrast, the black-white differential in 1987 was about

110

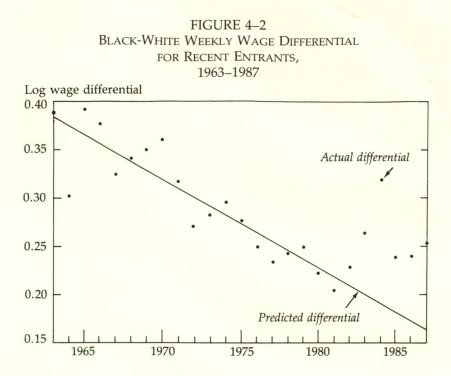

FIGURE 4–2
BLACK-WHITE WEEKLY WAGE DIFFERENTIAL
FOR RECENT ENTRANTS,
1963–1987

Log wage differential

Actual differential

Predicted differential

NOTE: See note to figure 4–1.
SOURCE: Authors' calculations.

the same as it had been in 1977. The present differential of about .30 is approximately 50 percent larger than the .20 differential one would predict based on the trend from 1963 through 1979. While year-to-year variation in the black-white differential makes it difficult to pinpoint the beginning of the slowdown within the 1975–1979 interval, it is clear that wage convergence in the past decade has been significantly smaller than it was in the preceding decade and a half.

Figure 4–2 plots the log-wage differential for white and black workers with fewer than ten years of potential experience. The story is similar. The black-white wage differential narrows from approximately .38 in the mid-1960s to about .23 by 1980. More recent observations show a differential of about .25, with the exception of 1984, when the differential was significantly higher. The recent differentials are once again about ten to twelve percentage points higher than the pre-1979 trend would have caused an analyst to project. The data in figure 4–2 are particularly informative, since much of the convergence documented in figure 4–1 reflects the retirement of older cohorts whose black-white wage differential was significantly greater than that of more recent cohorts. This effect could have caused wages for blacks and whites to continue converging over the sample period, even though wage differentials were constant or expanding between successive entering cohorts. In addition, the rate of convergence might also be expected to slow as the cohorts of men who entered the labor force before World War II leave the sample, even if stable convergence continues among the relatively new entrants. Given the similar patterns in figures 4–1 and 4–2, it appears the slowdown in black-white wage convergence is not simply an artifact of the retirement of older cohorts from the data. Rather, it appears that it does not matter qualitatively whether we choose the wage differential among young workers or among all workers as the barometer of black-white wage convergence.

The pervasiveness of the slowdown can be seen most clearly from the data in table 4–1. Panel A gives average log-wage differentials by five-year-experience intervals based on a division of the sample into five calendar-year intervals. The data in the table are simple averages across years of the wage differential for the indicated experience group. The data in the 1965 column are the averages of the differentials from the years 1963 through 1967; the 1970 column refers to 1968–1972, and so forth. The labels 1965, 1970, etc., refer to the mid-years of the calculations. The layout of the table allows the reader to follow given experience levels through time by reading across the rows; reading down the diagonals allows us to follow cohorts through time.[6]

Comparisons of the first, second, and third columns of panel A show a consistent pattern of wage convergence from the 1963–1967 interval to the 1973–1977 interval. In contrast, comparisons of the third and fourth columns of the table show that wages converged at some levels of experience, particularly for those with six to ten years of experience and those with sixteen to twenty years of experience, but they remained stable at other levels. It appears that wage convergence was significantly smaller between the 1973–1977 period and the 1978–1982 period than it had been in earlier years. Comparisons of the data from the final two columns reveal a pattern of either stable differentials or a slight divergence. Most important, the pattern of rapid convergence illustrated in the first two columns is no longer present. Following cohorts down the diagonals we see a similar story. Only four out of the possible twenty-one comparisons for the earlier periods show relative wages diverging within a cohort, but five out of the seven possible comparisons show blacks losing ground when the final two columns are compared. The evidence for a significant slowdown in convergence seems quite clear from these numbers.

112

TABLE 4–1
BLACK-WHITE DIFFERENTIALS BY EXPERIENCE LEVEL, 1965–1985

| | *Panel A. Wage Differentials* | | | | |
	1965	1970	1975	1980	1985
All experience					
levels	0.45	0.40	0.33	0.29	0.30
< 6	0.34	0.29	0.24	0.24	0.26
6–10	0.37	0.35	0.29	0.22	0.27
11–15	0.49	0.39	0.30	0.30	0.32
16–20	0.50	0.45	0.37	0.29	0.28
21–25	0.49	0.45	0.37	0.31	0.33
26–30	0.47	0.43	0.40	0.36	0.34
31–35	0.46	0.44	0.38	0.43	0.38
> 35	0.48	0.41	0.36	0.35	0.35
	Panel B. Residual Differentials				
	1965	1970	1975	1980	1985
All experience					
levels	0.30	0.25	0.21	0.21	0.23
< 6	0.21	0.15	0.14	0.18	0.21
6–10	0.26	0.24	0.18	0.16	0.22
11–15	0.34	0.27	0.21	0.21	0.26
16–20	0.34	0.30	0.27	0.21	0.21
21–25	0.32	0.28	0.23	0.22	0.26
26–30	0.30	0.29	0.25	0.25	0.25
31–35	0.29	0.27	0.23	0.28	0.26
> 35	0.29	0.24	0.19	0.22	0.23

NOTE: Standard errors for the "all experience levels" estimates are approximately 0.005 in each year. Standard errors for individual experience-level estimates range from 0.011 to 0.020.
SOURCE: Authors.

Panel B of table 4–1 makes analogous comparisons using differences in black and white residuals from a simple wage equation. The use of regression residuals allows us to control for differences between blacks and whites in education levels, experience levels, and regions of residence.[7] Since the regression used to calculate the residuals includes education effects, these calculations do not reflect changes in the black-white wage gap caused by schooling-completion changes and fluctuations in the return to schooling for whites. In spite of this difference the results are qualitatively similar to those shown in panel A. When the black-white differentials are compared at

FIGURE 4–3
TRENDS IN COLLEGE WAGE PREMIUMS,
1963–1986

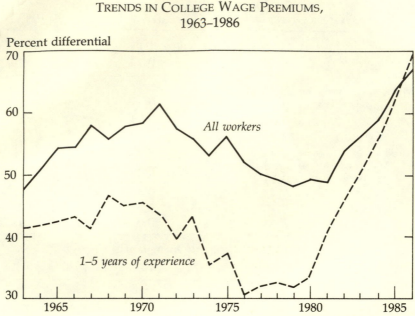

Percent differential

All workers

1–5 years of experience

NOTE: The college premium is the percentage difference between the average wages of workers with sixteen years of education and those with twelve years of education.
SOURCE: Kevin Murphy and Finis Welch, "Wage Premiums for College Graduates: Recent Growth and Possible Explanations," *Educational Researcher* (May 1989), pp. 17–26, figure 1.

a given level of experience through time, convergence occurs at all experience levels from 1965 to 1970 and again from 1970 to 1975. In contrast, comparisons of the third and fourth columns (1975 and 1980) show mixed results, and comparisons of the final two columns (1980 and 1985) show either no convergence or divergence for six of the seven comparisons. Whether we compare unadjusted differentials as in panel A or regression residuals as in panel B, clearly black-white wage convergence has slowed significantly since the mid- to late 1970s.

This slowdown, however, has not occurred in isolation. The slowdown in black-white convergence has been accompanied by other dramatic changes in relative wages. Perhaps the most dramatic change in relative wages in recent years has been the remarkable increase in the returns to a college degree. Figure 4–3 illustrates the change. In 1979 college graduates earned about 50 percent more on average than high school graduates. By 1987 this differential had increased to over 65 percent. When the calculations are restricted to those with one to five years of experience the changes are even more dramatic. The differential between young college and high school graduates was about 33 percent in 1979. It more than doubled to 68 percent by 1986.

Education is not the only dimension in which wage differentials have increased. Figure 4–4 plots real wages for the 10th, 50th, and 90th percentiles of the college and high school wage distributions for recent entrants from 1963 through 1987. Wages for each percentile are indexed to start at zero between 1963 and 1964. There is almost no divergence among the different percentiles for high school graduates from 1963 through about 1970, and very little divergence for college graduates from 1965 through 1970. Since 1970, however, the wage differential between the 90th percentile and the 10th percentile has increased by about 30 percentage points for both education groups.

This general increase in wage inequality based on both the observables and unobservables has caused wage differentials to expand considerably over the sample period. More significant for the slowdown, the expansion has been more rapid in recent years than in earlier years. Figure 4–5 gives the average annual rate of increase in wages by percentiles of the wage distribution (where wage growth is measured relative to mean growth) for two periods: 1965 to 1980, the decade and a half when blacks gained significantly on whites, and 1980 to 1985, the period after the slowdown.[8] As the figure makes clear, inequality rose significantly in both periods. The increase is far larger in the later period, however, particularly at the percentile extremes. Based on these results it appears that the tendency for wage differentials to expand has increased in recent years.

Changes in inequality such as those documented in figure 4–5 and changes in the return to schooling of the magnitude documented in figure 4–3 are likely to have a significant impact on the black-white wage gap. The magnitude of these effects depends on the differences in educational attainment and quality of schooling between blacks and whites, and on the size of the wage gap between blacks and whites at a given educational level.

Table 4–2 addresses differences in educational attainment between blacks and whites as of 1965, 1975, 1985, and for the sample as a whole. The most striking differences between blacks and whites emerge in comparisons of the numbers of each who graduated from college or who attained less than a high school degree. Across all experience levels about 20 percent of whites were college graduates, whereas only 8.4 percent of blacks received a college degree. The gap is actually slightly larger in absolute terms for new entrants, among

FIGURE 4-4
Cumulative Wage Growth by Percentile within Groups, 1963–1987

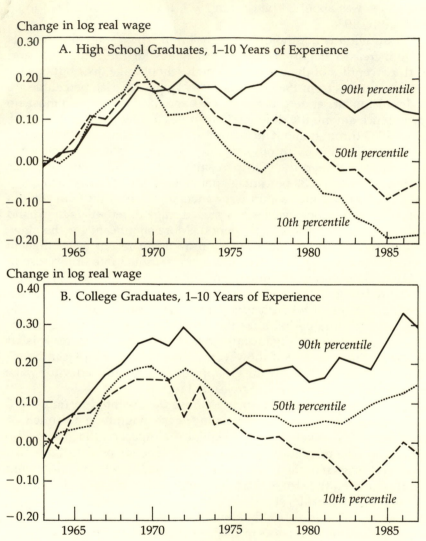

Change in log real wage

A. High School Graduates, 1–10 Years of Experience

90th percentile

50th percentile

10th percentile

Change in log real wage

B. College Graduates, 1–10 Years of Experience

90th percentile

50th percentile

10th percentile

NOTE: The series plot cumulative growth of wages at the median and the 10th and 90th percentiles of wage distributions for two demographic groups. Wage growth is measured relative to a 1963–1964 average.
SOURCE: Authors' calculations.

FIGURE 4–5
GROWTH RATES OF RELATIVE WAGE BY PERCENTILE,
1965–1980 AND 1980–1985

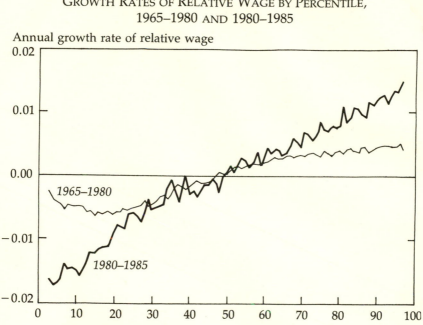

Annual growth rate of relative wage

NOTE: The series represent growth rates of wages at different percentiles of the wage distribution for two subperiods of the data. Both series are indexed relative to the period's average wage growth; by construction, relative wage growth of a worker with the average wage is zero.
SOURCE: Authors' calculations.

whom 25.5 percent of white men have college degrees but only 12.2 percent of young blacks do. The percentage of blacks with less than a high school degree exceeds that of whites by about twenty percentage points in the whole sample (45.1 versus 26.2 percent), and by ten percentage points among those with one to ten years of experience (24.4 percent versus 14.5 percent).

Based on these numbers the increase in returns on a college degree since 1979 of about 0.15 should have increased the black-white wage differential by about $11.5 \times 0.15 = 1.75$, which would account for a slowdown of $1.75/8 = 0.22$ percent per year. Calculations for the younger cohorts give significantly larger effects, since the profits of higher education have increased most for younger workers. These calculations illustrate how changes in the returns to education can have a significant effect on the black-white wage differential and thus in the way the turnaround from a period of moderate decline in

TABLE 4–2

Educational Attainment for Whites and Blacks, 1963–1987

Panel A. Blacks: All Experience Levels

	1965	1975	1985	1963–1987
Less than high school	65.5	45.8	26.7	45.1
High school graduates	23.5	35.0	41.8	34.1
Some college	6.3	11.9	18.2	12.4
College graduates	4.6	7.4	13.4	8.4

Panel B. Whites: All Experience Levels

	1965	1975	1985	1963–1987
Less than high school	40.0	25.8	17.0	26.2
High school graduates	35.2	38.6	39.6	38.4
Some college	11.1	15.9	18.1	15.6
College graduates	13.9	19.7	25.2	19.9

Panel C. Blacks: 1–10 Years of Experience

	1965	1975	1985	1963–1987
Less than high school	40.5	23.6	13.4	24.4
High school graduates	41.3	47.8	48.3	45.4
Some college	10.4	17.4	22.2	18.0
College graduates	7.7	11.2	16.0	12.2

Panel D. Whites: 1–10 Years of Experience

	1965	1975	1985	1963–1987
Less than high school	21.4	13.8	11.9	14.5
High school graduates	42.6	38.6	40.4	40.6
Some college	15.3	21.2	19.4	19.4
College graduates	20.7	26.4	28.3	25.5

Source: Authors.

education returns in the 1970s to rapidly increasing returns in the 1980s could contribute to the slowdown in black-white wage convergence. In addition, these numbers make no attempt to correct for differences in the quality of schooling received by blacks and whites, which may make the effective gap in schooling larger than the gap in educational attainment measured in table 4–2, and thus may increase the effect of higher schooling returns on the black-white wage gap.

In addition to the increase in wage differentials between education groups, the within-group comparisons shown in figure 4–4 and the inequality changes displayed in figure 4 point to a more general increase in wage inequality. Given the existing gap between blacks

FIGURE 4–6
LOCATION OF BLACKS IN THE WHITE WAGE DISTRIBUTION

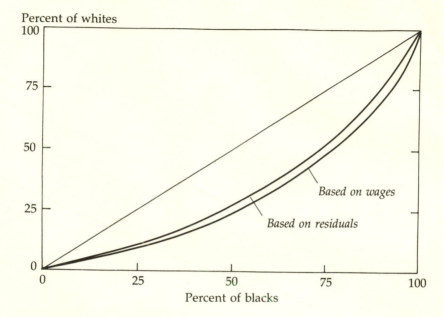

NOTE: The series relate the percentage of blacks with wages below the wage at any given point in the white wage distribution.
SOURCE: Authors' calculations.

and whites in weekly earnings, any increase in wage inequality is likely to expand the wage differential between blacks and whites. Figure 4–6 and the associated numbers given in table 4–3 illustrate the size of the black-white wage gap by finding the position of blacks in the white wage distribution over the full sample period. The figure and the calculations in the table compute the fraction of whites earning less than a given percentage of blacks. The number twenty-four in the "all years" column shows that on average over our sample, 24 percent of whites have wages lower than the median blacks', or alternatively that the median black is at the 24th percentile of the white wage distribution. Market forces that cause the lower quartile of whites to lose relative to the average white might well be expected to increase black-white wage inequality, because the same forces will cause the average black (with wages and perhaps marketable skills similar to someone at the 24th percentile of the white wage distribution) to lose relative to the average white.

TABLE 4–3

PERCENTAGE OF WHITES EARNING LESS THAN BLACKS
BY PERCENTILE, 1965, 1975, AND 1985

Panel A. Weekly Wages

Percentile of Black Distribution	1965	1975	1985	All Years
10	2	3	4	3
25	5	10	12	9
50	16	25	29	24
75	38	51	54	48
90	63	72	76	70

Panel B. Weekly Wage Residuals

Percentile of Black Distribution	1965	1975	1985	All Years
10	2	4	5	4
25	7	11	13	11
50	21	29	31	28
75	46	56	56	54
90	74	79	78	77

SOURCE: Authors.

The upper line in figure 4–6 and panel B of table 4–3 give the corresponding numbers based on weekly wage residuals from the white regression line. In terms of wage residuals, blacks do slightly better than for the wage level calculations. This does not follow simply from the fact that the observable differences between whites and blacks "explain" some of the wage gap. Rather, this reflects the fact that the gap in wages between blacks and whites is actually larger relative to the dispersion of wages than is the residual gap relative to the dispersion of the residuals. Hence the gap between blacks and whites based on the observables is larger relative to the dispersion of the observables than is the residual gap between blacks and whites relative to the dispersion of the residuals. Given the large increase in within-group inequality shown in figure 4–5, one would have expected blacks to lose ground relative to whites beginning around 1970. Whether changes in within-group inequality or changes in the returns to education can account for the recent slowdown are at this point open questions. It is clear that they both work in that direction. The next section attempts to give us an answer.

Accounting for the Slowdown

In order to talk sensibly about the slowdown we must first provide a useful definition of black-white wage convergence. In our opinion the most useful definition distinguishes between effects that are black-specific and effects that result from more pervasive relative wage changes in the economy. The black-specific category would include both observable and unobservable convergence in the skills of blacks and whites (such as convergence in either years of or the quality of schooling), as well as changes in relative wages generated by changes in black-specific prices (such as changes in market discrimination). The more pervasive changes would then consist of relative price changes in the labor market affecting the relative wages of whites and blacks, including those price effects affecting the "unexplained" or residual portion of the black-white wage differential.

In addition to distinguishing between black-specific and not black-specific, we would ideally distinguish the effects of skill convergence between blacks and whites from the effects of racial discrimination changes in the labor market. Our ability to do this is extremely limited, however, and we will only be able to attribute wage gap changes generated by relative schooling completion changes to the skill convergence category. Any residual convergence will be considered as simply reflecting some combination of skill convergence and changes in labor market discrimination.

We begin our analysis by performing a decomposition of the black-white wage differential into predicted and residual components, using yearly regressions of wages on measures of education, potential experience, and region of residence. Our approach along these lines is to divide the black-white differential in each year into two categories: the "predicted gap," the difference between the average wage of whites and the wage blacks would receive given their observable characteristics if they were paid like whites; and the "residual gap," the difference between the predicted and the actual wage for blacks. Figure 4–7 graphs the black-white differential as well as the residual gap calculated over all experience levels. Figure 4–8 replicates these calculations for workers with one to ten years of experience. As the figures make clear, the differences in observable characteristics account for a significant portion (about one-third) of the total black-white wage gap, and convergence in the predicted gap accounts for a significant amount of wage convergence, as evidenced by the decline in the vertical distance between the lines through time.

Analytically we can think of this exercise as follows. In each year we have a log weekly wage equation for whites so that

1

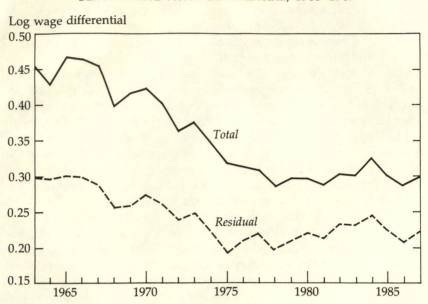

FIGURE 4–7
BLACK-WHITE WAGE DIFFERENTIAL, 1963–1987

Log wage differential

NOTE: The total series is as in figure 4–1. The residual series is that portion of the total differential not accounted for by observed differences in education, experience, and region of residence.
SOURCE: Authors' calculations.

$$Y_{it} = X_u \beta_t + u_{it} \qquad (4\text{–}1)$$

where X_{it} is a vector containing the observable characteristics of an individual white worker and β_t gives the coefficients on these characteristics in year t; as usual, we define $E(u_{it}|x_{it}) = 0$, so that this equation gives mean wages for whites with given characteristics. The actual wage differential between blacks and whites is then simply

$$\begin{aligned} D_t &= Y_{wt} - Y_{bt} = X_{wt}\beta_t + U_{wt} - (X_{bt}\beta_t + U_{bt}) \\ &= (X_{wt} - X_{bt})\beta_t - U_{bt} \\ &= \Delta X_t \beta_t - U_{bt} \end{aligned} \qquad (4\text{–}2)$$

Where $\Delta X_t = (X_{wt} - X_{bt})$, the term $\Delta X_t \beta_t$ is the predicted gap between blacks and whites, and $-U_{bt}$ is the residual gap. Using this formulation, wage convergence between blacks and whites between one year, such as year t, and another year, such as year t', can be written as

$$D_{t'} - D_t = (\Delta X_{t'} - \Delta X_t)\beta_t + \Delta X_{t'}(\beta_{t'} - \beta_t) - (U_{bt'} - U_{bt}) \qquad (4\text{–}3)$$

which decomposes wage convergence into convergence based on observable quantity changes at fixed prices, $(\Delta X_{t'} - \Delta X_t)\beta_{t'}$, price

FIGURE 4–8

BLACK-WHITE WAGE DIFFERENTIAL FOR NEW ENTRANTS, 1963–1987

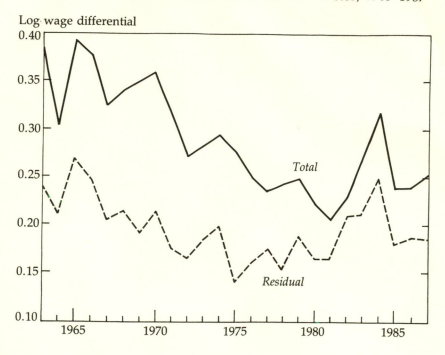

effects, $\Delta X_{t'}(\beta_{t'} - \beta_t)$, and changes in the residual gap, $-(U_{bt'} - U_{bt})$. Rather than pick some base year for measuring effects (year t in the example above), we pick the average over all years as the benchmark so that in our empirical implementation equation (4–3) becomes

$$D_{t'} - \bar{D} = (\Delta X_{t'} - \Delta \bar{X})\beta + \Delta X_{t'}(\beta_{t'} - \bar{\beta}) - (U_{bt'} - \bar{U}_b) \qquad (4\text{--}4)$$

where $\bar{D}$, $\bar{\beta}$, $\Delta \bar{X}$, and $\bar{U}_b$ are obtained using the data for all years together.

The results of such a decomposition are presented in table 4–4. Panel A presents the calculations for all experience levels and panel B presents calculations for workers with one to ten years of experience. For simplicity the results in the table divide the sample into three periods, 1963–1970, 1970–1979, and 1979–1987. These periods represent our attempt to distinguish the post-1979 slowdown period from the earlier periods of more rapid wage convergence. For each period we estimate the average annual rate of change in each component, such as the total gap or the predicted gap, by estimating a linear spline

TABLE 4-4
RATE OF BLACK-WHITE CONVERGENCE AND COMPONENTS, SELECTED PERIODS, 1963–1987

Panel A. All Experience Levels

	(1) 1963–70	(2) 1970–79	(3) 1979–87	Difference (2)–(3)
Total	.78	1.38	−.27	1.65
	(.22)	(.15)	(.19)	(.30)
Observables	.01	.81	.07	.74
	(.13)	(.09)	(.11)	(.18)
Prices	.07	.06	−.27	.33
	(.05)	(.03)	(.04)	(.07)
Quantities	−.06	.76	.34	.42
	(.12)	(.08)	(.10)	(.16)
Gap	.77	.57	−.34	.91
	(.20)	(.13)	(.17)	(.27)

Panel B. Experience Levels 1–10

	(1) 1963–70	(2) 1970–79	(3) 1979–87	Difference (2)–(3)
Total	.49	1.20	−.51	1.71
	(.36)	(.24)	(.30)	(.48)
Observables	−.41	.99	−.01	1.00
	(.24)	(.16)	(.20)	(.32)
Prices	.13	.14	−.37	.52
	(.06)	(.04)	(.05)	(.09)
Quantities	−.55	.85	.36	.48
	(.24)	(.16)	(.20)	(.32)
Gap	.91	.21	−.50	.71
	(.31)	(.20)	(.26)	(.42)

SOURCE: Authors.

with break points in 1970 and 1979. The numbers in the first row of panel A indicate that the total black-white wage gap narrowed at an average rate of 0.78 percent per year from 1963 to 1970. The gap then narrowed at a rate of 1.38 percent per year from 1970 through 1979, and the gap actually expanded at a rate of about .27 percent per year from 1979 to 1987. As we saw earlier, these numbers indicate that black-white convergence has been slower in the most recent years than it was during either of the previous periods. Here and for most of the remainder of the paper we define the slowdown as the difference between the rate of convergence during the 1970–79 period and the rate of convergence during the 1979–1987 period. As the last column shows, we estimate the slowdown in total wage convergence as 1.65 percent per year.[9]

This slowdown can be decomposed into a component explained by the observables, or predicted gap, of 0.74 and a residual, or unexplained slowdown, of 0.91 percent per year. The observable component of the slowdown can then be decomposed further into the part due to changes in prices, 0.33 percent per year, and a slowdown in measured skill convergence, 0.42 percent per year. The residual gap shown in figure 4–7 indicates a moderate decline in wage convergence from the 1963–1970 period to the 1970–1979 period, from 0.77 percent per year residual convergence to 0.57 percent per year. Residual convergence declines significantly more, from 0.57 to −0.34, when we compare the second and third intervals. In fact the residual slowdown of 0.91 shown in the final column accounts for about 60 percent of the total slowdown. As these calculations show, the increase in returns to education have had a significant effect on black-white convergence, lowering the rate of convergence by 0.33 percentage points, but this together with the slowdown in education convergence still explains somewhat less than half of the total slowdown.

The calculations for workers with one to ten years of experience presented in panel B of table 4–4 give only slightly different results. For this group the total slowdown is quite similar to that measured over all workers, 1.71 versus 1.65, and the observed changes account for slightly more than half of the slowdown—1.00 out of 1.71. The slowdown in measured skill convergence accounts for 0.48 percentage points of the predicted slowdown and the price effect accounts for another 0.52 percentage points. The larger price effect for the younger workers simply reflects the much greater increase in education differentials among younger workers. As in panel A, the residual gap accounts for a significant component of the slowdown—about 40 percent.

The basic message of table 4–4 is that the rise in education differentials and a slowing of black-white education convergence in the 1980s explain somewhat less than half of the decline for all workers and slightly more than one-half of the decline for younger workers. As we illustrated in the previous section, however, the expansion in education differentials has not been the only or even the largest source of relative wage changes among whites. Much of the increase in total inequality has been due to changes in relative wages within narrowly defined education and experience categories. As we saw above, the median black worker is at the twenty-eighth percentile of the white residual distribution; hence the slowdown in wage growth for blacks relative to whites within group (what is captured by the residual gap in table 4–4) may simply reflect the more pervasive losses suffered by other workers at the low end of the wage distribution, and not something black-specific.

A statistical framework useful in evaluating this hypothesis parallels that used above to decompose the effects of the observables. We simply write

$$Y_{it} = X_{it}\beta_t + \sigma_t\theta_{it} \tag{4–5}$$

where θ_{it} is a "standardized" residual (with mean zero and variance 1) and σ_t is the within-group standard deviation of wages in year t. Changes in σ_t through time reflect changes in within-group inequality. Using this notation the wage differential between blacks and whites is

$$D_t = Y_{wt} - Y_{bt} = \Delta X_t\beta_t + \sigma_t\Delta\theta_t \tag{4–6}$$

where $\Delta\theta_t$ is the difference in the average standardized residual for whites and blacks. The convergence in black-white wages from year t to year t' would then be

$$\begin{aligned} D_{t'} - D_t &= (\Delta X_{t'} - \Delta X_t)\beta_t + \Delta X_{t'}(\beta_{t'} - \beta_t) \\ &+ (\Delta\theta_{t'} - \Delta\theta_t)\sigma_t + \Delta\theta_{t'}(\sigma_{t'} - \sigma_t) \end{aligned} \tag{4–7}$$

where we have decomposed the change in the unobservables in a fashion identical to that used for the observables. The first two terms are identical to those in equation (4–3). The third term captures changes in the relative positions of blacks and whites—that is, whether blacks are moving up or down within the distribution of whites—while the fourth term captures the effect of changing inequality. Provided the $\Delta\theta_{t'}$ term is negative, meaning that blacks earn on average less than the mean, the fourth term implies that a rise in inequality would increase the black-white wage differential even if blacks maintained the same positions in the white distribution— $\Delta\theta_t - \Delta\theta_t' = 0$.

A decomposition such as that defined in equation (4–7) can easily be implemented empirically. The term $(\Delta\theta_{t'} - \Delta\theta_t)\sigma_t$ measures the change in the average black residual, evaluated using the year-t distribution of white earnings, due to blacks changing their position in the white wage distribution. Empirically this decomposition can be implemented by assigning to each black in each year a percentile number corresponding to his position in the white residual distribution for that year. For each individual in year t' we can then compute what his wage residual would have been in year t given his position in the wage distribution. The term $(\Delta\theta_{t'} - \Delta\theta_t)\sigma_t$ is then simply the difference between the average of these imputed residuals and the actual average residual for blacks in year t. Since both computations use the same year t residual distribution, this term only captures movements of blacks through the white residual distribution.

The final term can be calculated analogously. In this case we compare the same year t' individuals and allow only the white residual distribution to change. Once again we assign percentiles of the white distribution to each black in year t', compute what residual that black would have had in year t given that position in the white distribution, and subtract that from the actual year t' residual. Since the percentile locations of the blacks are held fixed in this calculation, the change in this index only reflects changes in residual inequality for whites.

While these terms are relatively straightforward to calculate, their interpretation can be more problematic. We have to decide whether these effects should be labeled black-specific or should be attributed to more general changes in relative prices. The term $(\Delta\theta_{t'} - \Delta\theta_t)\sigma_t$ reflects gains or losses for blacks relative to whites with the same level of earnings and hence would most likely be considered black-specific. Such a change could be due to either skill convergence of blacks and whites, causing blacks to move up in the white wage distribution, or a reduction in discrimination.

Whether the second term should be called a black-specific effect or a more general relative wage effect depends on the source of the difference in wage distribution locations for blacks and whites. To see this, it is instructive to look at one polar case where the wage gap between blacks and whites consists of a difference in marketable skills, due perhaps to market or pre-market discrimination in training or schooling. If we interpret the rise in wage inequality among whites as a rise in the market premium for skill, then the term $\Delta\theta_{t'}(\sigma_{t'} - \sigma_t)$ correctly represents a general relative price effect. It is simply the residual skill differential between whites and blacks times the change in the market prices for these skills, and it is completely analogous to the observable price change effects described in table 4–4. Including this term in the components of explained changes gives the convergence in the residual wage gap of

$$R_{t'} - R_t = -[(U_{bt'} - U_{bt}) - \Delta\theta_{t'}(\sigma_{t'} - \sigma_t)] \qquad (4\text{–}8)$$

which simply says that the true black-specific effect is the change in the regression residual gap minus the change in the gap that would be expected given the position of blacks in the white residual distribution. This can have two interpretations. First, since this second term represents a pure price effect, we can think of equation (4–8) as netting out the price change so as to leave a pure quantity change, which is the convergence term of interest. Second, we can think of

127

this expression as a comparison between the wage change for a given black and the wage change for a white with the same observable characteristics and comparable initial earnings—a white at the same point in the residual distribution. Since the difference in earnings between whites and blacks reflects a difference in skills in this hypothetical case, the comparison between whites and blacks at the same earnings level allows us to compare black wage changes with wage changes for white workers with comparable skills.

This analysis would not be completely appropriate when the black-white wage gap reflects both skill differences and market discrimination. To see this, let $\theta_{it} = \delta_{it} + d_{it}$, where δ_{it} is the skill level of individual i relative to the average, and d_{it} reflects market discrimination, so that $d_{it} = -d_t$ if the individual is black and $d_{it} = 0$ if he is white. In this case the decomposition from equation (4–8) can be written as

$$D_{t'} - D_t = (\Delta X_{t'} - \Delta X_t)\beta_t + \Delta X_{t'}(\beta_{t'} - \beta_t) +$$
$$(\Delta \theta_{t'} - \Delta \theta_t)\sigma_t + [\Delta \delta_{t'}(\sigma_t - \sigma_t) + d_{t'}(\sigma_{t'} - \sigma_t)] \qquad (4\text{–}9)$$

where $\Delta \delta_t$ is the skill gap between whites and blacks. The term in brackets is what would be calculated by the decomposition described above. In this case, however, only the first term in brackets represents something that is not black-specific. The first term here again gives the predicted change in the wage differential based on the skill difference between whites and blacks. The second term captures the fact that as the wage differentials increase among whites, the dollar cost to blacks rises for being moved down a given amount in the white distribution; in other words, the cost of a given value of d_t rises. Since this component of the differential is a consequence of market-specific treatment of blacks, it seems appropriate to include any increase in its cost in the black-specific category.

One can also think of the issue in terms of the choice of the proper white comparable. When some of the residual differential between whites and blacks reflects discrimination, blacks must be more skilled than whites earning the same wage. When we compare the wage change for a black with the wage change for a white at the same initial wage level we are comparing a typical black to a less-skilled white. This then causes us to overstate the extent by which any increase in the returns to skill should have lowered the wages of these blacks, thus leading to an overcorrection for the effect of skill prices. Hence, when discrimination is a significant component of the wage gap between whites and blacks, "correcting" for the residual inequality effect as we have shown will overstate the desired price change effect.

The opposite is equally true. When a significant portion of the residual wage gap between whites and blacks is accounted for by skill

TABLE 4–5
BLACK-WHITE CONVERGENCE CONTROLLING FOR RESIDUAL INEQUALITY CHANGES, SELECTED PERIODS, 1963–1987

	(1) 1963–70	(2) 1970–79	(3) 1979–87	Difference (2)–(3)
Total	.78	1.38	−.27	1.65
	(.22)	(.15)	(.19)	(.30)
Observables	.01	.81	.07	.74
	(.13)	(.09)	(.11)	(.18)
Prices	.07	.06	−.27	.33
	(.05)	(.03)	(.04)	(.07)
Quantities	−.06	.76	.34	.42
	(.12)	(.08)	(.10)	(.16)
Unobservable	−.10	−.22	−.33	.11
prices	(.05)	(.04)	(.05)	(.07)
Gap	.87	.79	−.01	.80
	(.19)	(.13)	(.16)	(.26)

SOURCE: Authors.

differences, the failure to make any correction would cause an understatement of the effects of an increase in skill differentials on the black-white gap. Since the truth is likely to lie somewhere between the extreme of a pure skill gap and a pure discrimination effect, it seems clear that one can use the computations with and without such a correction to obtain a range of reasonable estimates.

Table 4–5 supplements the observable decompositions from table 4–4 with an additional term, which we label an unobservable price effect.[10] The most noticeable effect of this addition is to increase the convergence of the residual gap in all three periods as compared with table 4–4. This increase results from the rise in residual wage inequality over most of the sample period and implies that actual black progress must be greater in order to overcome the negative effect of rising inequality. In addition, the accelerating rate of inequality growth over the sample implies that the slowdown in residual convergence from the first period to the second was cut in half and that the unexplained slowdown effect measured in the final column was reduced from .91 to .80. As these calculations make clear, however, correcting for the increase in white inequality does much more to the level of black-white convergence and to the difference between the first and final periods than to the comparison of the 1970s and 1980s. The basic reason for this is that growth in within-group inequality has been relatively steady since about 1970.

As this analysis shows, as long as a nontrivial portion of the black-white wage differential is accounted for by a difference in skills, such as differences in schooling quality, then it is necessary to make at least some adjustment beyond the usual regression adjustment based on observables to account for changes in skill prices. The approach we have outlined benchmarks the two extremes, of no skill gap and of a gap accounted for entirely by skill differentials, by using the wage differentials within whites at a given schooling level as a proxy for the price effect on the black-white skill gap. This is equivalent to tracking black-white convergence by comparing wages for blacks and for white comparables, defined as whites with the same observable characteristics and the same initial wage level. Such an analysis assumes that the part of the black-white gap accounted for by a difference in skills would move proportionately with wage differences among observationally equivalent whites. While it seems clear that such a skill price adjustment is necessary, it is by no means obvious that the wage differentials among whites at a given level of experience and education represent the best proxy.

If all skill differentials moved together then the choice of which observable skill price to use in such an analysis would be of no consequence. As we have documented elsewhere,[11] however, even though all skill differentials have increased by about the same amount since 1963 the timing of these increases within the interval shows significant differences. To illustrate, figure 4–9 gives the "price" of skill measured by the difference between the 90th and 10th percentiles within education and experience groups, and the price of skill as measured by the college–high school wage differential. Both series are indexed to equal 100 in 1963. As the figure shows, even though both prices rise by about the same amount over the sample period the time patterns are significantly different. The within-group inequality measure moves steadily upward after 1970, while the education premium actually goes down slightly during the 1970s before moving sharply upward after 1979. Given this difference in these two series it seems quite clear that the choice of which one to use as a proxy for the skill differential between whites and blacks might matter considerably.

In many ways the educational wage differential may be the most natural differential to use for looking at the black-white wage gap, given the emphasis on differences in schooling quality in much of the previous literature.[12] In order to evaluate this alternative we utilize the same framework as above and attempt to benchmark the two extremes. The case of little or no skill gap is the same as above, since with no gap the skill price is of no consequence. To pin down the

FIGURE 4–9
PRICES OF SKILLS, 1963–1987
(1963 = 100)

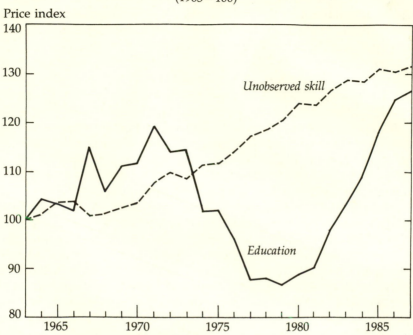

NOTE: The education skill price is the college–high school wage differential. The unobserved skill price is the difference between the 90th and 10th percentiles of the residual wage distribution.
SOURCE: Authors' calculations.

other end of the spectrum we assume that the skill gap is accounted for entirely by differences in the quality of schooling. We let the log-wage equation for whites be

$$Y_{it} = X_{it}\beta_t + U_{it}, \, E(U_{it}/X_{it}) = 0 \qquad (4\text{–}10)$$

When the gap is accounted for by schooling quality the true wage equation for blacks would be

$$Y_{it} = X^*_{it}\beta_t + U_{it}, E(U_{it}/X^*_{it}) = 0 \qquad (4\text{–}11)$$

where X^*_{it} gives the "quality adjusted" education level for blacks in equivalent average years of schooling for whites. The change in the wage differential between blacks and whites from year t to t' would then be

$$D_{t'} - D_t = [(X_{wt'} - X^*_{bt'}) - (X_{wt} - X^*_{bt})]$$
$$\beta_t + (X_{wr'} - X^*_{bt'})(\beta_{t'} - \beta_t) \qquad (4\text{–}12)$$

The first term reflects skill convergence due both to convergence in actual schooling and to convergence in average schooling quality. To see this we can write $X^*_{bt} = X_{bt} - Q_t$, where X_{bt} is actual years of schooling for blacks and Q_t measures the difference between measured and effective schooling for blacks. Using this notation and rearranging terms yields

$$D_{t'} - D_t = [(X_{wt'} - X_{bt'}) - (X_{wt} - X_{bt})]\beta_t + (X_{wt'} - X_{bt'})(\beta_{t'} - \beta_t)$$
$$+ (Q_{t'} - Q_t)\beta_t + Q_{t'}(\beta_{t'} - B_t) \qquad (4\text{--}13)$$

The first two terms are simply the decompositions of the observables used in tables 4–4 and 4–5. The third and fourth terms are more novel and represent the effect of convergence in schooling quality at fixed prices and the effect of the change in education returns at a fixed quality of schooling gap. In this case the final term represents a general price effect on the black-white wage gap which we would like to net out when measuring black-white convergence.

Empirically we calculated this term as follows. We estimated the average relationship between earnings and education over all years of the sample for both blacks and whites. The functional form used for both equations was a piecewise linear function with independently estimated linear segments from zero to twelve years of schooling, twelve to sixteen years of schooling, and more than sixteen years of schooling. In addition we allow for graduation premiums at both twelve and sixteen years of schooling.[13] Armed with these estimates we found effective schooling for blacks by finding the level of white schooling that gave the same level of earnings at a given level of black schooling. The price effect, $Q_t(\beta_{t'} - \beta_t)$, is then calculated as the difference in the predicted change in wages for blacks evaluated at actual education levels and at the education levels implied by the quality correction. In addition, since the education gap is not the same at all levels of schooling we obtain another term, which is the predicted change in education quality as the education composition of the black labor force changes (This is labeled as a composition effect in table 4–6.

The results of these calculations are presented in table 4–6. The price effect, $Q_{t'}(\beta_{t'} - \beta_t)$, labeled as unobservable prices in the table, is quite large and explains an additional .78 percentage points of the slowdown. After correcting for observable changes and making this adjustment for education quality, the slowdown in residual wage convergence is basically eliminated, although a larger slowdown occurs between the 1960s and 1970s than in table 4–4. The educational composition effect is quite small, but it also helps to explain a portion of the convergence slowdown. According to the results in panel A, if the level of the black-white wage gap is largely accounted for by

TABLE 4–6
BLACK-WHITE CONVERGENCE WITH ESTIMATED EDUCATION QUALITY EFFECTS, SELECTED PERIODS, 1963–1987

Panel A. All Experience Levels

	(1) 1963–70	(2) 1970–79	(3) 1979–87	Difference (2)–(3)
Total	.78	1.38	−.27	1.65
	(.22)	(.15)	(.19)	(.30)
Observables	.01	.81	.07	.74
	(.13)	(.09)	(.11)	(.18)
Prices	.07	.06	−.27	.33
	(.05)	(.03)	(.04)	(.07)
Quantities	−.06	.76	.34	.42
	(.12)	(.08)	(.10)	(.16)
Educational composition effect	−.03	.03	−.04	.07
	(.02)	(.01)	(.02)	(.03)
Unobservable prices	−.26	.02	−.76	.78
	(.14)	(.09)	(.12)	(.19)
Gap	1.06	.52	.46	.06
	(.20)	(.13)	(.17)	(.27)

Panel B. Experience Levels 1–10

	(1) 1963–70	(2) 1970–79	(3) 1979–87	Difference (2)–(3)
Total	.49	1.20	−.51	1.71
	(.36)	(.24)	(.30)	(.48)
Observables	−.41	.99	−.01	1.00
	(.24)	(.16)	(.20)	(.32)
Prices	.13	.14	−.37	.52
	(.06)	(.04)	(.05)	(.09)
Quantities	−.55	.85	.36	.48
	(.24)	(.16)	(.20)	(.32)
Educational composition effect	.08	.13	−.04	.17
	(.06)	(.04)	(.05)	(.08)
Unobservable prices	−.13	.00	−.65	.65
	(.18)	(.12)	(.15)	(.24)
Gap	.96	.07	.19	−.11
	(.28)	(.19)	(.24)	(.38)

SOURCE: Authors.

educational quality differences in the cross section, then it may be reasonable to attribute a large component of the slowdown in black-white wage convergence to the rise in returns to schooling in recent years. Under this interpretation, the existing gap in "effective" schooling has led to rising differentials between blacks and whites as the demand for a more educated work force has increased.

The results for younger workers, shown in panel B, are similar. In this case the total slowdown of 1.71 is slightly more than accounted for by these computations, leaving a residual slowdown of -0.11. The education quality adjustment for younger workers turns out to be about the same as for workers in general, reflecting the conflicting effects of a smaller gap in education quality and a larger change in educational prices for younger workers. As was the case in the calculations for all workers, however, the slowdown from the 1960s to the 1970s is now marginally larger than in table 4–4.

Figure 4–10 graphs the predicted black-white wage gap and the actual wage gap using the education quality model described above. The actual gap is the same as that shown in figure 4–1. The predicted gap is simply the predicted wage for whites in each year minus the predicted wage for blacks after the education quality adjustment and after adding a linear trend of $-.62$ percent per year, to make the total wage convergence the same for the actual and predicted series for the period as a whole; this simply proxies for a constant rate of black-white residual wage convergence. The similarity of the two lines is striking, given the fact that the scaling of the predicted differential is entirely determined by the cross-sectional wage differentials between whites and blacks and that the time series movements used are simply those for the education returns applied to our estimated quality gap. Figure 4–11 presents the same two series for new entrants. Once again the similarity of the two series is striking. These two figures demonstrate that the time series fluctuations in the black-white wage gap around trend are closely related to the observable differences between blacks and whites and the returns to schooling.

Figures 4–12 and 4–13 graph the residual gap from the regression decomposition and the predicted residual gap based on the education quality adjustment and trend only. Since the effects of observables are eliminated from both series, the comovement of these time series reflects only the strong association between the black-white wage gap within education and experience levels and the returns to schooling. Clearly the black-white wage differential appears to be well explained by a model in which the returns to education proxy for the price effects between races, overlaid on a smooth trend toward wage equal-

FIGURE 4–10
BLACK-WHITE WAGE DIFFERENTIAL BASED ON THE
EDUCATION QUALITY MODEL, 1967–1987

Log wage differential

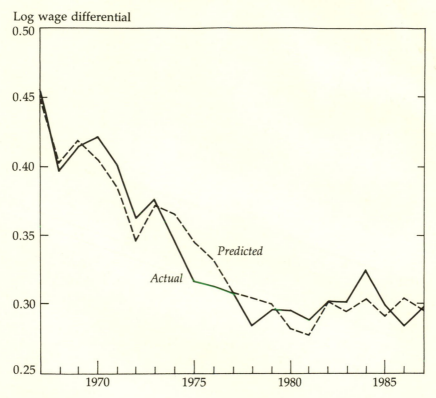

NOTE: The actual series is as in figure 4–1. The predicted series is the average predicted wage for whites minus the average predicted wage for blacks, after correcting for differences in educational quality. See the text for details.
SOURCE: Authors' calculations.

ity. The only significant variations appear for the earliest few years, for which data quality may in fact be suspect.

The basic idea underlying results such as those presented in table 4–5 and figures 4–10, 4–11, 4–12, and 4–13 is that relative price changes have led to significant fluctuations in the wage differentials within education levels. One way to test the validity of this hypothesis is to obtain additional observable measures of skills and skill prices to find proxies, such as occupational differentials, for such relative price effects. Table 4–7 presents relative wage changes by one-digit occupa-

FIGURE 4–11

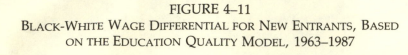

BLACK-WHITE WAGE DIFFERENTIAL FOR NEW ENTRANTS, BASED
ON THE EDUCATION QUALITY MODEL, 1963–1987

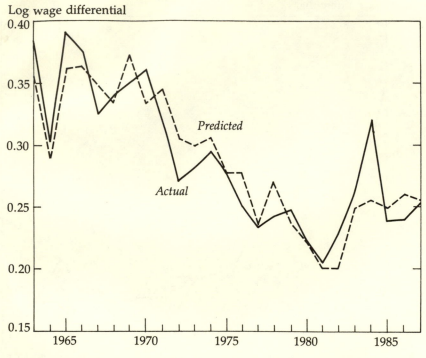

Log wage differential

Predicted

Actual

NOTE: See note to figure 4–10.
SOURCE: Authors' calculations.

tion categories for the 1970s and 1980s; data comparability limits our
ability to do these calculations for the 1960s. Clearly occupational
differentials have moved similarly to the returns to education, with
more highly skilled workers such as professionals, managers, and
salespeople losing ground during the 1970s and gaining significantly
during the 1980s. This is probably not surprising given the well-
known relationship between education and occupation. What interests us here is the additional information contained in occupation for
wage differentials within education levels.

Table 4–8 gives the average occupational distributions for whites
and blacks, as well as the difference in these distributions. This table
illustrates that expansions in occupational differentials such as those
shown in table 4–7 lead to a significant change in the black-white
wage differentials, given the large difference in occupation distribu-

FIGURE 4–12

Black-White Wage Residual Differential, 1963–1987

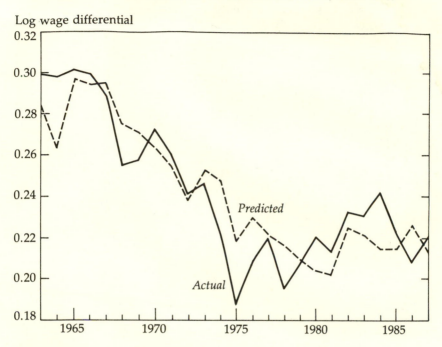

Log wage differential

NOTE: The series are constructed as in figures 4–10 and 4–11, except that wage residuals are utilized. See figure 4–7 and the text for details.
SOURCE: Authors' calculations.

tions. It remains to be seen whether these changes are already proxied by the education effects included in our previous decompositions. In order to see how much additional information is added by occupation we included three-digit occupation dummies along with the other observable variables included in the decomposition in table 4–4. We calculated the additional impact of occupation by taking the difference between the predicted values from regression equations using occupational effects and education controls, and the predicted values from regression equations containing only the education controls. Since this exercise can be performed for both the quantity change term (change in observables at fixed prices) and the price effect term (change in the wage gap given fixed education and occupation differences between whites and blacks), we decompose the occupation effect just as we did the education effects in table 4–4.

The results of this decomposition are summarized in table 4–9.[14]

137

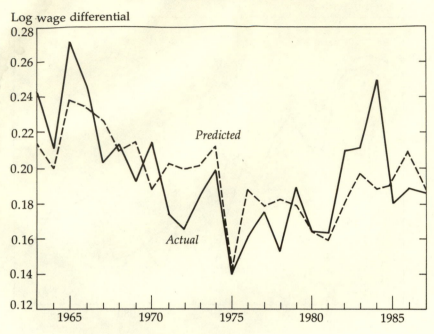

NOTE: See note to figure 4–12.
SOURCE: Authors' calculations.

Even after controlling for education, changes in occupational prices explain another 0.29 percentage points of the slowdown, and changes in occupation quantities explain another 0.32 percentage points. Based on these numbers it appears that a significant portion of the residual slowdown (0.29 out of 0.91) is attributable to shifts in relative wages across occupations within education levels. Our speculations that changes in skill prices within education levels have contributed significantly to the black-white slowdown seem to be confirmed. Table 4–9 also shows something else. Occupational progress within education levels, defined as the predicted change in the wage gap from the change in the black education and occupation distributions minus the predictions based on education changes alone, slowed significantly from the 1970s to the 1980s. This seems to suggest that at least some component of the slowdown in residual wage convergence reflects an actual slowdown in black economic progress and is not solely the result of relative price movements.

TABLE 4–7

RELATIVE WAGE GROWTH BY OCCUPATIONS, 1970–1979 AND 1979–1987

Occupation	1970–79	1979–87	Difference
Professionals	−.53	.95	1.48
	(.06)	(.07)	
Managers	−.55	.66	1.21
	(.11)	(.13)	
Sales	−.52	.46	.98
	(.20)	(.24)	
Clerical	.21	−.80	−1.01
	(.18)	(.21)	
Craftsmen	.17	−.54	−.71
	(.06)	(.07)	
Operatives	.81	−.82	−1.63
	(.09)	(.11)	
Transport operatives	.68	−.80	−1.48
	(.12)	(.14)	
Laborers	.63	.72	−1.06
	(.16)	(.19)	
Services	−.65	−.44	.21
	(.13)	(.15)	
Private household	1.92	−.85	−2.77
	(.31)	(.37)	

SOURCE: Authors.

Panel B presents the analogous estimates for workers with one to ten years of experience. For this group, occupation related changes capture slightly less of the slowdown, but more was already captured by education for this group. In addition the slowdown in occupational quantity convergence, or occupational progress for blacks, seems somewhat smaller than in the calculation for all workers.

If we add the amount explained by the changes in occupation prices to the amount explained by the observable prices and quantities, what is left over is simply the occupational quantity changes, which represent convergence, and the residual or unexplained rate of black-white convergence. These convergence rates as well as the slowdown in convergence are listed in the final row of each panel. Since the initial slowdown in panel A is 1.65 and the slowdown shown in the last row is .64, changes in education and occupation returns and changes in educational convergence explain about $61 = 100 \times (1 - .64/1.65)$ percent of the slowdown. For younger work-

139

TABLE 4–8

DISTRIBUTION OF BLACK AND WHITE WORKERS ACROSS OCCUPATIONS

Occupation	Whites	Blacks	Total
Professionals	16.06	7.61	15.38
Managers	14.45	4.92	13.69
Sales	5.73	1.68	5.41
Clerical	6.59	8.41	6.74
Craftsmen	24.28	16.58	23.66
Operatives	12.72	18.57	13.18
Transport operatives	6.38	10.33	6.69
Laborers	5.43	14.24	6.13
Services	6.84	15.28	7.52
Private household	1.51	2.31	1.57

SOURCE: Authors.

ers the combination of observed changes in education along with education and occupation price changes explain about $70 = 100 \times (1 - .51/1.71)$ percent of the slowdown. As we have stressed, these calculations are likely to understate the importance of relative price changes since they make no correction for price effects within occupational classifications.

Table 4–10 presents similar results using one-digit occupation classifications. These calculations avoid many of the problems in matching three-digit occupations across the 1970-1980 census definitions. They have significantly less detail, however, and one would expect them to pick up less of the occupational wage structure change. While this seems to be somewhat true, the similarity of the results with the three-digit calculations is reassuring. We believe that the occupation results lend significant support to to our view that the recent increase in returns to skill have had significant effects on the black-white wage gap within education groups. This could not be revealed by the usual regression decomposition methods. These calculations imply that most of the slowdown in black-white convergence is attributable to changes in the rate of educational convergence, or observable quantities, and more importantly to the effects of a rising premium on education and other forms of skill. At the same time these results show that there has been a real slowdown in the occupational convergence between blacks and whites, suggesting that prices cannot be the whole story.

TABLE 4–9
BLACK-WHITE CONVERGENCE WITH THREE-DIGIT OCCUPATION EFFECTS, 1970–1979 AND 1979–1987

Panel A. All Experience Levels

	(1) 1970–79	(2) 1979–87	Difference (1)–(2)
Total	1.38	−.27	1.65
	(.15)	(.19)	(.30)
Observables	1.11	−.25	1.36
	(.08)	(.09)	(.16)
Prices	.06	−.27	.33
	(.03)	(.04)	(.07)
Quantities	.76	.34	.42
	(.08)	(.10)	(.16)
Occupation prices	.11	−.18	.29
	(.04)	(.04)	(.07)
Occupation quantities	.18	−.14	.32
	(.05)	(.05)	(.09)
Gap	.29	−.03	.32
	(.15)	(.17)	(.28)
Gap + occupation quantities	.47	−.17	.64
	(.15)	(.17)	(.29)

Panel B. Experience Levels 1–10

	(1) 1970–79	(2) 1979–87	Difference (1)–(2)
Total	1.20	−.51	1.71
	(.24)	(.30)	(.48)
Observables	1.01	−.28	1.29
	(.21)	(.24)	(.39)
Prices	.14	−.37	.52
	(.04)	(.05)	(.09)
Quantities	.85	.36	.48
	(.16)	(.20)	(.32)
Occupation prices	.07	−.13	.20
	(.05)	(.06)	(.10)
Occupation quantities	−.05	−.14	.09
	(.08)	(.09)	(.16)
Gap	.19	−.23	.42
	(.23)	(.26)	(.43)
Gap + occupation quantities	.14	−.37	.51
	(.23)	(.27)	(.45)

SOURCE: Authors.

141

TABLE 4–10

BLACK-WHITE CONVERGENCE WITH ONE-DIGIT OCCUPATION
EFFECTS, 1970–1979 AND 1979–1987

Panel A. All Experience Levels

	(1) 1970–79	(2) 1979–87	Difference (1)–(2)
Total	1.38	−.27	1.65
	(.15)	(.19)	(.30)
Observables	1.12	−.10	1.22
	(.11)	(.12)	(.21)
Prices	.06	−.27	.33
	(.03)	(.04)	(.07)
Quantities	.76	.34	.42
	(.08)	(.10)	(.16)
Occupation prices	.13	−.10	.23
	(.03)	(.04)	(.05)
Occupation quantities	.17	−.07	.24
	(.04)	(.05)	(.08)
Gap	.25	−.17	.42
	(.16)	(.20)	(.32)
Gap + occupation quantities	.42	−.24	.66
	(.17)	(.19)	(.32)

Panel B. Experience Levels 1–10

	(1) 1970–79	(2) 1979–87	Difference (1)–(2)
Total	1.20	−.51	1.71
	(.24)	(.30)	(.48)
Observables	1.09	−.21	1.30
	(.21)	(.24)	(.41)
Prices	.14	−.37	.52
	(.04)	(.05)	(.09)
Quantities	.85	.36	.48
	(.16)	(.20)	(.32)
Occupation prices	.07	−.13	.20
	(.05)	(.06)	(.10)
Occupation quantities	−.05	−.14	.09
	(.08)	(.09)	(.16)
Gap	.19	−.23	.42
	(.23)	(.26)	(.43)
Gap + occupation quantities	.14	−.37	.51
	(.23)	(.27)	(.45)

SOURCE: Authors.

Conclusion

When relative wages are not constant among whites, the measurement of black economic progress is problematic. The selection of a particular segment of the white population to serve as the barometer of black progress has a direct bearing on results. Considering the large changes in the wage structure over the past decade and a half, this problem is particularly acute for the most recent period. Simply comparing raw averages for blacks and whites yields an enormous slowdown in black progress from the 1970s to the 1980s—1.65 percent per year. Controlling for observable changes in prices and quantities—that is, comparing blacks to whites with the same education and experience—lowers this slowdown by about 0.74 percentage points to 0.91 percent per year. If we compare wage growth for blacks with wage growth for whites with similar education and experience levels and similar initial wages, the slowdown falls further, to 0.80. Finally, if we compare the wages for blacks with the wages for less educated whites with the same earnings, thus controlling for differences in the quality of schooling, the slowdown is almost eliminated.

Which of these comparisons is valid depends crucially on the cause of the residual wage gap between whites and blacks. To the extent that it reflects only discrimination, the numbers after controlling for the observables provide the best estimate of the slowdown in true black progress. To the extent that it reflects a gap between whites and blacks in acquired skills such as education, one of the other estimates becomes more relevant. Even if the black-white wage gap has a large skill component, the type of skill differential and hence the relevant skill price must still be ascertained. To the extent that the skill gap reflects differences in the quality of schooling, as emphasized by research to date, a very large portion of the black-white slowdown can be attributed to the recent change in the market value of education. What is needed is further direct evidence concerning the size of the schooling quality gap and the way returns to schooling quality have changed within racial groups. Our analysis in this paper suggests that looking in that direction may be an excellent way to understand the slowdown in black-white convergence.

Wage Differences
and Racial Inequities

A Commentary by Albert Rees

The preceding chapter is a useful and instructive one, but I have some reservations about the last part of the analysis. The authors begin by showing that the weekly earnings of black and white male workers converged steadily between 1963 and 1979. This convergence stopped abruptly in 1980, and until 1987 there was no further convergence. The same pattern is found after controlling for experience.

The authors point out that this slowdown in convergence did not take place in isolation but was part of a general pattern of widening wage differentials in the 1980s. I have no quarrel with this observation. One could equally observe, however, that during the 1980s there was a slowdown or reversal of other trends toward equality between blacks and whites, in areas having nothing to do with wages. In the past few years, for example, the difference in life expectancy at birth between white and black men, a difference that had been narrowing in the long run, has begun to widen again. Similarly the fraction of black male high-school graduates who go on to college, which had risen rapidly in the 1970s, has begun to fall.

In the second part of the chapter the authors attribute about half of the slowdown in convergence to a rise in the rate of return to a college degree in the 1980s and to the fact that proportionally fewer black than white males are college graduates. This analysis is convincing.

In the last part of the chapter the authors make a correction for differences in the quality of education between blacks and whites, which in their view explains most of the remainder of the slowdown. This analysis is ingenious, but it raises serious, unanswered questions. The gauge used for measuring differences in educational quality, called effective schooling, is the level of white schooling that yields the same level of earnings as a given level of black schooling. Thus, if a black college graduate earns the same amount as a white with two years of college, this is taken as a measure of the quality difference between white and black education. Clearly it could be, and in a world with no race discrimination it probably would be. Other interpretations, however, are possible. Differences in earnings between blacks and whites with the same number of years of schooling could arise because discriminating employers prefer less-educated whites to more-educated blacks when their productivity is the same. Resolution of this issue will have to await the development of more direct measures of the quality of education and of the return on quality.

5
Achievement, Test Scores, and Relative Wages

John Bishop

During the postwar period the United States has experienced large gyrations in the academic achievement of high school graduates and in the return to a college education. The test scores of students completing high school, which had been rising continuously since World War I, peaked in 1965–1967 and declined 1.25 grade-level equivalents by 1979. At that point a recovery began, and test scores returned to the 1966 levels.[1] Trends in the payoff to college have followed a remarkably similar path. The college wage premium was quite low immediately following World War II, but once the market had digested the large cohort of GI Bill graduates, the college premium grew substantially during the 1950s and early 1960s. For men with one to five years of postschool work experience, the wage premium apparently peaked at 41 percent in the middle 1960s, after which a slow decline set in, with a trough at 28 percent in the late 1970s. Since then the college premium for men with one to five years of experience has boomed and has now reached 70 percent.[2]

This chapter examines the causal connections between these two phenomena: changes in the academic achievement of high school graduates and changes in the payoff to college graduates. Four specific questions are addressed:

1. Did the postwar cycles in the payoff to college contribute to the rise, then fall, then rise of academic achievement levels of students completing their high school education?

    Apparently, yes. The timing of the peaks and the troughs of these two series is remarkably coincident in the postwar period, and students living in communities with high rates of return to

The author thanks Tom Friedrich for help preparing the data on trends in college majors and John Gary and George Jakubson for assistance in creating the extract of the National Longitudinal Survey (NLS) of youth analyzed in this paper.

college are more likely to take college preparatory courses in high school.

2. Did the test-score decline slow the growth of the aggregate supply of well-educated workers? Did it contribute to the recent general escalation in the payoff to college?

   Yes. If a grade-level-equivalent metric is used for the calculation, the test-score decline caused almost as large a deceleration in the growth of work force quality during the 1980s as the slowdown in the growth of mean years of schooling. The deceleration in the growth of both the quantity and quality of schooling is one reason the college premium rose during the 1980s.

3. What has happened to the academic achievement of college graduates? Did the relative quality of college graduates fall during the 1970s and grow during the 1980s; did this in turn contribute to recent increases in the payoff to college for recent cohorts of college graduates?

   Yes. Test scores of college graduates did decline in the early 1970s but not as much as high school test scores. Consequently the relative quality of recent college graduates hit bottom in 1975 and has been increasing ever since. Shifts toward more remunerative majors have also improved the relative wage of recent college graduates during the 1980s.

4. Did the shortage of well-educated workers during the 1980s cause increases in the wage payoff to academic achievements not signaled by school credentials?

   Apparently, no. For workers under the age of thirty, the payoff to years of college and to work experience increased substantially during the 1980s, but the payoff to higher test scores did not.

The Impact of the Payoff to College on Effort and Achievement in High School

Probably the most important connection between relative-wage trends and test-score trends is the impact of the payoff to college on the incentive to study in high school. Academic achievement in high school has important effects on the probability of attending college, the quality of college attended, and the probability of completing college, but as discussed later, achievement in science, mathematical reasoning, reading, and vocabulary has almost no effect during the decade following graduation on the wage rates and earnings of those not going to college.[3] Consequently the payoff to the college degree is

147

a primary determinant of the economic payoff to studying in high school. This suggests that the magnitude of the payoff to college may influence course selection and effort in high school. This issue can be examined in both time-series and cross-section data.

Test-Score Trends. For the post–World War II era, the best data on trends in the general intellectual achievement of students nearing completion of compulsory schooling come from the Iowa Test of Educational Development (ITED). This data set is extremely valuable because it provides equated data since 1942 and annual data from 1960 to the present. Because about 95 percent of the public and private schools in the state of Iowa regularly participated in the testing program, the analyses of trends in ITED data for Iowa are not plagued by changing selectivity of the population taking the test. This feature of the data makes ITED trends for Iowa a better representation of national trends before 1970 than the American College Test (ACT), the Scholastic Aptitude Test (SAT), and the American Council on Education (ACE) Psychological Exam. Since these other tests were taken at first by a highly select group of students and only more recently by more representative samples of college-bound students, trends in these test scores are biased by the decreasing selectivity of those who took the test.

Figure 5–1 plots the trends of ITED composite scores for Iowa eleventh and twelfth graders combined. Through 1965 the trend was up: at first moderately, and then dramatically after Sputnik.[4] The gains for twelfth graders between 1942 and 1966 are all the more remarkable for they coincide with an increase in the high school graduation rate in Iowa, from 65 percent in 1941 to 88 percent in 1968.

In 1966 the educational achievement of high school students stopped rising and began a decline that lasted about thirteen years. On the ITED the composite scores of Iowa ninth graders dropped 0.283 SDs, and the scores of seniors dropped 0.35 SDs or about 1.25 grade-level equivalents. Comparable declines occurred throughout the country and for upper elementary and junior high school students as well.[5]

Recent efforts to improve the quality and rigor of the curriculum apparently have had an effect, as test scores are rising again. By 1988 Iowa twelfth graders recouped about three-quarters of their previous decline, and ninth graders surpassed their 1965 record by almost two-fifths of a grade-level equivalent. SAT and ACT scores have risen as well, though at a slower rate because of increases during the 1980s in the proportion of high school graduates taking these tests.

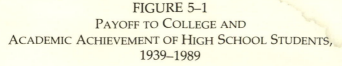

FIGURE 5–1
PAYOFF TO COLLEGE AND
ACADEMIC ACHIEVEMENT OF HIGH SCHOOL STUDENTS,
1939–1989

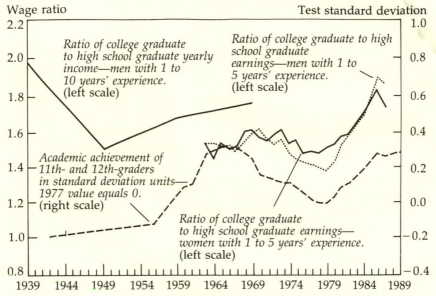

SOURCE: Author's calculations.

College Payoff Trends. The wage premium received by those with a college education has also varied a great deal over the past sixty years. The ratio of the weekly earnings of five high-level professional occupations to the weekly earnings of manufacturing production workers fell substantially during the depression and World War II from 3.3 in 1929 to 2.88 in 1939 and to 2.46 in 1950.[6] Professional wages then rebounded, and the ratio rose to 2.9 in 1964. Decennial census data on the payoff to college for men with limited amounts of postschool work experience exhibit a similar pattern. The ratio of the incomes of twenty-five- to thirty-five-year-old white males with four or more years of college to the incomes of twenty- to twenty-nine-year-old high school graduates was 1.99 in 1939, 1.45 in 1949, 1.68 in 1959, and 1.76 in 1969 (see figure 5–1).[7] Figure 5–1 also presents Lawrence Katz and Kevin Murphy's estimates of college–high school monthly earnings ratio for workers with less than five years of postschool work experience. Their carefully constructed series indicates that the wage

149

premium for college degree holders with less than five years of work experience fell from 51 percent in 1963–1964 to 44 percent in 1979–1980 and then rose to 84 percent in 1988.[8] Marvin Kosters's data on trends in the payoff to college tell the same story. He calculated that the college–high school hourly wage differential for workers of all experience levels fell from 49 percent in 1973 to 40–41 percent in 1979 for both men and women and then grew rapidly in the 1980s, reaching 82 percent for men and 52 percent for women by 1988 (see chapter 1).

Comparing Trends. The time-series data for the postwar period appear to suggest that changes in the economic payoff to college for young and inexperienced workers appear to influence the academic achievement of students in high school. Both the college payoff and test scores rose during the 1950s and peaked during the 1960s. The two series then decline together, and starting in 1979–1980 they start up together. When the average eleventh- and twelfth-grade ITED test score is regressed on a logarithm of the current college graduate–high school graduate weekly earnings ratio and a trend, one obtains the following results:

$$\text{ITEDav} = 22.07 + 1.41^*\log (\text{college wage/hs wage})$$
$$\phantom{\text{ITEDav} = }(5.56)(7.92)$$
$$- .0114^*\text{year} \quad R^2 = .78$$
$$(3.70) \qquad 1966\text{–}1987 \tag{5–1}$$

The results suggest that the decline in the payoff to college between 1969 and 1979 lowered test scores 15 percent of a standard deviation (about half the total decline in academic achievement at the end of high school), and the rise between 1979 and 1987 raised test scores 29 percent of a standard deviation.

As further support for the hypothesis, categories of students who have higher-than-average probabilities of attending college—white students, suburban students, and college-going students—experienced larger-than-average test-score declines between 1966 and 1979.[9] Test scores and the payoff to college did move in opposite directions during the 1930s and 1940s, and there are other plausible explanations of the post-1966 test-score decline and rebound. In the late 1960s and early 1970s, for example, a series of decisions by the courts and the Equal Employment Opportunity Commission (EEOC) forced most companies to abandon basic skills tests assessing verbal and mathematical competence as selection devices.[10] This probably lowered the rewards for studying for the non-college-bound and might have influenced their effort in high school. In addition graduation requirements and teacher expectations apparently followed the same kind of cycle. Consequently this examination of aggregate time-series data provides only suggestive evidence linking rates of return to college and academic performance in high school.

Cross-Section Evidence. Cross-section data provide a second opportunity to examine the influences of the college payoff on the behavior of high school students. There is spatial variation in the future payoffs to college education. If most young people intend to remain in the local labor market after school, one would expect geographic differentials in the payoff to affect (1) the number of college prep courses taken in high school, (2) the time spent studying, and (3) the probability of attending college. A rather crude measure of the college payoff—the average differential between accountant's, teacher's, and engineer's wages and operative wages—has significant positive effects on the college attendance rates of young men in the top 75 percent of the ability distribution.[11]

Table 5–1 presents linear regression estimates of the effect of college payoff, academic orientation of courses, and study time on the subsequent college attendance of 27,046 male high school juniors at Project Talent high schools in 1960. Separate models were estimated for students by family income. The control variables included in the regression are noted in the table. Academic orientation of courses has substantial positive effects on college attendance, and length of study has modest positive effects. The college payoff variable has significant direct effects on college attendance rates of students from low- and moderate-income families even when hours spent studying, the academic orientation of courses, and aptitude are controlled.[12] Since students probably base judgments about the reward to college on both local and national data, these results are a likely lower-bound estimate of the aggregate effect of a nationwide change in the payoff to college.

Do prospective payoffs to college, however, influence behavior of students while they are in high school? To explore this issue, the measure of the college payoff was included in models predicting the number of college preparatory courses taken through the junior year of high school and the weekly number of hours spent studying, including in-school study periods. The standardized regression coefficients (representing the effect of a 20 percent change in the payoff to college) are presented in table 5–2. Students living in labor markets with a large college payoff take additional academic courses, but they do not spend more time studying. The expected positive effect of payoff on hours studying may be absent because of the inclusion in the study time variable of in-school study periods, for college-bound

151

TABLE 5–1

DETERMINANTS OF COLLEGE ENTRANCE FOR MALE HIGH SCHOOL
JUNIORS, PROJECT TALENT HIGH SCHOOLS

Independent Variables	Income				
	Poverty	Lower Middle	Middle	Upper Middle	High
College payoff (SD = $570)	0.080[c] (2.86)	0.054[c] (3.44)	0.036[c] (2.89)	−0.033[a] (1.83)	−0.018 (1.14)
Academic orientation	0.163[c] (7.58)	0.201[c] (16.16)	0.256[c] (24.33)	0.227[c] (14.54)	0.227[c] (15.87)
Hours of study (SD = 5.5 hrs.)	0.092[c] (4.59)	0.043[c] (3.96)	0.116[c] (12.64)	0.057[c] (4.16)	−0.022 (0.12)
R^2	0.224	0.273	0.307	0.288	0.272
Number of observations	2,320	6,538	8,766	4,309	5,113

NOTE: Standardized regression coefficients with t statistics in parentheses under the coefficient. The coefficient on the payoff variable represents the effect of a $570 increase in the difference between professionals and operatives at a time (1959) when mean earnings of male high school graduates twenty-five to sixty-four years old was $6,132. The coefficient on the study hours per week variable represents the effect of a 5.5-hour increase in reported study time. Mean hours of reported study time including study halls was about 9 hours.
a. Significant at the 10 percent level on a two-tail test.
b. Significant at the 5 percent level on a two-tail test.
c. Significant at the 1 percent level on a two-tail test.
SOURCE: Weighted least-squares prediction of college attendance in fall 1961 from longitudinal data on 27,046 male high school juniors in the Project Talent data base. Students were categorized by family income, and separate models were estimated for each group. An extensive set of controls was included in the models: socioeconomic status, number of siblings, number of changes of school, academic aptitude, tuition at public universities and colleges in the state, cost (including travel costs) of attending the lowest-cost two-year and four-year colleges, distance to the lowest-cost college, selectivity of local colleges, opportunity cost of the student's time (the operative wage rate), and a dummy for being from an intact family and for the cheapest local postsecondary institution as a two-year vocational college. Data were collected by phone from a 5 percent sample of the nonrespondents to Project Talent's mail questionnaires. Because nonrespondents to the mail questionnaire were systematically different from those who responded, the people who were part of the nonrespondent sample were assigned weights of twenty in the weighted regression.

TABLE 5–2

EFFECT OF COLLEGE PAYOFF ON ACADEMIC ORIENTATION OF HIGH
SCHOOL COURSES AND HOURS OF STUDY TIME, MALE HIGH SCHOOL
JUNIORS, PROJECT TALENT HIGH SCHOOLS

	Beta Coefficient on Payoff Variable by Income Group				
Dependent Variable	Poverty	Lower Middle	Middle	Upper Middle	High
Regression predicting academic orientation	0.103c (4.01)	0.025a (1.81)	0.011 (0.98)	0.065c (4.26)	0.072c (5.19)
Regression predicting study time	−0.060c (2.14)	−0.002 (0.10)	−0.057c (4.33)	−0.081c (4.54)	0.004 (0.25)
Number of observations	2,320	6,538	8,766	4,309	5,113

NOTE: Standardized regression coefficients represent the effect of a $570 (in 1959 dollars) increase in the earnings differential between professionals and operatives. The payoff variable had a mean of $2,957 and a standard deviation of $570. Male high school graduates twenty-five to sixty-four years old earned an average of $6,132 in 1959. ($T$ statistics are in parentheses under the coefficient.)
a. Significant at the 10 percent level on a two-tail test.
b. Significant at the 5 percent level on a two-tail test.
c. Significant at the 1 percent level on a two-tail test.
SOURCE: Weighted least-squares models predicting the academic orientation of course taken and time spent in study halls and studying at home from data on 27,046 male high school juniors in the Project Talent data base. Students were categorized by family income and separate models were estimated for each group. An extensive set of controls was included in the models: socioeconomic status, parents' education, academic aptitude, religious activity, tuition at public universities and colleges in the state, cost (including travel costs) of attending the lowest-cost two-year and four-year colleges, distance to the lowest-cost college, selectivity of local colleges, opportunity cost of the student's time (the operative wage rate and the SMSA unemployment rate), and characteristics of the local high school—size, teacher salary, teacher experience, homogeneous grouping, hours of homework assigned, and dummies for race, being the eldest child, being from an intact family, and sports ability. Data were collected by phone from a 5 percent sample of the nonrespondents to Project Talent's mail questionnaires. Because nonrespondents to the mail questionnaire were systematically different from those who responded, the people who were part of the nonrespondent sample were assigned weights of twenty in the weighted regression.

TABLE 5–3

Slowdown in the Growth, Length, and Quality of the Education of the Employed Work Force, 1959–1988
(thousands)

	1959	1970	1980	1988
Years of schooling				
16+	6,381	10,185	19,192	26,814
13–15	6,123	10,501	18,875	24,080
12	20,213	30,792	42,285	47,760
9–11	13,037	13,659	16,345	14,535
0–8	20,082	13,817	8,752	6,534
Total	65,836	78,954	105,349	119,723
Ratio of 16+ to LE 12 years of school	0.1185	0.1746	0.2848	0.3896
Mean years of school	10.52	11.58	12.46	12.93
EQ index (1929 = 0)	0.3064	0.4267	0.5210	0.5619

Yearly Rates of Gain

	1959–69	1969–79	1979–87
Ratio of college to high school wages			
Men			
Murphy & Welch	—	−0.0046	0.0219[c]
Dean et al.	−0.0046	−0.0077	0.0208[b]
Kosters	—	−0.0093[a]	0.0282[d]
Women			
Dean et al.	0.0011	0.0030	0.0153[b]
Kosters		−0.0122[a]	0.0091[d]
Ratio of college to high school employment			
CPS-over age 16	0.0353	0.0488	0.0392
CPS-adjusted education overreport	0.0353	0.0488	0.0351
Mean years of schooling	0.0964	0.0915	0.0588
EQ index × 5	0.0602	0.0472	0.0256
Mean years of school equivalence	0.1566	0.1387	0.0844

a. Yearly growth 1973–79
b. Yearly growth 1980–86
c. Yearly growth 1980–85
d. Yearly growth 1979–88
Sources: Data on educational attainment of the labor force over the age of

students typically take heavier course loads and consequently schedule fewer study periods.

This evidence suggests that the decline in the payoff to college for young workers during the late 1960s and 1970s probably contributed to the test-score decline. A reliable estimate of the magnitude of this response does not appear feasible at this time, however. Turning to the effects of the test-score decline on wage profiles, the next section examines the impact of recent slowdowns in the improvement in the quality and the quantity of educated workers on trends in the total payoff to college.

The Effect of the Test-Score Decline on the Aggregate Supply and Relative Wage of Well-educated Workers

During the twentieth century a rapidly expanding supply of college graduates has raced a fast-growing demand for the skills developed at colleges and universities. When supply grows faster than demand, the payoff to college falls, as during the 1970s, when the payoff to college for males was declining at a rate of 0.46 to 0.93 percent per year (see table 5–3). When demand grows more rapidly than supply, the payoff to college rises. That happened during the 1980s, when the college payoff for males rose at an unprecedented rate of 2.08 to 2.83 percent per year.[13] What caused this change? Was there a deceleration in the growth of relative supply of college graduates, or was there an acceleration in the growth of the relative demand for college graduates?

In chapter 2 Kevin Murphy and Finis Welch suggest that the recent trade deficit and the resulting decline of U.S. manufacturing may have contributed significantly to the large real-wage declines suffered by high school graduates and the relative gains of college graduates. John Bound and George Johnson, in chapter 3, point out, however, that some of the major heavy employers of college graduates—education and government—also experienced declines in their employment share and that the net effect of all shifts in the industrial composition of employment on the relative demand for college graduates was essentially zero. Consequently, if the outward shift in relative

---

sixteen are from the *Handbook of Labor Statistics*, table 65, and unpublished BLS data. The EQ index is from John Bishop, "Is the Test Score Decline Responsible for the Productivity Growth Decline?" The data on rates of change in relative wage ratios are from the articles by Murphy and Welch and by Kosters in this volume and from Edwin Dean, Kent Kunze, and Larry S. Rosenblum, "Productivity Change and Measurement of Heterogeneous Labor Inputs," Bureau of Labor Statistics, March 1989.

FIGURE 5-2
BACHELOR'S DEGREES AWARDED, 1945–1986
(thousands)

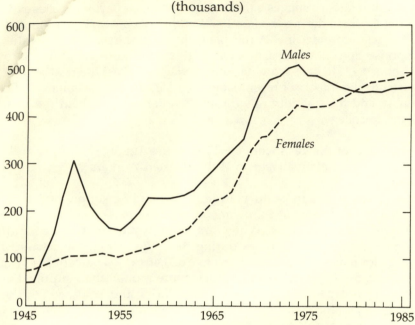

SOURCE: Author's calculations.

demand for college graduates indeed accelerated after 1979, its cause must be sought within industries. The two most likely causes of an acceleration of historical up-skilling trends are the microcomputer revolution and the transfer to Mexico and overseas of production activities that do not require a great deal of skill.

Another possible source of the pervasive increase in the payoff to college during the 1980s is the sudden deceleration during the late 1970s of the increase in the relative supply of college graduates and of skilled workers generally. An examination of figure 5–2 data on bachelor's degrees reveals a significant deceleration in the growth of the college-educated work force during the late 1970s and 1980s. Bachelor's degrees rose rapidly in the first three decades of the postwar period. The peak was reached, however, in 1974 for men; number of degrees awarded to men is still nearly 50,000 below that peak. Bachelor's degrees awarded to women has grown sluggishly since 1974. The deceleration in the growth of the college share for all men and women eighteen to sixty-five years old is rather modest—from 3.7 percent per year for 1973 to 1979 to 2.7 percent per year for 1979 to 1987—but it is larger for men and for younger workers, the groups that experienced the largest increases in the payoff to college.[14] Rates of growth of workers with twelve or fewer years of schooling also changed. The ratio of employed college graduates in the labor force to workers with twelve or fewer years of schooling, which rose 4.88 percent per year in the 1970s, grew at the slower rate of 3.92 percent per year between 1980 and 1988.[15]

The aggregate number of degrees granted by American colleges and universities during the 1980s, however, was significantly smaller than the growth in the numbers of people reporting sixteen or more years of schooling to interviewers for the Current Population Survey: the deceleration in the true growth of college graduate supply appears to be larger still.

Douglas Adkins has compared estimates of the stock of people with college degrees in census and CPS data to estimates based on cumulating degrees awarded and reconciled the differences for 1959, 1966, and 1970. He concluded that after appropriate adjustments are made, the two data sources yield remarkably similar estimates. When Adkins's reconciliation methodology is applied to the growth of college degrees after 1970, similar results are obtained for the 1970s. During the 1970s colleges awarded 8,523,000 bachelor's degrees, and the number of individuals born after 1925 claiming sixteen-plus years of schooling increased 10,675,000. Immigration probably accounts for about 809,000 of this discrepancy, and individuals with sixteen years of schooling but no degree for the rest.[16]

The growth in the number of bachelor's degrees awarded decelerated dramatically in the late 1970s and 1980s (see figure 5–2). Between 1980 and 1987 colleges awarded 6,543,000 bachelor's degrees. In CPS data, however, the numbers claiming to have sixteen-plus years of completed schooling rose 9,181,000. Immigration can account for no more than 734,000 of this increase, and individuals with sixteen years of schooling but no degree, for another 1,019,000. The remaining discrepancy of 885,000 is probably increased misreporting of years of schooling. If so, the annual growth rate of the ratio of college to high school workers between 1980 and 1988 in table 5–3 drops from 3.92 percent per year to 3.51 percent per year, and the implied deceleration in the growth of relative supply grows to 1.37 percentage points.

The second reason why CPS data on college graduates understates the true deceleration in the supply of well-educated workers is the post-1966 decline in the knowledge and skills of the students graduating from high school. This caused a substantial deceleration in the growth of effective supply of well-educated workers. The educational quotient (EQ) index describing the schooling constant average test scores (measured in population standard deviation units) of workers weighted by their share of compensation grew much more slowly in the late 1970s and 1980s than in the 1950s and 1960s (see table 5–3).[17]

The growth of mean years of schooling also decelerated during the 1980s. The annual growth rate of mean years of schooling, which was 0.0964 in the 1960s and 0.088 in the 1970s, fell to 0.0588 in the 1980s (see table 5–3). Since a population standard deviation on academic aptitude and broad spectrum achievement tests is approximately five grade-level equivalents, the changes in the EQ index can translate into years of equivalent schooling metric by multiplying by five. This way of equating test-score gains with years of schooling implies that during the 1960s the gain in the average quality of workers at given levels of education was about two-thirds of the gain in schooling quantity. The test-score decline resulted in a reduction in the contribution of improvements in educational quality to the growth of worker quality during the 1970s and an even larger drop in the 1980s. The next line of table 5–3 reports the rates of growth of an index combining the two effects. Clearly the rate of growth of the quantity and quality of the schooling embodied in the work force declined substantially in the 1980s. The annual rate of gain, which had been 0.157 years of schooling equivalent in the 1960s and 0.137 years of schooling equivalent in the 1970s, fell to 0.084 years of schooling equivalent during the 1980s.

Therefore, measured in efficiency units, the growth of the supply of well-educated workers slowed more substantially after 1980 than had been thought. Employers may have reacted to the declining quality of high school graduates by raising the minimum levels of schooling expected of new hires. Whether the deceleration in the growth of relative supply fully accounts for the rapid rise in the return to college during the 1980s depends on the elasticity of substitution between college and noncollege labor. If elasticities of substitution are no higher than one, the slowdown in the growth of the relative supply of college graduates can probably fully account for the growth of the college premium. If, however, elasticities of substitution are greater than one, the growth of the college premium must have been occasioned by an acceleration in the growth of relative demand as well as a deceleration in the growth of relative supply.[18]

Shifts in the Relative Quality of College Graduates during the 1960s, 1970s, and 1980s

Bound and Johnson have suggested that shifts in the quality of college graduates relative to high school graduates might be responsible for some of the growth of the wage differential between college and high school graduates for young workers (see chapter 3). The relative academic achievement of a cohort of college graduates will increase if college admission and completion become more contingent on initial levels of achievement or if colleges become better at promoting learning. It will also grow if college students shift from majors that offer little remuneration to majors that are well remunerated. All three possibilities are explored next.

Trends in the Impact of Academic Achievement on College Entrance Rates. Paul Taubman and Terence Wales examined trends in the impact of academic test scores on the probability of college entrance between 1924 and 1960 and concluded that ability became an increasingly important determinant of the probability of high school graduates entering college.[19] This trend might have reversed in the 1960s, however: the 1960s and early 1970s were a period of rapid growth for colleges with open-door admissions policies. Growing numbers of low-ability students pursuing vocational curricula in two-year institutions might have reduced the academic achievement differential between those entering college and those completing schooling with a high school degree.

To test this hypothesis, the calculations made by Taubman and Wales were replicated in two more recent nationally representative longitudinal studies of high school seniors: National Longitudinal Survey (NLS) Class of 1972, and High School and Beyond (HSB) (1980 graduates). Rates of college entrance for the year following graduation were calculated for each quartile of the ability distribution. The relationship between college entrance rates and a student's ability ranking was approximated by a series of linear segments, and mean ability rankings were calculated for college entrants and for non-college-going high school graduates.[20] The results are presented in table 5–4. The mean ability ranking of high school graduates not going to college was 0.47 in 1925, 0.43 in 1946, 0.42 in 1950, 0.40 in 1957, 0.35–0.36 in 1960–1961, 0.38 in 1972, and 0.364 in 1980. The class rank gap between those attending and those not attending college grew from 0.06 in 1925 to 0.20 in 1946 and then to 0.28 in 1960. The gap fell to 0.22 in 1972 and then returned to 0.25 in 1980. These calculations imply that the dependence of college entrance on ability did indeed fall between 1960 and 1972 but rose again between 1972 and 1980.

Correlations between test scores and college entrance are an alternative way of characterizing the dependence of college entrance on ability. The correlation between test scores (high school grades) and a zero-one dummy for college attendance eighteen months fol-

TABLE 5–4

AVERAGE ABILITY RANKING OF COLLEGE ENTRANTS AND HIGH SCHOOL
GRADUATES NOT ENTERING COLLEGE, 1925–1980

Source of Data	Year	College Average	Noncollege Average	Entrance Selectivity Differential
O'Brien	1925	53	47	6
Benson	1929	56	45	11
Barker	1934	58	43	15
Phearmon	1946	63	43	20
Berdie	1950	61	42	19
Little	1957	62	40	22
Talent	1960	63	35	28
Berke and Hood	1961	62	36	26
NLS Class of 1972	1972	60	38.9	22
High School and Beyond	1980	61.2	36.4	24.7

SOURCES: For the period before 1961, Paul Taubman and Terence Wales, "Mental Ability and Higher Educational Attainment in the 20th Century," Occasional Paper 118 National Bureau of Economic Research, 1972. For 1972 and 1980, Washington, D.C., John Gardner, *Transition from High School to Postsecondary Education: Analytical Studies* (Columbus; National Center for Research in Vocational, Ohio State University Research Foundation, February 1987), table 3–7.

lowing high school graduation was 0.399 (0.315) for 1972 high school graduates and 0.442 (0.384) for 1980 high school graduates.[21] Clearly the dependence of college entrance on ability was rising during the 1970s. Evidence of changes between 1961 and 1972 can be obtained by comparing the 0.399 correlation of NLS Class of 1972 data to the average correlation (for five family income strata) between test scores and college attendance eighteen months after graduation in Project Talent data on students who graduated in 1961. The correlation of the Project Talent achievement composite with college attendance was 0.458 circa 1961 and indicates a large decline in academic selectivity by 1972, when the comparable figure was 0.399.[22]

Data on the characteristics of college freshmen from the Cooperative Research Program of the American Council on Education (ACE) provide another look at trends in the degree to which college entrance depends on achievement levels. The percentage of freshmen who reported themselves in the bottom half of their high school graduating class first rose from 22 percent in 1968–1969 to 26.8 percent in

1970–1971 and then dropped to 20.2 percent in 1978. Although the wording of the question changed then, the trend apparently has continued after 1978. The percentage of freshmen who reported being in the bottom 60 percent of the high school graduating class dropped from 38.8 percent in 1979 to 36.0 percent in 1986.[23] When combined with rising college entrance rates in the 1980s, these data suggest that the impact of high school achievement on the likelihood of entering college rose during the 1970s and 1980s after falling during the 1960s.

Since 1980, the final source of data on trends is a 1985 survey of college admissions directors. The 2,203 institutions responding to the survey represented 74 percent of the institutions admitting freshmen students into bachelor's and associate degree programs. The admissions directors were asked about changes in admissions selectivity between 1980 and 1985. Only 2 percent of the institutions reported that they had become less selective. The proportion reporting they had become more selective was 42 percent at four-year private colleges, 49 percent at four-year public colleges, 30 percent at two-year private colleges, and 8 percent at two-year public colleges.[24] All of these data sets tell a consistent story of first declining, then rising influence of academic achievement on college entrance probabilities.[25]

Trends in the Relative Test Scores of College Graduates. The differential in academic achievement between high school graduates and college graduates will also increase if college graduation becomes more conditional on initial achievement levels and if students learn more while in college.

A natural way to assess trends in the selectivity and value added of college is to compare the trends on tests taken by recent college graduates to the trends on tests taken at the end of high school. Such comparisons face difficulties, however, because the tests taken by college graduates—the Graduate Record Examination (GRE), the Law School Admission Test (LSAT), the Graduate Management Admissions Test (GMAT), and the Medical College Admission Test (MCAT)—are not taken by representative samples of college graduates. These tests are taken primarily by applicants to graduate and professional schools. The share of college graduates entering such programs and the selectivity of these programs have changed. In 1966, the first year for which data are available for all four graduate tests, the number of graduate exams taken (uncorrected for multiple test taking) equaled 42 percent of the bachelor's degrees awarded that year (see column 5 of table 5–5). By 1971 the ratio had risen to 62.7 percent. Since that

TABLE 5–5

TRENDS IN TEST SCORES OF COLLEGE GRADUATES, 1960–1989

	Graduate Test Average[a]	ITED High School Graduate Average 4–9 Years Earlier[b]	Difference between College Graduate and High School Graduate	Ratio of BAs Awarded to High School Graduates 4–9 Years Earlier[c]	Ratio of Graduate Test Takers to BAs
1960				0.261	
1962				0.274	
1964		−0.049		0.281	
1966	0.116	0.023	0.083	0.290	0.422
1967	0.121	0.067	0.054	0.301	0.461
1968	0.124	0.141	−0.018	0.305	0.498
1969	0.103	0.197	−0.094	0.313	0.486
1970	0.046	0.232	−0.186	0.329	0.564
1971	0.008	0.265	−0.257	0.338	0.627
1972	−0.014	0.283	−0.297	0.345	0.618
1973	0.007	0.283	−0.290	0.341	0.606
1974	0.001	0.285	−0.284	0.338	0.631
1975	−0.014	0.245	−0.259	0.325	0.666
1976	0.000	0.211	−0.211	0.319	0.654
1977	0.000	0.186	−0.186	0.311	0.666
1978	−0.005	0.164	−0.169	0.307	0.674
1979	0.021	0.139	−0.118	0.301	0.677
1980	0.025	0.119	−0.094	0.301	0.682
1981	0.047	0.091	−0.044	0.300	0.680
1982	0.075	0.064	0.011	0.306	0.652
1983	0.119	0.034	0.085	0.311	0.664
1984	0.121	0.021	0.100	0.315	0.633
1985	0.118	0.016	0.102	0.319	0.637
1986	0.154	0.037	0.117	0.325	0.636
1987	0.150	0.052	0.098	0.333	0.666
1988	0.171	0.074	0.097	0.344	0.684
1989	0.213	0.110	0.103	0.362	0.696

a. An index of scores on the tests that students applying for graduate and professional schools take. All tests were deviated from their mean in 1977 and divided by their standard deviation before being averaged.

b. An index of eleventh- and twelfth-grade ITED test scores (deviated from their value in 1977 and divided by the standard deviation for that grade) for the cohort of students who graduated from high school four to nine years previously. The weights are 0.5 for t-4 and 0.1 for t-5, t-6, t-7, t-8, and t-9.

date, the ratio has fluctuated between 60 and 70 percent. An additional problem with the data is the return to school of many test takers years after completing a bachelor's degree.

Still another problem arises because foreign nationals are a large share of GMAT test takers (about 20 percent) and an increasing share of GRE test takers.[26] A time series of GRE scores for U.S. citizens was therefore used for the period 1972–1973 through 1988–1989, and earlier data on average scores were spliced onto this. On the GMAT, foreign nationals obtain comparable scores on the quantitative section but substantially lower scores on the verbal section. Because data on GMAT scores of foreign nationals before 1983 were unavailable, it is not clear how GMAT trends would change if foreign nationals were not included. Because of these problems, comparisons of graduate test scores and high school test scores must be done cautiously.

The time series constructed from these data is intended to measure trends in the general academic achievement of recent college graduates. Scores of the four different tests were deviated from their value in 1977, divided by their standard deviation, and averaged.[27] The weights used in constructing the average were 0.253 for the GMAT, 0.182 for the LSAT, 0.077 for the MCAT, and 0.488 for an average of GRE verbal and quantitative scores. The weighted average of the four graduate tests is presented in column 1 of table 5–5. An index of these college graduate test scores (with a value of 1 in 1966) was generated by adding .8845 to this average, and the result is plotted in figure 5–3.

The academic achievement of graduate test takers apparently declined during the late 1960s. Between 1966 and 1972 there was a 0.20 SD decline on the quantitative GRE, a 0.28 SD decline on the verbal GRE, and a 0.215 SD decline in the GMAT. There were small increases of 0.06 SD on the MCAT and of 0.09 SD on the LSAT. The comprehensive average declined by 0.13 SD. The decline of the grad-

c. Ratio of bachelor's degrees awarded in year *t* to the number of high school diplomas awarded four to nine years previously. Weights were 0.5 for *t*-4 and 0.1 for *t*-5, *t*-6, *t*-7, *t*-8, and *t*-9.
SOURCES: Data on twelfth-grade ITED and graduate GRE, GMAT, LSAT, and MCAT test scores and the number of graduate test takers were obtained from Clifford Adelman, "The Standardized Test Scores of College Graduates," 1983, table A; Nabeel Alsalam, ed., *The Condition of Education 1990: Postsecondary Education* (Washington, D.C.: U.S. Department of Education, National Center for Education Statistics, 1990), indicator 2:12; and correspondence with the testing organizations. Data on numbers of BAs and high school diplomas are from *Digest of Educational Statistics 1989* (Washington, D.C.: U.S. Department of Education, National Center for Education Statistics, 1989), tables 89 and 200.

FIGURE 5-3
Academic Achievement of High School Graduates versus Proportion Graduating from College and College Graduate Test Scores, 1965–1990

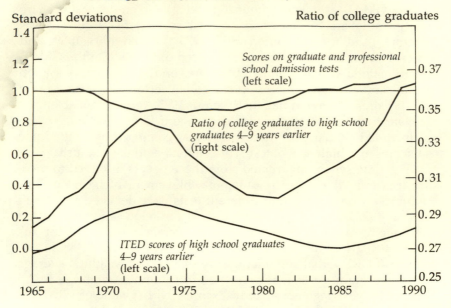

SOURCE: Author's calculations.

uate test average during this period was probably in part a result of the substantial increase in the proportion of high school graduates completing college (see column 4 of table 5–5 and figure 5–3). In addition the proportion of BA recipients who took graduate exams rose substantially (see column 5 of table 5–5). Consequently the average quality of all college graduates probably declined less than is indicated by the graduate test series.

As with high school graduates, there appears to have been a rebound in the test scores of college graduates planning to continue their schooling. The general index remained essentially flat between 1972 and 1980 but has since risen 0.23 SD above the 1972 level. Trends have differed substantially across tests. Between 1977 and 1989 there were declines of 0.095 SD on the MCAT but increases of 0.146 SD on the verbal GRE, 0.24 SD on the quantitative GRE, 0.337 SD on the GMAT, and 0.179 SD on the LSAT.

The index of trends in the academic achievement of high school graduates to which the college graduate test score time series is compared is a weighted average of ITED test scores for the high school graduating classes of four to nine years earlier.[28] Figure 5–3 plots high school test scores on the same graph as the college graduation rate. Clearly there is a strong positive association, suggesting that the test score decline may have helped cause the fall of college graduation rates during the 1970s.

A rough summary statistic describing changes in the gap between college and high school test scores—constructed by adopting test score standard deviations as a common metric and then subtracting the high school index from the college graduate index—can be found in column 3 of table 5–5. Given that caution must be exercised in drawing inferences from this data series, what does a comparison of these two time series tell us about changes in the selectivity and value added of a four-year college education during the past twenty-five years? The test scores of high school graduates rose rapidly during the early 1960s. Selectivity of college entrance fell, and the proportions of high school graduates completing college rose (from 0.281 in 1966 to 0.327 in 1972). Value added appears to have declined possibly because of the disruptions associated with the Vietnam War period. As a result the improvements in the quality of students graduating from high school did not produce gains on the tests taken by college graduates four years later. In fact the test scores of these college graduates were declining during the late 1960s. The index of the gap between college graduate test scores and high school graduate test scores four years earlier fell 0.37 standard deviations between 1966 and 1972. The trough of this series occurs three years after Woodstock (indicated by the vertical line on figure 5–3) and two years after four students demonstrating against the Vietnam War were killed at Kent State University. This figure exaggerates the magnitude of the true decline, however, since some of this measured decline in the relative quality of college graduates is a spurious result of the rise in the number of college graduates seeking admission to graduate school and taking the graduate tests.

At this point we entered a decade of declining test scores for entering students and stable scores for college graduates. Value added probably underwent a recovery as the disruptions associated with the Vietnam War ended. In addition the selectivity of college entry and graduation increased. Ratios of bachelor's degrees awarded to high school graduates four to nine years earlier fell from 0.345 in 1972 to 0.301 in 1979. Thus the decline in the quality of the students entering college resulted in an increase in attrition but no further decline in standards for graduation.

Then starting about 1979 first graduate and then high school test scores began to rise. By 1984 the index of the gap between college graduate and high school graduate test scores increased 0.41 standard deviations from its low in 1972. Since then the gap has remained stable.

To sum up, the test score gap between college graduates and high school graduates has fluctuated violently. It fell 38 percent of a standard deviation between 1966 and 1972 and has since risen 41 percent of a standard deviation. Test-score fluctuations of this magnitude have probably had significant effects on the wage premium received by young college graduates. An estimate of their magnitude may be obtained by multiplying the changes in the test score gap by 0.1406, Bishop's estimate of the effect of a one high school standard deviation test-score differential on the logarithm of the weekly wage. This implies that changes in the test score gap lowered the college wage premium for young college graduates during the 1970s about 5 percent and then raised it by a similar amount during the 1980s.[29] It would appear that growing academic achievement differentials between college and non-college youth have contributed significantly to the growing wage differential between the groups during the past decade.

Trends in the Distribution of College Majors. The wages received by college graduates depend on what the student studied while in school. The first four columns of table 5–6 present data from periodic surveys of random samples of recent college graduates on the effects of the field of study on salaries received one year after graduating from college.[30] The differences across fields are sometimes as large as the wage gains accruing to those obtaining higher level degrees. During the 1980s engineers were receiving 64 to 78 percent higher starting salaries than humanities majors, and business majors were receiving 29 to 34 percent higher starting salaries than humanities majors.

Data on the earnings of college graduates years after leaving college solidify the finding that majors in humanities, education, biological sciences, and social sciences other than economics earn far less than business, physical science, and engineering majors. The salaries of business majors tend to catch up with the engineers, but education and liberal arts majors remain far behind those with engineering and business degrees even when the quality of one's college is controlled. The seventh and eighth columns of table 5–6 present data on the relationship between college major and yearly earnings of men aged twenty-one to seventy from the 1967 Survey of Economic Opportunity. With college rank constant, undergraduate business majors earned 32 percent more and engineers 51 percent more than humanities majors and education majors.[31] The ninth column of table 5–6 presents 1984 data on monthly earnings by major for men and women combined. Physical science majors earned 93 percent more, engineers earned 114 percent more, and business majors earned 103 percent more than humanities majors.[32]

The fifth and sixth columns of the table present estimates of the effects of college major on 1979 hourly earnings of young men and women who had graduated from high school in 1972 while controlling for family background and the student's preferences regarding life goals (for example, the importance of being wealthy and of helping others).[33] Humanities, social science, and education majors received the lowest wage rates. Male engineers obtained 34 percent more than male humanities majors; male business majors were paid 13 percent more. Female engineers were paid 27 percent more than female humanities majors, and female business majors were paid 25 percent more. Clearly the market values some of the skills developed in college much more highly than others.

During the past two decades the life goals of entering college students and the fields of study shifted dramatically. "Develop[ing] a meaningful philosophy of life," which was considered essential or very important by 82 percent of entering freshmen in 1967–1969 is now [1987] considered very important by only 39.1 percent of entering freshmen. "Be[ing] very well-off financially," which in 1967–1969 was considered essential or very important by only 43 percent of freshmen, is now considered essential or very important by 75.6 percent of freshmen.[34]

Shifts of this magnitude in the priority attached to making money could be expected to result in students shifting out of fields of study leading to low-paid occupations (such as education and the humanities) into fields (such as business and engineering) leading to more remunerative occupations. A second factor that has shifted student demand toward business and technical majors has been changing attitudes regarding occupations appropriate for women. The rapid growth in numbers seeking access to programs in computer science, engineering, and business has been further sustained by continuing strong market demand for students prepared in these fields.

The shifts in college major have been quite substantial. Figures 5–4 and 5–5 present cumulative proportions of the bachelor's degrees awarded by college majors arranged in a hierarchy that roughly corresponds to the average wage of males or females who received their bachelor's degree in that field. Starting at the bottom of figure 5–4 for males, the fields are education, humanities and social science, natural

TABLE 5–6

WAGE RELATIVES BY COLLEGE MAJOR
(RELATIVE TO HUMANITIES MAJOR), 1966–1985
(percent)

	Earnings of Full-Time Workers 1 Year after BA, Both Sexes[a]				Hourly Earnings of 25-Year-Olds in 1979[b]		Median Earnings, Males, Age 21–70, BAs in 1966[c]		Average Monthly Earnings in 1984,[a] Both Sexes
	1976	1981	1985	1987	Male	Female	Medium-Rank College	All Colleges	
BA in Low-Wage Major									
Humanities	0	0	0	0	0	0	0	0	0
Social sciences	16	11	13	25	2	5	15	14	—
Excluding economics	ns	ns	ns	ns	ns	ns	ns	ns	28
Education	9	−9	−1	−2	−4	5	2	−9	−6
Psychology	—	−1	4	7	ns	ns	ns	ns	ns
Biological sciences	12	15	8	1	0	28	4	−11	12
Agriculture	ns	ns	ns	ns	ns	ns	ns	ns	45
Health	48	37	49	40	ns	ns	—	—	12

BA in High-Wage Major

Physical science, mathematics, computer science	21	29	25	39	—	—	31	28	—
Physical science	ns	ns	ns	ns	15	35	ns	ns	93
Mathematics	ns	ns	ns	ns	ns	ns	ns	ns	68
Computer science	ns	ns	ns	ns	19	13	—	—	ns
Engineering	110	78	72	64	34	27	51	52	114
Business	76	29	34	30	13	25	32	28	103
Economics	ns	ns	ns	ns	ns	ns	ns	ns	111

a. Percentage differential between the earnings one year after receiving a bachelor's degree of full-time workers who pursued the designated major over that received by humanities majors. Data are based on a probability sample of recent graduates. *Digest of Education Statistics: 1989* (Washington, D.C.: U.S. Department of Education, 1989), table 331, p. 375.

b. Percentage differential implied by regressions predicting hourly wage rate of college graduates who have been out about three years, controlling for degree and preferences using 1,835 observations from Class of 1972 data. Thomas N. Daymont and Paul J. Andrisani, "Job Preferences, College Major, and the Gender Gap in Earnings," *Journal of Human Resources*, Summer 1984, pp. 408–28.

c. Percentage differential for median yearly earnings of male BA holders with designated major relative to median earnings of humanities majors. Current Population Reports, P-20, No. 201.

d. Percentage differential for mean monthly earnings of BA holders with designated major relative to earnings of humanities and liberal arts majors. Current Population Reports, P-70, No. 11, p. 13.

FIGURE 5–4
Proportion of Bachelor's Degrees Awarded to Males, by Subject, 1945–1986

Cumulative proportion

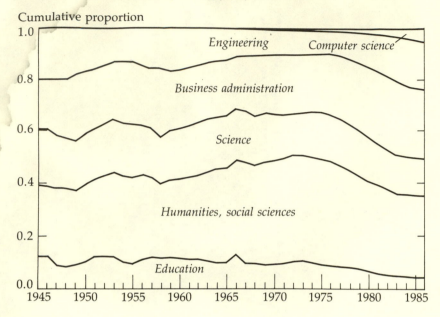

SOURCE: Author's calculations.

science, business administration, engineering, and computer science. From the bottom of the figure we see that in 1973 degrees in education, humanities, and social science accounted for 50.5 percent of bachelor's degrees awarded to men and for 83.5 percent of the bachelor's degrees awarded to women. By 1986 these percentages had dropped to 35.1 percent and 54.7 percent, respectively. From the top, degrees in engineering, computer science, and business accounted for 33.2 percent of the bachelor's degrees awarded to men in 1973 and for 50.8 percent awarded to men in 1986. For women, degrees in engineering, computer science, and business grew from 3.5 percent to 26.6 percent of degrees awarded.

Since the most rapidly growing fields are also the highest paid, the shifts in subjects studied in college probably account for a portion of the growth in the return to college for the most recent cohorts of college graduates. An index of the effect of the composition of college majors on the payoff to college was obtained by calculating a weighted average of the logged percentage differentials relative to humanities majors reported in columns 5 and 6 of table 5–6 using numbers of

FIGURE 5-5
Proportion of Bachelor's Degrees Awarded to Females, by Subject, 1945–1986

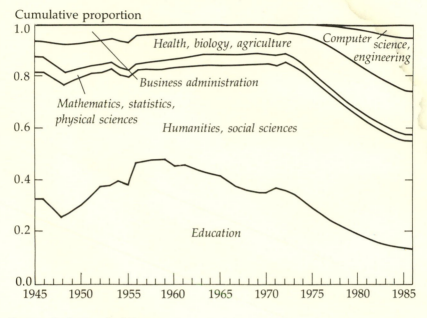

SOURCE: Author's calculations.

degrees awarded in that field as weights. Figure 5–6 presents the index for men and women with exactly sixteen years of schooling and one to five years of experience. The value of the index is 0 if everyone studies the humanities and 0.22 [In(1.25)] if all women major in business.

In 1953 the value of the index was 0.088 for males and 0.080 for females. The indexes remained reasonably stable for the following decade but then fell after 1963, reaching a value of 0.071 for both males and females in 1973. At this point the indexes diverged. The shift of women into more remunerative college majors began in earnest in 1973, and the index started a steady climb to 0.100 in 1981 and 0.120 in 1987.

For males the gradual shift toward lower-paying college majors did not end until 1976, with an index for that year's degree recipients of 0.066. After 1977 the shift toward more remunerative majors was rapid, and the index for those with one to five years of experience grew to 0.074 in 1981 and 0.100 in 1987. The decline, then rise of this index are consistent with observed trends in the payoff to college for

FIGURE 5-6
INDEX OF PAYOFF TO COLLEGE MAJORS FOR BACHELOR'S
DEGREE–HOLDERS WITH
ONE TO FIVE YEARS' EXPERIENCE, 1950–1987

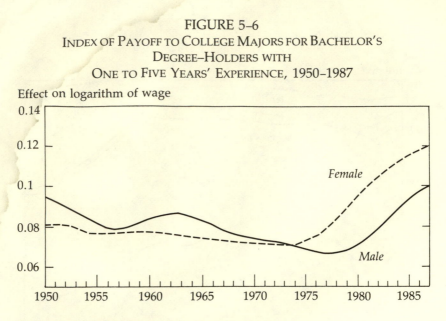

Effect on logarithm of wage

those with little labor market experience relative to the college payoff for workers of all experience levels.

The Return to Academic Achievement during the 1980s?

The payoffs to visible indicators of skill such as the college degree and to postschool work experience have risen substantially during the 1980s. Visible though it may be, however, length of schooling is an imperfect measure of skill. What has happened to the payoff to direct measures of skill such as tests assessing various types of competency? How substantial was the payoff to academic competencies at the beginning of the 1980s? How substantial is it now? The availability of data sets containing direct measures of academic competence for random samples of the population has made possible studies of the impact of academic competencies on wages and earnings for specific points in time. Comparisons over time are difficult because paired surveys of random samples of adults collected a decade or so apart, containing both wage information and test scores for the *same* test battery, are not to be found. In the absence of such a paired data set, analysis of longitudinal data provides the only feasible way of assessing possible trends in the payoff to academic competency. The youth cohort of National Longitudinal Survey is a data set that may be able to shed some light on this issue.

Data. An analysis of the effects of test scores on wage rates is possible in the NLS Youth because the Armed Services Vocational Aptitude Battery (ASVAB) was administered to the youth cohort of the NLS in 1980. At the time the NLS youth were between fifteen and twenty-three years of age. The ASVAB is a three-hour battery of tests used by the armed forces for selecting recruits and for assigning them to occupational specialties. The primary purpose of the ASVAB is to predict the success of new recruits in training and their subsequent performance in their occupational specialty. Eighty percent of the jobs held by enlisted personnel in the military have civilian counterparts, and the ASVAB is a valid predictor of job performance in the civilian sector.[35] During the summer of 1980, all members of the NLS Youth sample were asked to take this test and offered a $50 honorarium as an inducement. The tests were successfully administered to 94 percent of the sample.[36]

To reduce measurement error and to simplify the specification of interaction variables, the youth's learning achievements were represented by three composite variables: general academic achievement, computational speed, and technical competence. The academic composite was defined by averaging normalized subtest scores for arithmetic reasoning, mathematics knowledge, word knowledge, paragraph comprehension, and general science and then by renormalizing to give the variable a standard deviation of one. Factor analysis of the ASVAB has found that the speeded tests constitute a separate factor. Consequently, computational speed—the number of correct answers on a three-minute fifty-problem arithmetic computation test—was defined as a separate achievement variable. The measure of technical competence was constructed by averaging the mechanical comprehension, auto and shop information, and electronics subtest scores of the ASVAB.

All of these competencies are highly correlated with years of schooling. When these composites are regressed on age, ethnicity, proportion of 1980 spent in school, region, work experience, occupation of parents, and schooling, the coefficients on years of high school range between 0.19 for math and 0.28 for verbal for males and between 0.12 for technical and 0.24 for verbal for females.

Specification. In the basic model the log of the hourly wage in the current or most recent job is regressed on test scores, years of schooling, years of college, school attendance, work experience, and a variety of other control variables:

$$W_t = a_t A + b_t T + c_t R + d_t S_t + e_t C_t + f_t E_t + g_t N_t + h_t Z_t + u_t \quad t = 1979\ldots 1986 \quad (5\text{--}2)$$

where

W_t is the log of the worker's wage in the current or most recent job at the time of the interview in year t.

A is a composite of ASVAB subtest scores measuring competence in reading, vocabulary, mathematical reasoning, and science knowledge.

T is the ASVAB technical composite measuring mechanical comprehension and electronics, auto, and shop knowledge.

R is a measure of speed in simple arithmetic computation.

S_t is years of schooling completed by the interview date in year t.

C_t is years of college completed by the interview date in year t.

E_t is cumulated weeks of work experience since 1975 divided by 52. Actual experience and its square both enter the models.

N_t is age on the interview date in year t minus 16. Both age and (Age-16)^2 enter the cross-section models.

Z_t is a vector of control variables such as school attendance, marital status, parenthood, Hispanic, race, region, past and current military service, residence in an SMSA, and current local unemployment rate.

u_t is the disturbance term for year t.

Trends over time in the payoff to various academic competencies are assessed in two different ways. The first method is to estimate repeated cross sections and then to examine whether the coefficients on test scores are exhibiting a trend. This approach has the advantage of simplicity and transparency. The problem with this approach, however, is that since the effects of academic achievement grow as the individual ages, the estimated effect of test scores on wages is larger in 1986 than in 1979 even if there are no secular trends in the reward for academic achievement. Consequently, no conclusions regarding secular change in the payoff to academic competency can be drawn from simple comparisons of cross-section regressions estimated in the NLS Youth. The repeated cross-section analysis is therefore just a first look at the data, not a test of hypotheses regarding trends in the returns to indicators of skill. In the second method, data for the full 1981 to 1986 period are used to estimate a single regression equation that explicitly tests for trends in the coefficients on skill variables in the context of a model that allows the payoff to academic competency also to vary with age, student status, and advanced education.

Repeated Cross-Section Results. Let us turn first to an examination of the repeated cross-section estimates of equation 5–1 that are reported in table 5–7. The effects of schooling on wage rates appear to have changed substantially during the 1980s. The impact of high school appears to have been smaller at the end of the sample period than it was around 1980. The effect of college appears to have grown substantially.

The most powerful determinant of the wage rates of young men and women is the cumulated weeks of work experience.[37] With age and schooling constant, each additional year of actual work experience raises 1986 wages 6.4 percent for males and 5.7 percent for females. Age has substantially smaller effects. The coefficients on the age and actual work experience variables apparently do not exhibit any trend.

Test scores have important effects on wage rates. As one might anticipate, technical competence has a strong positive effect on the wage rates of young men but not on the wage rates of young women.[38] Computational speed is related to higher wage rates for both men and women.[39] Academic competence has a modest positive effect on the wage rates of women but a negative effect on the wage rates of men.

While the absence of a positive wage response to a male's academic skills (and the small size, 0.7 percent wage increase per grade level equivalent, for females) may appear surprising, it is quite consistent with the findings of other studies of recent high school graduates using data sets such as High School and Beyond and NLS Class of 1972.[40] It is also consistent with data on hiring practices. Only 3 percent of new hires with a high school degree at small and medium firms were administered basic skills tests before hiring in 1987.[41]

Employers have been avoiding such tests largely because in 1971 the EEOC started requiring costly validity studies at the firm before a basic skills test could be used for selection.[42] Research has found that these tests are positively related to job performance in almost all jobs. The fear of litigation, however, as well as the costs of doing a special validity study, induced all but a few firms to drop testing.[43]

The effects of test scores on wage rates appear to have grown over time. An increase of one standard deviation in all three test composites, which raised wage rates of males only 4.3 percent in 1980–1981, raised 1985–1986 wage rates 12.5 percent. A similar increase in test scores for females, which raised wage rates only 5.3 percent in 1980–1981, raised wages 10.8 percent in 1985–1986.

The results presented in table 5–7, however, may overstate

TABLE 5-7

Effect of Skill Indicators on the Hourly Wage, 1979–1986

Year	Academic Test	Technical Test	Computational Speed	Years of Education	Years of College	Actual Experience	Actual Experience Sq.	Age	Age Sq.	R^2	Number of Observations
Male											
1986	−.028[a] (1.76)	.078[c] (5.93)	.068[c] (6.82)	.016[b] (2.54)	.027[c] (3.14)	.064[c] (5.11)	−.0009 (.76)	.007 (.23)	−.0005 (.31)	.264	4160
1985	−.012 (.77)	.073[c] (5.63)	.071[c] (7.19)	.011[a] (1.74)	.025[c] (2.82)	.068[c] (5.21)	−.0017 (1.27)	.028 (1.05)	−.0018 (1.12)	.271	4100
1984	−.023 (1.43)	.065[c] (4.83)	.073[c] (7.17)	.012[a] (1.84)	.013 (1.42)	.064[c] (4.45)	−.001 (.04)	.011 (.45)	−.0005 (.32)	.238	4099
1983	−.040[b] (2.50)	.066[c] (5.03)	.067[c] (6.72)	.025[c] (3.84)	.004 (.46)	.064[c] (4.15)	−.0017 (.81)	.011 (.47)	.0003 (.20)	.249	3994
1982	−.036[b] (2.30)	.052[c] (3.96)	.046[c] (4.63)	.026[c] (3.85)	.002 (.24)	.075[c] (4.42)	−.0046[a] (1.74)	.0006 (.03)	.00015 (.85)	.224	4100
1981	−.035[b] (2.28)	.033[b] (2.56)	.051[c] (5.14)	.036[c] (5.30)	−.017 (1.58)	.100[c] (5.20)	−.0113[c] (3.26)	−.053 (2.72)	.0076[b] (3.85)	.241	3617
1980	−.047[c] (3.06)	.048[c] (3.70)	.035[c] (3.54)	.034[c] (4.88)	−.012 (.94)	.052[b] (2.40)	−.0059 (1.25)	−.018 (1.06)	.0048[b] (2.26)	.229	3392
1979	−.025 (1.34)	.034[b] (2.16)	.036[c] (3.00)	.034[c] (4.18)	−.042[b] (2.36)	.000 (.03)	.009 (1.09)	.026[a] (1.68)	.0015 (.64)	.247	2205

176

Female

1986	.072c (4.22)	−.003 (0.87)	.040c (3.87)	.054c (5.48)	.057c (4.70)	.0014 (1.15)	.032 (1.04)	−.0025 (1.53)	.272	4072
1985	.076c (4.58)	−.016 (.92)	.040c (3.97)	.049c (4.92)	.082c (6.43)	−.0016 (1.18)	.031 (1.11)	−.0019 (1.16)	.254	3960
1984	.048c (2.83)	.005 (.27)	.045c (4.33)	.063c (6.18)	.098c (6.98)	−.0037 (2.17)	.026 (1.03)	−.0015 (.86)	.233	3985
1983	.039b (2.42)	−.014 (.80)	.052c (5.30)	.056c (5.59)	.083c (5.49)	−.0021 (1.01)	.015 (.68)	−.0010 (.59)	.209	3894
1982	.005 (.33)	.014 (.85)	.048c (5.07)	.037c (3.80)	.092c (5.76)	−.0039 (1.52)	−.004 (.19)	.0007 (.43)	.187	3894
1981	.019 (1.23)	.013 (.78)	.32c (3.39)	.050c (4.75)	.085c (4.49)	.0026 (.73)	.024 (1.27)	−.0022 (1.17)	.195	3400
1980	.034b (1.96)	−.024 (1.32)	.032 (3.03)	.006 (.47)	.085c (3.64)	−.0038 (.72)	.060c (3.14)	−.0060c (2.67)	.150	3124
1979	−.012 (.58)	.012 (.54)	.041c (3.14)	−.035b (1.97)	.045 (1.26)	.0000 (.00)	.129c (6.97)	−.014c (5.36)	.235	2061

a. Significant at the 10 percent level on a two-tail test.
b. Significant at the 5 percent level on a two-tail test.
c. Significant at the 1 percent level on a two-tail test.

SOURCE: Least-squares estimation of equation 5–1 predicting the log of the hourly wage rate on one's current or most recent job separately for each year. The sample included individuals in the NLS Youth data set who were not in the military in 1979 and who answered questions about wages in the yearly interviews from 1981 to 1986. The coefficient on the variables included in this table were constrained to be the same in all years while the coefficients on control variables were not. Controls not shown in the table included school attendance (four variables), minority status, past and current military service, marital status, having one or more children, four census regions, rural residence, residence outside an SMSA, and the local unemployment rate.

positive trends in the returns to skill for at least four reasons. First, the apparent trend in the coefficient on test scores may be due to the aging of the sample. A number of studies have found that the return to comprehensive academic achievement increases with the age of the worker.[44] This would occur if achievement in academic and technical fields improves access to jobs offering considerable training and enables the worker to benefit more from training. Another probable cause of positive interactions between age and test scores is employer ignorance of the academic achievements measured by test scores and the resulting long delays before workers with strong academic achievement are discovered to be more productive and remunerated accordingly.

Second, the number of the sample participants who were in school diminished as time passed. Students working during the summer or part time during the school year generally have a narrower choice of occupations than young people who have completed their schooling. The high turnover rates and the necessity of scheduling work around school may prevent students from receiving the full wage benefits of their greater schooling and academic competence. If so, the decline in the proportion who are students in the sample would tend to cause the estimated effects of schooling and test scores in table 5–7 to exhibit a spurious positive trend.

Third, the proportion of NLS Youth who had completed a few years of college grew substantially between 1979 and 1986. It has often been hypothesized that the return to academic competency is larger for college graduates than for high school graduates. If so, the average impact of test scores on wages would grow as larger proportions of the sample complete their college education. Whether there is such a positive interaction in models predicting the log of the wage rate is controversial. Analyses of the National Bureau of Economic Research/ Thorndike data on men who were in the air force during World War II tend to support the hypothesis, but analyses of other data sets have been more equivocal.[45]

Fourth, interactions between work experience and years of schooling are likely. If cumulated actual work experience can substitute for schooling in some jobs, the return to cumulated work experience would be expected to be lower for young workers with greater amounts of schooling. Since schooling and work experience of the NLS Youth were growing between 1979 and 1986, trends in the effects of these variables might have been influenced by such an interaction.

Time-Series–Cross-Section Results

To test the hypotheses just discussed and obtain an unbiased estimate of the trend in the wage payoff to the skills of young men and women, wage rate models containing the hypothesized interactions were estimated by joint generalized least squares for years 1981 through 1986.[46] Coefficients on skill variables were not allowed to vary freely from year to year. Instead the estimation allows the coefficients on test scores, years of schooling, and actual work experience (a through f in equation 5–2) to exhibit a linear trend. In addition, interactions were specified between age and the three ASVAB composites, between student status and both academic achievement and years of schooling, and between years of college and both academic achievement and actual work experience.

The models were estimated using seemingly unrelated regression on a sample of young men and women who were not in the military in 1979 and who reported on a current or recent job in each interview between 1981 and 1986.[47] Data from 1979 and 1980 were not included because this would have excluded from the analysis many of the youngest members of the NLS Youth data base.

Main Effects of Skill Indicators. The results are presented in table 5–8. The specification of the skill variables and interactions is described in the notes to the table. The main effects of the test variables changed only slightly. The coefficients of main effects on the technical competence and computational speed (b_0 and c_0 in the notes to the table) provide estimates for the year 1983 of the effect of the competency on labor market outcomes of twenty-two-year-old high school graduates. As before, computational speed had a positive effect on the wages of both men and women while technical competence affected only the wages of men. Academic competence had a small positive effect on female wages but a significant negative effect on male wages. While test score effects are highly significant, they are modest in magnitude. An increase of one grade-level equivalent in all three test composites raised 1983 wages of twenty-two-year-olds only 1 to 1.5 percent.

The main effects of a year of high school for nonstudents in 1983 (d_0) were 0.03 for males and 0.025 for females. The coefficient of main effects on years of college, e_0 (0.058 for males and 0.034 for females), provides an estimate for 1983 of the amount by which the payoff to a year of college exceeds the payoff to a year of high school for workers with average academic test scores and four years of cumulated work experience.

TABLE 5–8
Effects of Skills on Wage Rates, 1981–1986

	Males		Females	
	Coefficient	T statistic	Coefficient	T statistic
Main Effects				
Academic test (a_0)	$-.038^b$	(2.49)	.020	(1.36)
Technical test (b_0)	$.053^c$	(4.36)	.004	(.24)
Computational test (c_0)	$.057^c$	(6.06)	$.039^c$	(4.43)
Years of schooling (d_0)	$.030^c$	(4.74)	$.025^c$	(3.19)
Years of college (e_0)	$.058^c$	(3.84)	$.034^b$	(2.37)
Actual experience (f_0)	$.1076^c$	(7.64)	$.0822^c$	(5.54)
Actual experience sq. (f_1)	$-.0048^c$	(2.99)	$-.0013$	(.74)
Potential experience (g_0)	$.048^c$	(5.45)	$.0345^c$	(3.69)
Potential experience sq. (g_1)	$-.0036^c$	(5.25)	$-.0033^c$	(4.23)
Interaction of Date with				
Academic test (a_1)	.0030	(.39)	.0011	(.14)
Technical test (b_1)	.0034	(.59)	$-.0036$	(.42)
Computational test (c_1)	$-.0067$	(1.31)	$-.0027$	(.55)
Years of schooling (d_1)	$-.0055^c$	(2.74)	$-.0033$	(1.11)
Years of college (e_1)	$.0184^c$	(5.20)	$.0101^b$	(2.50)
Actual experience (f_1)	$.0053^a$	(1.80)	.0020	(.66)
Interactions of Age with				
Academic test (a_2)	$-.0048$	(.76)	.0041	(.64)
Technical test (b_2)	.0027	(.54)	.0032	(.82)
Computational test (c_2)	$.0097^b$	(2.29)	.0058	(.87)
Interactions of actual experience with				
Years of college (e_4)	$-.0139^c$	(5.11)	$-.0072^c$	(2.71)
Academic test (e_5)	.0050	(.99)	.0045	(.72)
Interactions of academic test and college (d_5)	$.0124^b$	(2.22)	$.0148^c$	(2.70)

TABLE 5–8 (Continued)

	Males		Females	
	Coefficient	T statistic	Coefficient	T statistic
Interactions of student status with				
Years of schooling				
(d_3)	$-.0327^c$	(3.80)	$-.0163^b$	(1.99)
Academic test (a_3)	.0262	(1.47)	$-.0173$	(.94)
R^2 (pooled 1981–86 data)	.1295		.1218	
Number of observations per year	2,155		1,920	
F test on sum of trend x test interactions	.004		.57	
F test on sum of age x test interactions	2.85^a		5.78^b	
F test on sum of trend x schooling interactions	19.91^c		6.24^b	

NOTE: Joint generalized least-squares estimation of equation 5–1 predicting the log of the hourly wage rate on one's current or most recent job. The sample included individuals who were not in the military in 1979 and who answered questions about wages in the yearly interviews from 1981 through 1986. The coefficient of the variables included in this table were constrained to be the same in all years while the coefficients on control variables were not. Controls not shown in the table included school attendance (four variables), minority status, currently in the military, marital status, having one or more children, four census regions, rural residence, residence outside an SMSA, and the local unemployment rate. Potential experience, P, was substituted for age in these models. Potential experience is defined as max$\{0, age - max[16, (years of schooling + 6)]\}$. The model estimated was

$$W_t = aA + bT + cR + dS_t + eC_t + fE_t + gP_t + h_tZ_t + u_t, \text{ jointly for } t = 1981...1986$$

where
$a = a_0 + a_1(\text{year-1983}) + a_2(\text{age}_t\text{-22}) + a_3(\text{student}_t)$
$b = b_0 + b_1(\text{year-1983}) + b_2(\text{age}_t\text{-22})$
$c = c_0 + c_1(\text{year-1983}) + c_2(\text{age}_t\text{-22})$
$d = d_0 + d_1(\text{year-1983}) + d_3(\text{student}_t) + d_5A$
$e = e_0 + e_1(\text{year-1983}) + e_4(E_t\text{-4}) + e_5A$
$f = f_0 + f_1(\text{year-1983}) + f_4E_t$
$g = g_0 + g_4P_t$
$\text{student}_t = $ share of calendar year t in school

a. Significant at the 10 percent level on a two-tail test.
b. Significant at the 5 percent level on a two-tail test.
c. Significant at the 1 percent level on a two-tail test.

Both measures of work experience have large effects on wage rates. The existence of diminishing returns to actual and to potential experience was tested by entering square terms into the model. Actual cumulated work experience exhibits significant diminishing returns in the model predicting the wage rates of men but not significantly so in the models predicting the wage rates of women. The effect of actual experience is substantial. With potential work experience constant, the fourth full year of actual work experience raised wage rates of male and female high school graduates 7.3 to 7.4 percent. These results are no doubt in part caused by unobserved heterogeneity, but it is still quite remarkable that one year of actual work experience had a slightly larger effect on wages than a five-grade-level equivalent (that is, a one-population standard deviation) increase in all three test composites. Potential postschool work experience exhibited strong diminishing returns. Holding actual work experience constant, the first year of potential postschool experience raised the wage of males 4.8 percent (females, 3.45 percent) while the fourth year raised it only 2.3 percent (1.1 percent).

Trends in the Payoff to Skill. The coefficients on the interactions of year with the skill variables (a_1 through f_1) provide estimates of the effect of trends in the estimated wage payoff to various dimensions of skill in a model that allows the effects of skills to vary with age, experience, and student status. Clearly there is a strong positive trend in the payoff to college. Between 1981 and 1986 the ratio of the wage of college and high school graduates increased 29 percent [exp(0.258), where $0.258 = (1986-1981)*4*(0.0176-0.0056)$] for males and 14.6 percent for females. The payoff for four years of high school fell during this period 10.4 percent for males and 6.4 percent for females. These results are consistent with the results presented in table 5–7 and the findings reported in other chapters of this volume.

For returns to test scores, however, the results presented in table 5–7 are overturned. When the effect of schooling on wages is allowed to grow with time and interactions of student status and age with test score are included in the model, the F tests on the sum of the test-score trend coefficients indicate that there is no tendency for the estimated payoff to test scores to increase over the 1980s. Other specifications do not alter this conclusion as long as test scores are interacted with age and student status as well as with a time trend. For women, the point estimate for the sum of the test score trend coefficients is negative. Since scores on tests taken in 1980 become less reliable indicators of the worker's current academic competency as time passes, this result might have been caused by rising errors in the measurement of true competence as years pass. Consequently the absence of positive coefficients on test score trends is not a decisive refutation of the hypothesis that the return to true competencies rose in the 1980s. Better data are required before the issue can be finally settled.

There is a significant positive trend in the payoff to cumulated actual work experience for men but not for women. Models not reported here also tested for trends in the return to potential work experience; none were found.

Lifecycle Determinants of the Payoff to Skill Indicators.

Age. The findings regarding the effect of age on the payoff to the competencies measured by the ASVAB are presented in rows 16 to 18 of table 5–8. An *F* test was conducted on the sum of the coefficients on age interactions with the three test composites. The sum of the coefficients was significantly positive in both regressions ($p = 0.09$ for males and $p = 0.016$ for females from two-tail tests). *Ceteris paribus* a differential of one standard deviation in all three test composites raised the wage rates of male high school graduates not in school 4.8 percent at age nineteen, 7.2 percent at age twenty-two, and 9.6 percent at age twenty-five. For comparable women, a one-SD increase in all three tests raised wage rates 2.4 percent at age nineteen, 6.3 percent at age twenty-two, and 10.2 percent at age twenty-five.

This finding of a positive interaction between age and test scores is consistent with previous studies.[48] For males, the competency interacting most positively with age is computational speed. Also noteworthy, age has a larger positive effect on the payoff to test scores than cumulated work experience. Tests for interactions between actual work experience and test scores typically obtain small insignificant positive coefficients when age times test score interactions are in the model. Since the impact of test scores on wages grows even when the individual is not working, it would appear that differential investment in or payoffs to on-the-job training are not the only cause of the interaction between age and test scores. This result is supported by the findings in both NLS and High School and Beyond data that high test scores are not associated with the receipt of greater amounts of on-the-job training when schooling is held constant.[49] These results suggest that signals of academic competency may not at first be available to employers of high school graduates. Over time, however, the greater competence of the individuals with high test scores is revealed to the market partly by signals generated on the job (for example, promotions) and also by signals generated by further schooling (for example, college reputation and grades) and by unemployment (for example, reasons for turnover and for nonemployment), and wage rates increasingly reflect this knowledge.[50] More research is needed on this issue.

Student status. As hypothesized, the jobs occupied by students do not reward years of schooling as well as the jobs occupied by nonstudents. Being a student reduces the yearly payoff to schooling 3.3 percent for males and 1.6 percent for females.

College-test-score interactions. High academic test scores do appear to have the hypothesized significant positive effects on the wage payoff to attending college. The payoff to four years of college in 1983 was a 26.6 percent increase in wages for women (42 percent, men) at the 43rd percentile in the academic test score distribution, a 34 percent increase for women (49 percent, men) at the 80th percentile in the test-score distribution and a 42.5 percent increase for women (57 percent, men) at the 96.7th percentile in the test-score distribution. College quality and major, however, were not controlled in these models. Including these two variables in the model probably would substantially reduce the positive interaction between test scores and years of college.

Education and experience interactions. As hypothesized, the interaction between college and work experience is negative and significant. Each year of college lowers the male payoff to fifty-two weeks of cumulated work experience 1.39 percent (female, 0.72 percent). Apparently these alternative mechanisms for developing skill are substitutes.

Summary and Implications

Four kinds of interaction between the fluctuations in academic achievement of those completing their schooling and fluctuations in the payoff to a college education have been examined. In three cases evidence of interaction appears:

1. The decline, then the rise in the payoff to college appear to have contributed to the decline in academic achievement in high school between 1966 and 1980 and the subsequent rise in that achievement. A reliable estimate of how much of the test-score decline was caused by declines in the payoff to college does not, however, appear to be feasible.

2. The test-score decline contributed to the deceleration of the growth of the supply of well-educated workers and is thus one

of the causes of the general increase in the payoff to skill during the past decade.

3. The quality of college graduates relative to high school graduates from the same birth cohort has changed substantially over the past forty years for three reasons. The selectivity of college admissions rose through 1961, declined between 1961 and 1972, and rose again after 1972. Second, the gap between the test scores of college graduates and high school graduates appears to have declined in the late 1960s and to have risen continuously since 1972. Finally, the proportions of students pursuing the more remunerative technical and business majors have been changing—first declining during the 1960s and then rising during the last fifteen years. These three forces have tended to raise the productivity and wages of the latest cohorts of college graduates substantially above that of high school graduates with similar levels of experience.

The one exception to the general finding of interactions is the apparent lack of evidence that the general shortage of skilled and well-educated workers has bid up the return to achievements measured by test scores. The analysis of NLS Youth data implies that school credentials produce large payoffs immediately after leaving school and that these payoffs have grown substantially during the 1980s. The rewards for learning the material being taught in school, if they are not well signaled by a credential, are small at first but grow as the individual ages. But the rewards for such learning do not appear to have risen in the 1980s. Apparently the shift in the relative demand for skill has bid up wages only where skills are well signaled to the labor market. Society's tendency to reward credentials rather than learning appears to have remained strong during the period of skill shortage.

The threat of litigation brought under the 1971 Griggs interpretation of title 7 of the Civil Rights Act of 1965 deterred many employers from using tests measuring competence in reading and mathematics and grades in high school to help select new employees. This is one of the important reasons why youth do not on average receive significantly higher wage rates when they learn more English, science, and mathematics in high school. Recent court decisions have made it easier to defend using such tests as part of a selection process, but only a few of the larger employers have reintroduced basic skills tests into their selection procedures for clerical and factory jobs. If current interpretations of title 7 remain in force, the number of employers assessing competence in reading and mathematics before hiring is likely to increase slowly and the payoff to basic skills is likely to increase as well, albeit slowly. If, however, the language contained in the civil rights bill vetoed by President Bush becomes law, the legal impediments to the use of high school grades and scores on basic skills tests in employer hiring decisions will probably grow, and the payoff to basic skills competencies uncorrelated with years of schooling will probably not increase.

A Curious Hypothesis of Supply

A Commentary by Sherwin Rosen

John Bishop illuminates the problem of wages and workers by examining whether the intertemporal pattern of relative college quality can help account for the large increase in the rate of return to college in the 1980s. The reversal in the rate of return in the 1980s from its downward trend in the 1970s probably has been caused by a variety of forces. They are difficult to identify because few, if any, of the plausible explanatory variables follow the same intertemporal path. Bishop has put together an impressive array of facts from a diverse set of sources. The work supports the hypothesis that changes in school quality are one such contributory cause. An important strand in this chapter and in his related work is the economic idea that the quality of education and students' performance at school is influenced by the expected return from education. The intertemporal pattern of high school achievement scores certainly supports this kind of causation and sheds important new light on educational production. It helps in understanding why school quality changes from time to time.

Table 5–3 presents estimates of the average quantity and quality of schooling (indexed by school achievement test scores) embodied in the employed labor force for every decade since 1959. The numbers show a clear deceleration in the rate of growth in the 1980s. If the demand for skill grew in the 1980s at its previous pace, this relative retardation in supply would cause the skilled wage premium to rise.

Nonetheless, the hypothesis of exogenous decreases in supply, which must be the point of the calculations, is rather curious. The trend toward early retirement of males during this period would raise the average schooling of employed older cohorts over time because more-educated workers retire later than the less-educated and are less prone to disability. The calculation in the table probably is greatly affected by the changing role of women in the labor market, and it would be useful if the calculation could be done for each sex. Indeed the increase in the market supply of women remains to be investigated thoroughly as a separate contributory cause of the increasing return to skill. Although the exogenous entry of less-skilled women might account for some of the patterns in table 5–3, it surely cannot account for all of it because the trend of female labor force participation is too smooth. It also would be useful to have some indication of how the changing size of successive cohorts affects these calculations. The number of bachelor's degrees awarded, for example, has remained fairly flat in recent years because recent cohorts are smaller than previously.

Even after all these details are examined, the question of what caused the 1980s retardation found in the table remains. Shouldn't the supply of educated and skilled labor in the more recent cohorts have increased in response to these high prices in the 1980s? This more traditional aspect of supply response at the extensive margin is not examined in this chapter, or in others in this volume, for that matter. It is an important piece of unfinished business for understanding this problem and should be examined in greater depth soon. The evidence on improvements in college achievement in table 5–5 as well as the shifts of college majors in response to economic rewards is part of this bigger story of endogenous supply response, but the response of numbers and college enrollment rates should be at least as important.

The results in table 5–4 on college selectivity are thought-provoking. The 1960s and 1970s saw enormous growth in public colleges that were increasingly stratified by academic abilities and achievement. There was substantial growth in two- and four-year colleges catering to the middle to lower tail of the college-going population. Colleges seem to have become increasingly selective and stratified in allocating students among schools within the college system. Yet colleges as a whole have become less selective because more lower-ability students have been admitted to the system over the years. These things seem to cut in opposite ways for the measured return to schooling, although the second effect is probably more important than the first. It would be useful to fill in the numbers in table 5–4 for the middle and late 1960s and throughout the 1970s and 1980s. As such, the table suggests that college selectivity might have more explanatory power for the declining skill premiums of the 1970s than for the rising skill premiums of the 1980s.

The picture is further clouded by the finding late in the chapter that implicit prices of abilities did not rise in the 1980s among NLS youth. This is surprising in light of the general increase in the value of job market skills to which these ability measures are related. A youth sample is difficult to study in this regard because the transitions between school and work are lengthy and complicated. For instance, jobs held by more-able persons still in school are less likely to be connected to long-run careers and skills because they are used to finance further education, whereas less-able persons are less likely to be enrolled and more likely to hold jobs more closely connected to their long-run prospects. Examining the interactions between ability and current school enrollment in the earnings regression would begin to inform this point. There may be interactions between ability and completed schooling in that regression as well. Perhaps ability prices may have increased for college-educated workers but not for those with less schooling. It would be useful to see if that is true.

Notes

CHAPTER 1: WAGES AND DEMOGRAPHICS, *Marvin H. Kosters*

1. For examples of recent analyses and references, see Robert E. Litan, Robert Z. Lawrence, and Charles L. Schultze, eds., *American Living Standards: Threats and Challenges* (Washington, D.C.: Brookings Institution, 1988); Barry Bluestone and Bennett Harrison, "The Growth of Low-Wage Employment: 1963–86," *American Economic Review, Papers and Proceedings,* vol. 78, no. 2 (May 1988), pp. 124–28; and Frank Levy, *Dollars and Dreams: The Changing American Income Distribution* (New York: W.W. Norton, 1988).

2. The public attention that was given to the decline in returns to higher education in the 1970s was probably enhanced by books such as Richard B. Freeman, *The Overeducated American* (New York: Academic Press, 1976). For documentation of the decline in returns to higher education and analysis of the decline in relative wages of younger workers, see Finis Welch, "Effects of Cohort Size on Earnings: The Baby Boom Babies' Financial Bust," *Journal of Political Economy,* vol. 87, no. 5, pt. 2 (October 1979), pp. 565–97.

3. See, for example, Kevin Murphy and Finis Welch, chapter 2 in this volume; John Bound and George Johnson, chapter 3 in this volume; June O'Neill, "The Wage Gap between Men and Women in the United States," in Steven L. Willborn, ed., *Women's Wages: A Legal and Economic Analysis of Stability and Change in Six Industrial Countries* (Greenwich, Conn.: JAI Press, forthcoming); and June O'Neill, "Women and Wages," *The American Enterprise* (November/December 1990), pp. 24–33.

4. Trends in work experience of women are discussed in James P. Smith and Michael P. Ward, *Women's Wages and Work in the Twentieth Century* (Santa Monica, Calif.: RAND Corporation, 1984); June O'Neill, "The Trend in the Male-Female Wage Gap in the United States," *Journal of Labor Economics,* vol. 3, no. 1, pt. 2 (January 1985), pp. S91–S116; O'Neill, "The Wage Gap between Men and Women"; and Claudia Golden, "Life-Cycle Labor-Force Participation of Married Women: Historical Evidence and Implications," *Journal of Labor Economics,* vol. 7, no. 1 (January 1989), pp. 20–47.

5. The trends in figure 1–2 are quite similar when they are calculated using the composition of the work force in 1988, although the decline in real wages is somewhat less pronounced for males.

6. It is also possible that a growing share of workers with less than twelve years of schooling has completed much less than twelve years. Net immigration has apparently accounted for more than 20 percent of labor force growth

191

during the 1980s and a much larger share of recent adult immigrants have completed only elementary school than the native-born adult population. Although median years of schooling for recent immigrants and native-born adults are not very different, about 30 percent of adult immigrants have completed eight years of schooling or less compared with only about 17 percent of native-born adults. Declining relative wages of workers with less than twelve years of schooling may be attributable in part to the influence of immigration. See *The Effect of Immigration on the U.S. Economy and Labor Market,* Immigration Policy and Research, Report 1, U.S. Department of Labor, Bureau of International Labor Affairs, 1989.

7. Changes in wages of college graduates relative to high school dropouts are examined for cohorts by McKinley L. Blackburn, David E. Bloom, and Richard B. Freeman, "The Declining Economic Position of Less Skilled American Men," in Gary Burtless, ed., *A Future of Lousy Jobs? The Changing Structure of U.S. Wages* (Washington, D.C.: Brookings Institution, 1990), pp. 31–76.

8. See John Bishop, chapter 5 in this volume, for an analysis of various measures of schooling quality and the influence on wages of changes in schooling quality.

9. The effects of changes in the rate of growth of college graduates as a fraction of the work force are examined in Lawrence F. Katz and Ana L. Revenga, *Changes in the Structure of Wages: The U.S. versus Japan,* Working Paper no. 3021 (National Bureau of Economic Research, July 1989).

10. The trend toward earlier retirement in recent years is very clear. At sixty-one years of age, just before male labor force participation drops off sharply, the rate of men declined from 77 to 68 percent from 1973 to 1983, according to data reported in Philip L. Rones, *Monthly Labor Review,* February 1985, p. 47. Early retirement may have been concentrated disproportionately among men with less schooling in the 1980s.

11. The timing of the increase in the fraction of workers near retirement with college degrees suggests that the increase might be attributable to a sharp rise in college training resulting from the GI Bill. According to the most detailed study I have seen of the effect of the GI Bill on college enrollment, however, the post-World War II bulge in college attendance made no net addition to the fraction of that cohort completing college but instead approximately made up for deferral of college during the war years. See Keith Olson, *The GI Bill, the Veterans and the Colleges* (Lexington: University Press of Kentucky, 1975).

12. Kevin Murphy and Finis Welch, chapter 2, in this volume.

13. See, for example, Bound and Johnson, chapter 3 in this volume and Katz and Revenga, "Changes in the Structure of Wages."

14. This approach to calculating potential work experience was employed by Jacob Mincer in *Schooling, Experience, and Earnings* (New York: National Bureau of Economic Research, 1974).

15. Sandra A. West, "Estimation of the Mean from Censored Income Data," *Proceedings of the Royal Statistical Society Meeting,* 1986, Survey Research Methods Section, pp. 665–70; and "Measures of Central Tendency," *Proceedings of*

the Royal Statistical Society Meeting, 1987, Business and Economics Section, pp. 751–56.

PAYOFF TO EDUCATION, *A Commentary by Gary Burtless*

1. McKinley L. Blackburn, David E. Bloom, and Richard B. Freeman, "Why Has the Economic Position of Less-Skilled Men Deteriorated in the 1980s?" in Gary Burtless, ed., *A Future of Lousy Jobs? The Changing Structure of U.S. Wages* (Washington, D.C.: Brookings Institution, 1990).

CHAPTER 2: INTERNATIONAL TRADE AND WAGES, *Murphy and Welch*

1. Richard Freeman, *The Overeducated American* (New York: Academic Press, 1976).

2. Richard Freeman, "The Effect of Demographic Factors on Age-Earnings Profiles in the U.S.," *Journal of Human Resources,* vol. 14, no. 3 (1979), pp. 289–313; Finis Welch, "Effects of Cohort Size on Earnings: The Baby Boom Babies' Financial Bust," *Journal of Political Economy,* vol. 87, no. 5, pt. 2 (October 1979), pp. S65–S97; Mark C. Berger, "The Effect of Cohort Size and the Earnings Growth of Young Workers," *Industrial and Labor Relations Review,* vol. 37 (July 1984), pp. 582–91; Mark C. Berger, "The Effect of Cohort Size on Earnings Growth: A Reexamination of the Evidence," *Journal of Political Economy,* vol. 93, no. 3 (June 1985), pp. 561–73; and Kevin Murphy, Mark Plant, and Finis Welch, "Cohort Size Earnings in the U.S.A.," in Ronald D. Lee, ed., *Economics of Changing Age Distributions in Developed Countries* (Oxford: Oxford University Press, 1988).

3. June O'Neill, "The Trend in the Sex Differential in Wages" (Paper presented at Conference on Trends in Women's Work, Education and Family Building, White House Conference Center, Chelwood Gate, Sussex, England, May 31–June 3, 1983) and James P. Smith and Michael P. Ward, *Women's Wages and Work in the Twentieth Century* (Santa Monica, Calif.: RAND, September 1984).

4. See James P. Smith and Finis Welch, "Affirmative Action and Labor Markets," *Journal of Labor Economics,* vol. 2, no. 2 (April 1984), pp. 269–301, for a notable exception. Black-white wage ratios did not increase at earlier or subsequent rates during the 1950s. Smith's explanation is that a majority of black workers during this period were products of educational and political disfranchisement that started in the South at the end of the nineteenth century.

5. Richard Freeman, "Black Economic Progress After 1964: Who Has Gained and Why?" in Sherwin Rosen, ed. *Studies in Labor Markets* (Chicago: University of Chicago Press, 1981), pp. 247–94, and Wayne Vroman, "Changes in Black Worker's Relative Earnings: Evidence from the 1960s," in

George von Furstenburg, ed., *Patterns of Racial Discrimination*, vol. 2, *Employment and Income* (Lexington, Mass.: DC Heath, 1974).

6. Smith and Welch, "Affirmative Action and Labor Markets."

7. At any time there are important differences in employment patterns of workers classified by age or potential experience, but these differences are related to cohorts through long-run shifts in industrial structure. When data are mixed over the full 1963–1986 period, the age relationships disappear.

8. *Economic Report of the President* (Washington, D.C.: Government Printing Office, various years).

9. Kevin Murphy and Finis Welch, "The Structure of Wages" (Los Angeles: Unicon Research Corporation, May 1989, unpublished).

10. Wage calculations reflect earnings of those who are not yet self-employed, who usually work at least thirty-five hours per week, and who worked at least twenty-six weeks in the year preceding the survey. Observations showing average earnings per week below $10 or above $1,875 are excluded, as are workers coded as in school or retired (as reason for working less than fifty weeks) and those who work without pay.

11. High school graduates in figure 2–2 and subsequent discussion refer to those who completed twelve years of school; college graduates are those completing sixteen years of school.

12. Murphy and Welch, "The Structure of Wages."

13. The 1963–1986 mean values of transformed variables are 0.94 for R_1, 1.02 for R_2, and 0.71 for R_3.

14. The CPS data used for wage illustrations can be divided into four periods: (1) 1963–1966, (2) 1967–1970, (3) 1971–1980, and (4) 1981–1986. The CPS samples for the first period are publicly available from the Bureau of the Census as are the remaining surveys. For this period we used tapes secured privately from the University of Wisconsin. Although the original data includes three-digit 1960 census industrial detail, the files distributed by the university are processed for general compatibility with later years. The resulting two-digit industrial taxonomy does not translate easily into the two-digit mapping we use. The second period uses industry identification from the 1960 census, the third period uses 1970 census definitions, and the fourth period uses 1980 census definitions. We use three-digit detail for the second and fourth periods to approximate the 1970 census two-digit definitions.

15. James S. Coleman, Sara D. Kelly, and John A. Moore, "Trends in School Segregation, 1968–73" (Washington, D.C.: Urban Institute, 1975).

16. For two groups designated as 1 and 2, let N_1 refer to the number in group 2. Weights for averages are proportional to $N_1N_2/(N_1+N_2)$.

17. *Economic Report of the President, 1988* (Washington, D.C.: Government Printing Office, 1988).

CHANGING STRUCTURE OF RELATIVE WAGES, *A Commentary by Walter Y. Oi*

1. The Nadiri-Rosen study identified three factors of production (production workers, nonproduction workers, and capital) and directed attention to adjustment costs. My dictionary defines a "factor" as "a person who carries

194

out business transactions for another" or "an element or constituent that makes a thing what it is." A factor in the Murphy-Welch study refers to workers who are of the same gender, race, years of education, and age. M. Ishaq Nadiri and Sherwin Rosen, *A Disequilibrium Model of the Demand for Factors* (New York: Columbia University Press, 1974).

2. Finis Welch, "Effects of Cohort Size on Earnings: The Baby Boom Babies' Financial Bust," *Journal of Political Economy*, vol. 87 (October 1979), pp. 565–97.

3. The authors assume a background production function exhibiting constant returns to scale in the labor inputs alone. Thus their unit cost functions, $c_k(w_1, \ldots w_J)$, are homogeneous of degree one in the J wage rates. Changes in imports can affect product prices by their impact on wages.

4. John H. Bishop, "Achievement, Test Scores, and Relative Wages," this volume.

5. Nancy Garvey and Cordelia Reimers, "Predicted vs. Potential Work Experience in an Earnings Function for Young Men," in Ronald Ehrenberg, ed., *Research in Labor Economics*, vol. 3 (Greenwich, Conn.: JAI Press, 1980), pp. 99–127.

6. June O'Neill, "The Trend in the Male-Female Wage Gap in the United States," *Journal of Labor Economics*, vol. 3 (January 1985), pp. S91–S116. James P..Smith and Michael P. Ward, *Women's Wages and Work in the Twentieth Century* (Santa Monica, Calif.: RAND Corp., 1984).

7. This trend was examined by Rebecca Blank, "Part-time and Temporary Work," in *Investing in People*, Paper 29 (Commission on Work Force Quality and Labor Market Efficiency, Washington, D.C., September 1989), pp. 1519–88. Blank also pointed out that the length of the work year (weeks worked a year) increased in the postwar period.

8. Jacob Mincer and Yoshio Higuchi, "Wage Structures and Labor Turnover in the United States and Japan," *Journal of the Japanese and International Economies*, vol. 2 (June 1988), pp. 97–133.

9. Henry Ludwell Moore, *Laws of Wages: An Essay in Statistical Economics* (New York: Macmillan, 1911; reprinted by Augustus M. Kelley, 1967): see especially chap. 6, pp. 140–68. R. A. Lester, "Pay Differences by Size of Establishment," *Industrial and Labor Relations Review*, vol. 7 (January 1967), pp. 57–67. Wesley Mellow, "Employwer Size and Wages," *Review of Economics and Statistics*, vol. 64 (August 1982), pp. 495–501.

An excellent review of the literature on this subject is provided by Charles Brown, James Hamilton, and James Medoff, *Employers Large and Small* (Cambridge: Harvard University Press, 1990). An explanation for the firm-size effect can be found in W. Y. Oi, "Employment Relations in Dual Labor Markets," *Journal of Labor Economics*, vol. 8 (January 1990), S124–S149.

10. Donald O. Parsons, "The Decline in Male Labor Force Participation," *Journal of Political Economy*, vol. 88 (February 1980), pp. 117–34. Jonathan S. Leonard, "The Social Security Disability Program and Labor Force Participation," Working Paper 392 (National Bureau of Economic Research, Cambridge, Mass., 1979).

11. The reasons for including a marital status dummy are ad hoc and not

terribly persuasive. Kathryn Shaw contends the lower labor turnover of married men is caused by risk aversion. She finds that as the wife's share of family income rises, the married man exhibits less risk aversion, and his quit propensity climbs. See K. Shaw, "The Quit Propensity of Married Men," *Journal of Labor Economics*, vol. 5 (October 1987), pp. 533–60.

12. The Welch-Smith paper was not published, but the discussant's comments were. See Donald B. Rubin, "Imputing Income in the CPS: Comments on 'Measures of Aggregate Labor Cost in the United States,' " in J. E. Triplett, ed., *The Measurement of Labor Costs* (Chicago: University of Chicago Press, 1983), pp. 333–43.

13. Sanford Jacoby, *Employing Bureaucracy* (New York: Columbia University Press, 1985).

CHAPTER 3: THE 1980s AND BEYOND,
Bound and Johnson

1. The sample includes persons in the annual Current Population Survey between the ages of eighteen and sixty-four whose principal activity was working (excluding full-time students) in nonagricultural industries (excluding private household services). The wage rate is defined as the ratio of the response to the question concerning usual weekly earnings and usual weekly hours. Potential experience is defined as age less years of schooling, minus six for those with educational attainment in excess of nine years; otherwise, potential experience equals age minus sixteen. One problem is that the response to the question on usual weekly earnings was capped at \$999.99, which was relevant for many highly educated males in 1987. Based on data from the March 1989 CPS, David Card has estimated that the actual earnings of those at the cap were on average 1.165 times the maximum recorded value, and we used this adjustment for the 1987 data. The average log wages that we use throughout the chapter refer to regressions for each of our thirty-two demographic groups in which log wages were regressed on potential experience, education (where relevant), dummy variables for major region, residing in an SMSA, race, and full-time status. Reported average log wages are for particular values of education and experience (as reported), for a weighted average of the regional dummies, and for white full-time workers residing in SMSAs.

2. Daniel S. Hammermesh, "The Demand for Labor in the Long Run," in Orley Ashenfelter and Richard Layard, eds., *Handbook of Labor Economics*, vol. 1 (Amsterdam: North-Holland, 1986), pp. 429–71.

3. Kevin Murphy and Finis Welch, chap. 2 in this volume. See also "The Structure of Wages" (Los Angeles: Unicon Research, May 1988), mimeograph.

4. Ibid.

5. Jean Baldwin Grossman, "The Substitutability of Natives and Immigrants in Production," *Review of Economics and Statistics*, vol. 64 (July 1982), pp. 596–603; George Borjas, "Immigrants, Minorities, and Labor Market Competition," *Industrial and Labor Relations Review*, vol. 40, no. 3 (April 1987), pp. 382–92; and Joseph Altonji and David Card, "The Effects of Immigration on the

Labor Market Outcomes of Natives," Working Paper 256 (Princeton University, August 1989).

6. This idea is based on our reading of David Card, "The Impact of the Mariel Boatlift on the Miami Labor Market," Working Paper 3069 (National Review of Economic Research, Washington, D.C., August 1989). Card does not necessarily subscribe to the interpretation set forth here.

7. Murphy and Welch, chap. 2 in this volume. See also "Structure of Wages."

8. Barry Bluestone and Bennett Harrison, *The Great U-Turn* (New York: Basic Books, 1988).

9. George Johnson, "Work Rules, Featherbedding, and Pareto-Optimal Union-Management Bargaining," *Journal of Labor Economics*, vol. 8, no. 1, pt. 2 (January 1990), pp. S237–59.

10. H. Gregg Lewis, "Union Relative Wage Effects," in Orley Ashenfelter and Richard Layard, eds., *Handbook of Labor Economics*, vol. 2 (Amsterdam: North-Holland, 1986), chap. 20.

11. Bluestone and Harrison, *Great U-Turn;* and McKinley L. Blackburn, David E. Bloom, and Richard B. Freeman, "The Declining Economic Position of Less Skilled American Men," in Gary Burtless, ed., *A Future of Lousy Jobs?* (Washington, D.C.: Brookings Institution, 1989), pp. 31–76.

12. James Smith and Michael Ward, *Women's Wages and Work in the Twentieth Century* (Santa Monica, Calif.: RAND Corp., 1984).

13. John Bishop, "Is the Test Score Decline Responsible for the Productivity Growth Decline?" *American Economic Review*, vol. 79, no. 1 (March 1989), pp. 178–97.

14. Kenneth Arrow, "The Theory of Discrimination," in Orley Ashenfelter and Albert Rees, eds., *Discrimination in Labor Markets* (Princeton: Princeton University Press, 1973), pp. 3–33; and Gary S. Becker, *The Economics of Discrimination* (Chicago: University of Chicago Press, 1957).

15. Bishop, "Is the Test Score Decline Responsible."

16. John Bound and George Johnson, "Changes in the Structure of Wages during the 1980s: An Evaluation of Alternative Explanations," Working Paper 2983 (National Bureau of Economic Research, Washington, D.C., May 1989).

17. Richard Freeman, "Demand for Education," in Orley Ashenfelter and Richard Layard, eds., *Handbook of Labor Economics*, vol. 1 (Amsterdam: North-Holland, 1986), pp. 357–86.

18. Finis Welch, "Education in Production," *Journal of Political Economy*, vol. 78 (January/February 1970), pp. 35–59.

REINTERPRETATION OF SUPPLY SHIFTS, *A Commentary by*
Lawrence F. Katz

1. Chinhui Juhn, Kevin M. Murphy, and Brooks Pierce, "Wage Inequality and the Rise in the Returns to Skill" (University of Chicago, November 1989, mimeograph).

2. Lawrence F. Katz and Kevin M. Murphy, "Changes in Relative Wages,

1963–1987: Supply and Demand Factors" (Harvard University, April 1990, mimeograph).

3. Juhn, Murphy, and Pierce, "Wage Inequality."

4. Katz and Murphy, "Changes in Relative Wages."

5. George J. Borjas, Richard B. Freeman, and Kevin Lang, "Undocumented Mexican-Born Workers in the United States: How Many and How Permanent" in J. Abowd and Richard B. Freeman, eds., *Immigration, Trade, and the Labor Market* (Chicago: University of Chicago Press and NBER, forthcoming).

6. George J. Borgas, Richard B. Freeman, and Lawrence F. Katz, "On the Labor Market Effects of Trade and Immigration" (Harvard University, January 1989, mimeograph).

7. Lawrence F. Katz and Ana L. Revenga, "Changes in the Structure of Wages: The United States vs. Japan," *Journal of the Japanese and International Economies*, vol. 3 (December 1989), pp. 522–53.

8. Mark Adams, Ruth Maybury, and William Smith, "Trends in the Distribution of Earnings, 1973 to 1986," *Employment Gazette*, vol. 96 (February 1988), pp. 75–82.

CHAPTER 4: SLOWDOWN IN BLACK-WHITE CONVERGENCE, *Juhn, Murphy, and Pierce*

1. See, for example, James P. Smith and Finis Welch, "Black-White Earnings and Employment: 1960–1970," *American Economic Review*, vol. 67 (June 1977), and Richard Freeman, "Black Economic Progress after 1964: Who Has Gained and Why?" in Sherwin Rosen, ed., *Studies in Labor Markets* (Chicago: University of Chicago Press, 1981), pp. 247–94.

2. Kevin M. Murphy and Finis Welch, "Wages Premiums for College Graduates: Recent Growth and Possible Explanations," *Educational Researcher* (May 1989), pp. 17–26.

3. Kevin M. Murphy and Finis Welch, "The Structure of Wages" (Paper presented at a meeting of the Population Association, Chicago, May 1987).

4. Chinhui Juhn, Kevin M. Murphy, and Brooks Pierce, "Wage Inequality and the Rise in Returns to Skill" (University of Chicago, Graduate School of Business, 1989).

5. For survey years 1964 through 1976, weeks worked are only available on a bracketed basis. We imputed means to these cells based on average weeks worked in each cell from the later sample years.

6. These cohorts are actually averages of five consecutive five-year cohorts. Since the weight on each cohort in the average stays fixed, however, the numbers can still be given a strict cohort interpretation.

7. The regressions include dummies for regions, as well as a quartic in experience fully interacted with education dummies for less than high school, high school graduates, some college and college graduates, and with linear education terms within the education categories.

8. As in the earlier table these calculations actually refer to five-year

averages so that 1965 is really the average of 1963–1967 and 1985 is really the average of 1983–1987.

9. The numbers for total convergence would seem to indicate that blacks gained more during the 1970s than during the 1960s. Such an interpretation, however, may not be correct. First, this difference is more than accounted for by the difference $(.82 = .76 - (-.06))$ in observable quantity convergence. Second, the majority of the quantity of skill convergence numbers is most likely a result of the change in sample composition from the first four years of data (1963 through 1967), which were generated at the University of Wisconsin, and the data from the public release tapes used in later years. Hence it is quite likely that the composition effects do not represent skill convergence for the U.S. population as a whole.

10. Here as in the observable decomposition presented in table 4–4, we actually chose a single base year (the average of all years). Hence year t in the formulas is actually a composite of all years in the sample.

11. Chinhui Juhn et al., "Wage Inequality."

12. See, for example, James P. Smith and Finis Welch, "Closing the Gap: Forty Years of Economic Progress for Blacks," Paper R-3330-DOL (RAND Corporation, Santa Monica, Calif., February 1986), and Finis Welch, "Black-White Earnings and Employment: 1960–1970," *American Economic Review*, vol. 67 (June 1977).

13. As we note below, the use of such a flexible functional form is actually critical in this case since the changes in education premiums have not been the same at all schooling levels. In particular the college–high school premium has risen much more than other education-based wage premiums.

14. The change in occupation codes from 1981 to 1982 in the Current Population Survey (CPS) prevented us from computing the fixed price or quantity change over this interval so that we had to interpolate this year. We chose to use the remaining years from 1979 through 1987 to estimate the average allocation between components over the period, and we assigned these to the 1981–1982 change using a regression. Provided the other years are representative of the 1981–1982 change, the interpolation should not yield misleading results. The similarity of these results with the one-digit results presented seems to suggest that the procedure worked well.

Chapter 5: Achievement, Test Scores, and Wages, *John Bishop*

1. Iowa Test of Educational Development composite scores of eleventh-grade students in Iowa declined from 18.9 in 1965 to 16.8 in 1977 and then rose to 19.2 in 1989. Composite scores for twelfth graders fell from 20.8 in 1966 to 18.4 in 1979 and then rose to 20.2 in 1989. During the 1970s and 1980s, twelfth-grade scores on the ITED composite averaged about 5.5 points higher than ninth-grade scores, implying that a grade-level equivalent was roughly equal to 1.835 points. Consequently in terms of grade-level equivalents the decline was 1.31 for seniors and 1.14 for juniors. Data on ITED trends were provided by Robert Forsyth of the Iowa Testing Program.

2. Kevin Murphy and Finis Welch, "Wage Premiums for College Graduates: Recent Growth and Possible Explanations," *Educational Researcher*, May 1989, pp. 17–26.

3. John H. Bishop, "The Productivity Consequences of What Is Learned in High School," *Journal of Curriculum Studies*, vol. 22, no. 2 (1990), pp. 101–126. In another study the effect of math, reading, and vocabulary test scores on the wage rates and earnings of high school graduates for both 1972 and 1980 was estimated in a model that contained controls for grade point average and the number of credit hours of academic and vocational courses. In both these years none of the variables representing academic performance—the three test scores, GPA, and the number of academic courses—had a significant (at the 10 percent level) effect on the wage rate of the first post–high school job. Only one variable (the vocabulary test for female members of the class of 1972) had a significant effect on the wage 18 months after graduation. John Bishop, Arthur Blakemore, and Stuart Low, "High School Graduates in the Labor Market: A Comparison of the Class of 1972 and 1980" (Columbus, Ohio: National Center for Research in Vocational Education, 1985).

4. Data on ITED trends was kindly provided by Robert Forsyth (personal communication). "Achievement Trends for the Iowa Tests of Educational Development in Iowa: 1942–1985," internal memorandum, Iowa City: Iowa Testing Programs, 1987. ITBS data were obtained from A. N. Hieronymus, E. F. Lindquist, and H. D. Hoover, *Iowa Test of Basic Skills: Manual for School Administrators* (Chicago: Riverside Publishing, 1979). Other tests that have been administered for long spans of time to stable test-taking populations also exhibit a positive trend during this period. Roger Farr and Leo Fey, "Reading Trend Data in the United States: A Mandate for Caveats and Caution," in eds. Gilbert Austin and Herbert Garber, *The Rise and Fall of National Test Scores* (New York: Academic Press, 1982), pp. 83–142. Between 1958 and 1966 Minnesota high school juniors gained 0.39 SDs on the Minnesota Scholastic Aptitude Test. See Edward O. Swanson, "Fashions in Test Scores, or What Goes Up Must Come Down?" *Student Counseling Bureau Review* (University of Minnesota) vol. 25, no. 1 (September 1973). The periodic national standardizations of the ITED also exhibit an increase during the 1960s.

5. From peak to trough the decline for seniors was 0.38 SDs on the SAT and 0.32 SDs on the ACT. For eleventh graders it was 0.28 SDs in the Illinois decade study, 0.24 SDs on the Preliminary Scholastic Aptitude Test, and 0.22 SDs on the California Achievement Test. The scores of ninth- and tenth-graders declined 0.42 SDs on the Metropolitan Achievement Tests. The scores of fifth- through eighth graders declined 0.33 SDs on the Stanford Achievement Test and 0.32 SDs on the ITBS. Daniel Koretz et al., *Trends in Educational Achievement* (Washington, D.C.: Congressional Budget Office, 1986) and Brian K. Waters, *The Test Score Decline: A Review and Annotated Bibliography*, Technical Memorandum 81–2, Directorate for Accession Policy, Office of the Secretary of Defense, (Washington, D.C., April 1981).

6. U.S., Department of Commerce, Bureau of the Census, *Historical Statistics of the United States* (Washington, D.C.: Government Printing Office, 1975). For 1929 through 1953 the index for high-level professionals is a geometric

average of yearly mean incomes of engineers, college teachers, dentists, physicians, and lawyers divided by fifty-two (D913–D916, D920). Because data on the net income of lawyers were not available after 1954, the geometric average of college teacher salary, engineer salary, and median incomes for physicians and dentists was calculated and spliced onto the series (D913, D918–D920). The data on weekly earnings of all manufacturing workers were taken from D804 of the same document.

7. Dieter Marenbach, "Rates of Return to Education in the United States from 1939 to 1959" (PhD Diss., Stanford University, 1973), pp. 89–90.

8. Lawrence Katz and Kevin Murphy, "Changes in Relative Wages, 1963–1987: Supply and Demand Factors" (National Bureau of Economic Research, Washington, D.C., April 1990), pp. 1–61.

9. Daniel Koretz et al., *Trends in Educational Achievement*.

10. Toby Friedman and Belvin E. Williams, "Current Use of Tests for Employment," in Alexandria K. Wigdor and Wendell R. Gardner, eds., *Ability Testing: Uses, Consequences, and Controversies, Part II: Documentation Section* (Washington, D.C.: National Academy Press, 1982), pp. 99–169.

11. John H. Bishop, "The Effect of Public Policies on the Demand for Higher Education," *Journal of Human Resources*, vol. 12, no. 3 (Summer 1977).

12. The payoff variable for this analysis was the earnings differential between professional workers and operatives measured in 1959 dollars deflated for the local cost of living. The local labor market is either the SMSA of residence or the non-SMSA portion of the state. In 1959, male high school graduates twenty-five- to sixty-four-years-old earned an average of $6,132. The payoff variable had a mean of $2,957 and a standard deviation of $570.

13. Since the college wage premium was rising at all experience levels, there must have been a rise in the price paid for skill during the 1980s. Changes in the relative quality of college and high school graduates in the cohorts entering the labor market directly effect the relative wages of the youngest workers but not the relative wages of workers who have been in the labor market at both points in time.

14. Lawrence Katz and Anna Revenga, "Changes in the Structure of Wages: The U.S. versus Japan," Working Paper 3021 (National Bureau of Economic Research, Washington, D.C., July 1989).

15. The source of data on the educational attainment of the labor force was the 1983 *Handbook of Labor Statistics*, table 65 and unpublished BLS data for 1988. Before 1972 the tabulations were for workers over the age of eighteen. After that date, tabulations were for workers over the age of sixteen. Consequently rates of change of educational attainment for the 1970s are for the eight-year period from 1972 to 1980 for which data is consistent over time.

16. Adkins assumes that 11.1 percent of people reporting sixteen or more years of schooling have completed sixteen years of schooling but lack either a bachelor's or first professional degree; Douglas L. Adkins, *The Great American Degree Machine* (Carnegie Foundation for the Advancement of Teaching, 1975), p. 65. Data on the share of immigrants with a college degree were kindly provided by George Borjas.

17. John H. Bishop, "Did the Test Score Decline Cause the Productivity

Growth Decline," *American Economic Review,* March 1989, pp. 178–97.

18. For the formal development of a model in which changes in rates of growth of wage differentials are equal to changes in relative supply growth times the inverse of the elasticity of substitution plus shifts in relative demand, see McKinley L. Blackburn, David E. Bloom, and Richard B. Freeman, "The Declining Economic Position of Less Skilled American Men," in Gary Burtless, *A Future of Lousy Jobs?* (Washington, D.C.: Brookings Institution, 1990), p. 41. Their empirical work suggests that the elasticity of substitution between college graduates and high school graduates twenty-five to sixty-four years of age is approximately 4.

19. Paul Taubman and Terence Wales, "Mental Ability and Higher Educational Attainment in the Twentieth Century," Occasional Paper 118 (National Bureau of Economic Research, Washington, D.C., 1972).

20. John A. Gardner, *Transition from High School to Postsecondary Education: Analytical Studies* (Columbus, Ohio: National Center for Research in Vocational Education, February 1987). This paper provides data on fall 1981 college entrance rates by ability quartile. The shape of the continuous relationship was derived from the quartile data as follows: the linear line segment characterizing the relationship between the twenty-fifth and seventy-fifth percentile was assumed to pass through the mean college entrance rates for the second and third quartiles. This produces estimates of entrance rates of 0.762 for the seventy-fifth percentile and 0.35 for the twenty-fifth percentile. The line segment characterizing the relationship in the top quartile was assumed to pass through the mean (0.816) for the quartile and connect with the 0.762 at the seventy-fifth percentile. The relationship in the bottom quartile was derived in a similar manner. Once the shape of the relationship was defined the mean ranking of those entering college and those not entering college was calculated.

21. Gregory Jackson, "Did College Choice Change during the Seventies?" *Economics of Education Review,* vol. 7, no. 1 (1988), pp. 15–27.

22. Since the tests used to construct the Project Talent achievement composite were different from the tests used in NLS 72, the difference between the correlations for 1961 and 1972 might be caused by differences in the test or differences in the representativeness of sample. If the Project Talent aptitude composite had been used instead of the achievement composite for calculating the 1961 correlation, the correlation would have been 0.41, and a much smaller reduction in selectivity between 1961 and 1972 would have been implied. Comparison with the achievement composite, however, is more appropriate because the mathematics, reading, and vocabulary tests available in NLS 72 and HSB appear at the achievement end of the aptitude-achievement continuum.

23. For twenty-three years the ACE has sponsored yearly surveys of the freshman classes of 500 to 600 two- and four-year colleges and universities. In 1985, invitations to participate went to all 2,741 institutions of higher education listed in the Department of Education's *Education Directory* with freshman classes of at least 50. The low institutional participation rate and the changing character of participating institutions threaten the validity of the trend data

generated by this survey. To minimize this problem, ACE stratifies colleges by size, control, and selectivity, and the attained sample is then reweighted to construct a profile of all freshman at American colleges and universities. Data are also available on the grade point average of entering freshman. Because trends in GPAs are affected by grade inflation, they tell us little about how the effect of academic performance in high school on college entrance is changing over time. In 1966, 30.5 percent of college freshman reported they had a high school GPA of C+ or below. This percentage fell to 26.8 percent in 1970–1971 and has continued to fall, reaching 20.2 percent in 1986. Alexander Astin, Kenneth Green, William S. Korn, and Marilynn Schalit, "The American Freshman: National Norms for Fall 1986" (Los Angeles: University of California, Los Angeles, Cooperative Institutional Research Program, Higher Education Research Institute, December 1986), and Alexander Astin, Kenneth C. Green, and William S. Korn, "The American Freshman: Twenty Year Trends" (Los Angeles: University of California, Los Angeles, Cooperative Institutional Research Program, Higher Education Research Institute, January 1987).

24. Hunter Breland, Gita Wilder, and Nancy J. Robertson, *Demographics, Standards, and Equity: Challenges in College Admissions* (Report sponsored by the American Association of Collegiate Registrars and Admissions Officers, the American College Testing Program, the College Board, Educational Testing Service, and National Association of College Admissions Counselors, November 1986).

25. Data on trends in high school GPAs and class rank are also available for SAT test takers in Educational Testing Service, *College-Bound Seniors: Eleven Years of National Data from the College Board's Admissions Testing Program* (College Board, 1984). Unfortunately the SAT data are not reliable indicator of trends in the relative quality of all college-bound students because the proportion of college-bound students taking the SAT has risen. The number of entering freshmen can be estimated by multiplying Hauser's estimates of the proportion of high school graduates entering colleges derived from the October interview of the Current Population Survey by the number of high school graduates; Robert Hauser, "College Entry among Black High School Graduates: Family Income Does Not Explain the Decline," Working Paper 87-19 (Center for Demography and Ecology, University of Wisconsin, 1987). Then the ratio of SAT test takers to entering freshmen was estimated by dividing the number of respondents to the SAT's Student Descriptive Questionnaire by the estimated number of freshmen. This ratio was 56 percent in 1973, 54.5 percent in 1976–1978, 61.2 percent in 1981, and 61.6 percent in 1985. The percentage of SAT test takers reporting themselves to be in the bottom 60 percent of their high school graduating class was 26 percent in 1973, 24 percent in 1976, 28 percent in 1978, 30 percent in 1982, and 32 percent in 1985. These patterns are clearly at odds with the data from HSB, NLS Class of 1972, and the ACE Cooperative Research Program. The growing proportion of high school graduates entering college and the growing share of them taking the SAT creates an appearance of deteriorating selectivity in SAT data during the late 1970s and the 1980s that is probably spurious.

26. Clifford Adelman, *The Standardized Test Scores of College Graduates, 1964–*

1982 (Study Group on the Condition of Excellence in American Higher Education, National Institute of Education, 1983).

27. Data on trends for these tests were obtained by correspondence with the organizations that administer these exams and from Clifford Adelman, *The Standardized Test Scores of College Graduates, 1964–1982.* The weights for the three professional school tests were the total numbers of test takers between 1976 and 1986. There are breaks in the comparability of the LSAT and MCAT. The one-year gaps in these series were filled in by assuming no change in mean scores during the interval.

28. The time series of SAT and ACT test scores is not used because there have been changes in the share of high school seniors who take these two tests during the period. Separate time series of ITED composite scores for high school juniors and seniors in the state of Iowa were deviated from the value in 1977 and divided by the 1977 standard deviation of the test for each group. Since the ITED is given in the fall of the year, the mean for high school graduates in year *t* was an average of senior scores for *t*-1 and junior scores for *t*-2. To calculate an index of the quality of the cohort of high school graduates who reach college graduation age in year *t*, a weighted average was calculated with *t*-4 receiving a weight of one-half and each of the five previous years (*t*-5 to *t*-9) receiving a weight of one-tenth.

29. John H. Bishop, "Test Score Decline," p. 181. Test-score standard deviations for populations of high school seniors on which the Iowa tests are normed are about 0.74 of the standard deviations for random samples of adults. The coefficient was obtained by multiplying 0.74 by 0.190. Bishop's estimate of the effect of academic achievement on weekly wages is for adult males. The wage rate effects of test scores are smaller for young workers, so using a coefficient from a study of adult earnings may exaggerate the estimated effect of changes in the relative quality of college graduates on young workers. Conversely there is evidence that across individuals, the productivity effects of academic achievement are larger than the wage effects; John H. Bishop, "Productivity Consequences" and "Information Externalities and the Social Return to Schooling," Discussion Paper 1987-04 (Cornell University Center for Advanced Human Resources Research, Ithaca, N.Y.). If this is the case, differences in academic achievement across recognizable groups might generate group or cohort reputations that in turn cause large mean wage differentials between groups. This would mean that our method underestimates the effect of changes in the test score gap on the college premium for young workers.

30. National Center for Education Statistics, *Digest of Education Statistics: 1989*, table 331, p. 375.

31. U.S., Department of Commerce, Bureau of the Census, *Characteristics of Men with College Degrees: 1967*, Current Population Reports, Population Characteristics, Series P-20, No. 201 (Washington, D.C.: Government Printing Office, 1970), p. 23.

32. U.S., Department of Commerce, Bureau of the Census, Current Population Reports, Series P-70, No. 11, *What's It Worth? Educational Background and*

Economic Status: Spring 1984 (Washington, D.C.: Government Printing Office, 1987). The large differentials between college majors found in these data reflect both differences in wage rates and in hours worked per month. If gender were controlled, the differentials would be smaller.

33. Thomas N. Daymont and Paul Andrisani, "Job Preferences, College Major, and the Gender Gap in Earnings," *Journal of Human Resources*, Summer 1984, pp. 408–28.

34. Astin et al., "The American Freshman: 1986" and "The American Freshman: Twenty Year Trends."

35. The ASVAB manual reports:

> Extensive research demonstrates that the ASVAB composites used in military selection and classification predict performance in training for a variety of military occupations. For example, validity coefficients for electrical and mechanical equipment repair specialties range from .36 to .74; those for communication specialties range from .36 to .52; those for data processing specialties range from .39 to .77; and those for clerical and supply specialties range from .53 to .73. These coefficients have been corrected for restriction of range.

U.S., Army, Military Entrance Processing Command, *Counselor's Manual for the Armed Services Vocational Aptitude Battery, Form 14* (North Chicago, Ill.: U.S. Military Entrance Processing Command, July 1984), p. 18. The test is highly correlated with the cognitive subtests of the General Aptitude Test Battery, a personnel selection test battery used by the U.S. Employment Service, the validity of which has been established by studies of more than 500 occupations. A validity generalization study funded by the armed forces concluded "that ASVAB is a highly valid predictor of performance in civilian occupations"; John E. Hunter, James J. Crossen, and David H. Friedman, "The Validity of the Armed Services Vocational Aptitude Battery (ASVAB) for Civilian and Military Job Performance" (Washington, D.C.: U.S., Department of Defense, August 1985), p. ix.

36. The 1980 version of the ASVAB (Form 8A) was administered by staff of the National Opinion Research Corporation according to strict guidelines conforming to standard ASVAB procedures. Testing was generally conducted in groups of five to ten persons. Dr. R. D. Bock, an authority on educational and psychological testing, evaluated the quality of the resulting ASVAB data for the Department of Defense. He concluded: "Data from responses of [the NLS Youth Sample] to the ASVAB are free from major defects such as high levels of guessing or carelessness, inappropriate levels of difficulty, cultural test-question bias, and inconsistencies in test administration procedures"; cited in U.S. Military Entrance Processing Command, *Counselor's Manual*, p. 19). A fuller description of the test battery can also be found in this document.

37. Models containing the actual cumulated work experience outperform models using both the more conventional potential work experience and its square and age and age squared. The corrected R squares of the wage models average 0.2426 for males and 0.2129 for females when age and actual experi-

ence appear in the model in a linear form. When the experience variables are potential experience and its square, the corrected R squares average 0.2257 for males and 0.1837 for females.

38. This result is consistent with previous research on the impact of trade and technical vocational course work on the wage rates and earnings of young men. Technical skills appear to pay off only when used. John Bishop, "Vocational Education for At-Risk Youth: How to Make It More Effective," Discussion Paper 88-12 (Cornell University, Center for Advanced Human Resource Research, Ithaca, N.Y., 1988). The returns to technical skills are likely to be gender specific. Few young women have jobs for which knowledge of electronics, mechanical principles, auto mechanics, and shop tools are essential: one should not expect technical knowledge to have a positive effect on the wage rates of women.

39. Computational speed has a significantly larger impact on wage rates of males than the academic composite in all eight of the cross-sections. This is somewhat of a puzzle, however, for computational speed is something that calculators do better than people and is not viewed by most educators as an appropriate goal for a high school mathematics curriculum; National Council of Teachers of Mathematics, *An Agenda for Action: Recommendations for School Mathematics of the 1980s* (Washington, D.C.: National Council of Teachers of Mathematics, 1980).

40. Paul Taubman and Terence Wales, "Education as an Investment and a Screening Device," in F. T. Juster, ed., *Education, Income and Human Behavior* (New York: McGraw-Hill, 1975); Robert Willis and Sherwin Rosen, "Education and Self-Selection," *Journal of Political Economy*, vol. 87, October 1979, pp. S7–S36; Robert Hauser and Thomas Daymont, "Schooling, Ability, and Earnings: Cross-Sectional Evidence 8–14 Years after High School Graduation," *Sociology of Education*, vol. 50, July 1977, pp. 182–206; Suk Kang and John Bishop, "Effects of Curriculum on Labor Market Success Immediately after High School," *Journal of Industrial Teacher Education*, vol. 23, no. 4 (1986), pp. 15–29.

41. This estimate is based on a survey of a stratified random sample of 2,000 members of the National Federation of Independent Business conducted in 1987.

42. Friedman and Williams, "Current Uses of Tests for Employment." Because they appear to be more job-related, mechanical aptitude tests like the three ASVAB technical tests have been much more likely to survive court challenge than tests assessing competence in English and mathematics. This is probably a major reason why technical subtests have large positive effects on wages of men even while basic skills tests have negative effects.

43. Bishop, "The Productivity Consequences" and "Information Externalities"; and John A. Hartigan and Alexandra Wigdor, *Fairness in Employment Testing* (Washington, D.C.: National Academy Press, 1989), p. 169.

44. Taubman and Wales, "Education as an Investment and a Screening Device"; Willis and Rosen, "Education and Self-Selection," pp. S7–S36; and Hauser and Daymont, "Schooling, Ability, and Earnings," pp. 182–206.

45. Taubman and Wales, "Education as an Investment and a Screening Device"; Willis and Rosen, "Education and Self-Selection," pp. S7–S36; John

C. Hause, "Ability and Schooling as Determinants of Lifetime Earnings, or If You're So Smart, Why Aren't You Rich," in F. T. Juster, ed., *Education, Income, and Human Behavior* (New York: McGraw-Hill, 1975).

46. In a data set that merges six separate cross sections for a nine-year birth cohort, age and date are not highly collinear, so separate main and interaction effects may be estimated for each variable. While biases caused by the correlation between date and age, student status and years of college can be purged from the estimates there is unfortunately no way of breaking the perfect confound between date and the time elapsed since the ASVAB test was taken. If the true model is a relationship between current academic competence and wages, the ASVAB test scores obtained in 1980 become an increasingly imperfect measure of true competence as time elapses. This will tend to give the interaction between test score and date a negative coefficient. If, despite this bias, the coefficient on the interaction is significantly positive, we have strong evidence for growing payoffs to true competency during the 1980s. If, however, the coefficient is zero or negative, the result is inconclusive.

47. Data for 1979 and 1980 were not included because requiring individuals to have a job for the entire 1979 to 1986 period would have greatly reduced the size of the sample.

48. Taubman and Wales, "Education as an Investment and a Screening Device"; Willis and Rosen, "Education and Self-Selection," pp. S7–S36; Hauser and Daymont, "Schooling, Ability, and Earnings," pp. 182–206.

49. Donald O. Parsons, "Wage Determination in the Post-Schooling Period: The Market for On-the-Job Training," *Pathways to the Future*, vol. 7. (Columbus: Ohio State University, Center for Human Resources Research) and John Bishop and Suk Kang, "A Bonding/Sorting Model of Employer Finance of General Training," (Cornell University, Center for Advanced Human Resources, Ithaca, N.Y., 1989). Working Paper.

50. This is an implication of a formal model developed by Henry Farber and Robert Gibbons, "Learning and Wage Determination," National Bureau of Economic Research, Washington, D.C., November 1990.

A NOTE ON THE BOOK

This book was edited
by the publications staff of the AEI Press.
The text was set in Palatino, a typeface designed by
the twentieth-century Swiss designer Hermann Zapf.
Coghill Book Typesetting, of Richmond, Virginia,
set the type, and Edwards Brothers Incorporated,
of Ann Arbor, Michigan, printed and bound the book,
using permanent acid-free paper.

The AEI PRESS is the publisher for the American Enterprise Institute for Public Policy Research, 1150 17th Street, N.W., Washington, D.C. 20036: *Christopher C. DeMuth,* publisher; *Edward Styles,* director; *Dana Lane,* assistant director; *Ann Petty,* editor; *Cheryl Weissman,* editor; *Susan Moran,* editorial assistant (rights and permissions). Books published by the AEI PRESS are distributed by arrangement with the University Press of America, 4720 Boston Way, Lanham, Md. 20706.